THE NEW AMERICAN BACKYARD

THE NEW AMERICAN BACKYARD

Easy, Organic Techniques and Solutions
for a Landscape You'll Love

KRIS MEDIC

RODALE

WE INSPIRE AND ENABLE PEOPLE TO IMPROVE THEIR LIVES AND THE WORLD AROUND THEM

We're always happy to hear from you. For questions or comments concerning the editorial content of this book, please write to:

Rodale Book Readers' Service
33 East Minor Street
Emmaus, PA 18098

Look for other Rodale books wherever books are sold. Or call us at (800) 848-4735.

For more information about Rodale Organic Gardening magazine and books, visit our World Wide Web site at:

www.organicgardening.com

Editor: *Karen Costello Soltys*
Interior Book Designer: *Marta Mitchell Strait*
Cover Designer: *Nancy Smola Biltcliff*
Contributing Designer: *Dale Mack*
Illustrators: *Robin Brickman (how-to), Jeni Webber (site plans)*
Photography Editor: *Lyn Horst*
Photography Assistant: *Jackie L. Ney*
Layout Designer: *Daniel MacBride*
Researcher: *Diana Erney*
Copy Editors: *Nancy N. Bailey, Candace Levy*
Manufacturing Coordinator: *Patrick T. Smith*
Indexer: *Nan Badgett*
Editorial Assistance: *Kerrie A. Cadden, Claudia Curran*

RODALE ORGANIC GARDENING BOOKS

Executive Editor: *Kathleen DeVanna Fish*
Managing Editor: *Fern Marshall Bradley*
Executive Creative Director: *Christin Gangi*
Art Director: *Patricia Field*
Production Manager: *Robert V. Anderson Jr.*
Studio Manager: *Leslie M. Keefe*
Copy Manager: *Nancy N. Bailey*
Book Manufacturing Director: *Helen Clogston*

Library of Congress Cataloging-in-Publication Data
Medic, Kris.
    The new American backyard : easy, organic techniques and solutions for a landscape you'll love / Kris Medic.
        p.   cm.
    Includes bibliographical references (p.) and index.
    ISBN 0–87596–833–3 (hardcover)
    1. Landscape gardening. 2. Organic gardening.   I. Title.
SB473 M394 2001
635.9'87—dc21   2001000006

Distributed in the book trade by St. Martin's Press

2   4   6   8   10   9   7   5   3   1   hardcover

FOR CAMPBELL, FOR HIS GENERATION, AND FOR THOSE THAT WILL FOLLOW.

Rodale
Organic Gardening Starts Here!

Here at Rodale, we've been gardening organically for more than 50 years—ever since my grandfather J. I. Rodale learned about composting and decided that healthy living starts with healthy soil. In 1940 J. I. started the Rodale Organic Farm to test his theories, and today the nonprofit Rodale Institute Experimental Farm is still at the forefront of organic gardening and farming research. In 1942 J. I. founded *Organic Gardening* magazine to share his discoveries with gardeners everywhere. His son, my father, Robert Rodale, headed *Organic Gardening* until 1990, and today a fourth generation of Rodales is growing up with the magazine. Over the years we've shown millions of readers how to grow bountiful crops and beautiful flowers using nature's own techniques.

In this book, you'll find the latest organic methods and the best gardening advice. We know—because the author and our editors are passionate about gardening! We feel strongly that our gardens should be safe for our children, pets, and the birds and butterflies that add beauty and delight to our lives and landscapes. Our gardens should provide us with fresh, flavorful vegetables, delightful herbs, and gorgeous flowers. And they should be a pleasure to work in as well as to view.

Sharing the secrets of safe, successful gardening is why we publish books. So come visit us at the Rodale Institute Experimental Farm, where you can tour the gardens every day—we're open year-round. And use this book to create your best garden ever.

Happy gardening!

Maria Rodale

Maria Rodale
Rodale Organic Gardening Books

Contents

An Easy Choice for Gardeners

Everyone wants an attractive home landscape. But spending lots of money on lawn care products and lots of hours each week watering, fertilizing, and mowing is so unnecessary. I often see smart, well-meaning people guided by an apparent belief that a green landscape is a healthy and responsible one—regardless of what it takes to create it. I'm saddened by what I see as a sense that a green lawn comes only from a truck with a spray rig. I'm committed to helping people understand their own power to create vibrant, useful landscapes that truly enrich the environment and to help them to avoid practices that pollute or degrade it.

This book is about creating a landscape that gives back. One that will give you pleasure, add to your property value, and won't require all your free time or tempt you to use harmful methods. Now that's what I call an attractive landscape! Rather than spending money unnecessarily on lawn care supplies, you can turn your property into a yard that practically takes care of itself. When you care for your yard organically, you can use the grass clippings to fertilize the grass instead of buying and hauling bags of unneeded stuff. When you plant trees and shrubs, you'll find your yard is shadier and a more enjoyable place to spend time. You'll be delighted by the sound of songbirds who take cover in your trees and charmed by the butterflies that visit your plantings for nectar. Your kids will learn to appreciate nature close at hand—right in their backyard. It will be a place that your whole family can enjoy.

Creating a Landscape You'll Love

The New American Backyard offers so many ideas—old and new, high-tech and low-tech—that can help you to create a home landscape that works in harmony with nature. You'll save time, effort, and money while conserving and protect natural resources. Whether you're growing paradise on earth or just a simple lawn, using sustainable practices rather than harsh chemical ones is an easy choice.

This book is divided into two parts to help you find exactly what you need. Part One gives you great information on making design changes and decisions that will make your yard more beautiful and less demanding. Whether you have a brand new home and no landscaping or you've been in your house for years and you want to make some changes, this section is for you.

You'll find design ideas—large and small—that can help you establish an enjoyable landscape that's easy on the budget and the environment. And, since plants aren't the only thing in your yard, I also take an in-depth look at hardscape, those nonliving elements that can sometimes make or break your yard's appearance and usability. Pick up some great tricks for hardscape details that can save you lots of time and trouble down the line and some advice on how to handle old or worn-out features. Finally, you'll find tips for reducing your home's energy costs and ways to make your backyard more comfortable.

Part Two is the place to go for great ideas on savvy yard maintenance. You might be surprised to discover that many common maintenance practices can be expensive and damaging to the environment. Learn how to create a smart, beautiful, chemical-free lawn, how to reduce your yard's watering needs without reducing its beauty, discover the least-toxic ways to discourage and control pests, and how to prune so you won't have to keep coming back.

Inspired by the Trees

Whether your goal is to conserve time, money, the environment, or all three, I hope you'll use this book as a resource for landscape design and maintenance tricks that work with nature for effective results.

Personally, I find the companionship of green growing things to be a constant and lifelong blessing. My fondness for plants—and the benefits that come with them—had an early start during summers spent among the towering hemlocks at my family's lake cabin. As a teenager, I spent much of my spare time volunteering in wilderness search and rescue, awed by the forest surroundings no matter how many days I'd been out or in what kind of weather.

When I grew up in suburban Philadelphia, an impressive overstory of oak trees shaded and graced our modest neighborhood. I was familiar enough with the streets of the city, as well, to observe how plantings—or their absence—could make or break the scene. I became determined to make trees my life's work.

I work in arboriculture and horticulture because I am convinced of the tremendous good that these professions can do in the world when they are practiced well. Creating beautiful gardens and wonderful spaces has been a delightful bonus in what, for me, has become a pursuit for environmental quality, one property at a time. To my way of thinking, there's no higher calling. If I can help my clients and their employees to understand, appreciate, and continue those sustainable practices, all the better!

Now it's your turn. My dream is for you to find the ideas, techniques, and guidance you need in *The New American Backyard* so that you, too, can turn your property into a natural haven for your family to enjoy.

Even a mundane storage area can be turned into a pretty corner of your yard. My family enjoys canoeing, but storing the canoe when we weren't using it was a problem—until we stored it in plain sight. We simply made it the centerpiece of a bed of native, spring-blooming plants. When summer comes, we have easy access to the canoe.

PART ONE

Simple and Elegant—
A New Way to Landscape

A Great **Landscape** and **How** to Get There

Do you live in a brand new house with an expanse of lawn that's just waiting for your **creative touch?** Or perhaps you've been in the same home with the same old landscape for years, and it's time to **make some changes.** Either way, a **truly great** landscape is awaiting you! In this chapter you'll start on the road to a **beautiful new** backyard by taking stock of what you already have. While you stroll around your yard, **think carefully** about what you **really enjoy** about it—and also about what bothers you. Then imagine what you'd like your yard to become. Whatever the size or shape of your yard, it has the potential to be a **haven** for birds and other wildlife, a **peaceful retreat** for your family, **a play area** for your children, and so much more.

Think of **All** Your Yard **Can Be**

Whether your backyard is nothing but lawn, has only a young shade tree or two, or sports a few too many overgrown landscape plants, it's already something special—it's your personal haven from the rest of the world. But just imagine all that your yard could be. If you enjoy welcoming friends and family over for a cookout, wouldn't it be so much more pleasurable if you had some comforting shade to keep the sun out of everyone's eyes as the sun begins to set? Would your children be more apt to play on their jungle gym if it weren't situated all alone in the beating sun in the farthest corner of the yard? And wouldn't your entire family enjoy the sight of birds and butterflies flitting through your little corner of the world, stopping to enjoy your plants or take a drink?

Unfortunately, what many of today's homeowners face is a yard without shade, privacy, or the soothing sounds of nature. So many new homes are built on land that was once farm fields, where there are no mature shade trees, no old fencerows, and no native plantings to add color, shade, privacy, or any real character. Quite often, the only thing taller than grass in our backyards is a shed built to house a lawn mower (or that jungle gym).

A Backyard as Cozy as a Family Room

Having a place to play and to store tools are two important uses of a backyard. But it can also be so much more. Relaxing, reading, entertaining, gardening, bird watching, or other rejuvenating activities can all go on in your own backyard. And it's so much nicer to do these things outdoors when your backyard is as comfortable as your family room. The good news is—it can be!

Even if your backyard merely features lawn and not much more, don't despair. The ideas in this book can help you to make it attractive and delightful. A perennial garden that you and the local birds and but-terflies can all enjoy, an evergreen planting that can screen out unwanted views and provide shady relief, or even a garden room that becomes your favorite retreat are just some of the possibilities. You'll find lots of ideas throughout this book to help you plan for the backyard of your dreams.

Good Looks Only Go So Far

While everyone wants a nice-looking landscape, this book is about creating a yard that goes beyond the typical neat and tidy foundation planting. For a usable,

Your new backyard will be more a source of pleasure than one of endless chores.

needs of your household—from a safe place to play to a secluded spot for relaxing to quick access for deliveries, trash removal, or reading meters—you'll realize that not every square inch of your backyard needs to be covered in grass. A typical backyard can have many uses, so planning to make the most of the space you have is quite important. You'll find much more about how to plan for your backyard needs—along with many landscape makeover plans—in Chapter 2.

Goal 2: Make Your Backyard More Economical

By economical, I don't mean buying bargain-bin plants. I'm referring to a landscape that doesn't waste. When you choose plants that are suited to your climate and growing conditions, for instance, they won't require lots of extra water, pampering, or power equipment to main-

family-friendly backyard, you'll want your yard to be an outdoor living space that's a haven for whatever you enjoy—curling up in the hammock with a favorite book, digging in the garden, playing catch, or sizzling steak or fish on the barbecue. And it's not that hard. If you plan for each of the five landscape goals below, your backyard can become the envy of all the neighborhood. Your yard won't only feel like a natural extension of your home, but it will also be a source of pleasure that doesn't eat up all your spare time or money to maintain.

Goal 1: Make Your Backyard Family-Friendly

While lots of turfgrass makes a nice soccer field or ball lot, it's not always the best choice for other outdoor activities. When you think about all the daily

Using plants to enclose spaces is an attractive way to make your yard more livable and help to reduce heating or cooling costs for your home.

tain them. As a result, your backyard won't waste natural resources and it won't cause undue air pollution. What's more, the time and money it takes to maintain this natural type of backyard are both minimal. An economical backyard helps to reduce heating and cooling costs, too, which in turn can add to your property value.

Goal 3: Turn Your Backyard into a Living Landscape

A living landscape is a thriving one that gives back more than it takes. It's not dependent on artificial chemical products to keep it green. Instead, it suc-

Composting is one of the most important steps in developing a living landscape. Decomposed plant material in compost can nourish growing plants rather than taking up space in a landfill.

ceeds on the amount of water and nutrients that are available naturally on your property. For instance, rather than lugging in bags of store-bought fertilizers to keep your grass green and then hauling all the bags of grass clippings to the curb for trash pickup, you can simplify the whole process. Just leave the grass clippings on the lawn when you mow. They'll decompose and release organic nitrogen right back into the soil where your grass can benefit from it. The waste products from one process become the fuel for another—the plants sustain themselves. And it means no more bulging bags of fertilizer to haul, no more yard waste to put out with the trash, and a lot less work for you!

Using grass clippings is just one example of easy maintenance techniques you can use to improve your yard and save you time. You'll find many more ideas for saving time, money, and resources in Part Two, "Timesaving Lawn and Garden Techniques."

Goal 4: Transform Your Backyard into a Productive Space

In addition to suiting the needs of your family, a great backyard can also give back more than it takes from you and the environment. If you enjoy gardening, for example, why not add some vegetables to the mix of plants you grow? A backyard is also a perfect place to grow fruits and nuts. Another way your backyard can give back is to provide a habitat for birds or other wildlife. Not only will they appreciate the space, but your family will also enjoy having them there. Birds are fun to watch and listen to. Add a birdbath to your plantings, and you're bound to have hours of enjoyment. Other simple benefits you can reap from your landscape are cooling, sheltering shade and clean, breathable oxygen—things we tend to take for granted.

Goal 5: Create a Beautiful, Enjoyable, and Comfortable Landscape

Once you plan for the first four goals, you can't help creating a backyard living space that is all these things: beautiful, enjoyable, and comfortable to be in. Your backyard will work for you, extend your living space, and probably end up being a place where you spend much of your time. It will be full of the plants and other things that you enjoy and full of the wonders and pleasures of the natural world.

Making the **Transition** to a **Great Backyard**

Although I've listed five goals for a great backyard, as you can see, they tend to overlap. That's because when you make one type of change for the better, it often yields other benefits. For instance, when you change your mowing habits and mow the grass higher and leave the clippings on the lawn, you've improved your lawn maintenance program without any extra work. In fact, you'll probably be doing *less* work because in addition to grass clippings providing nitrogen to your lawn for free, they also help hold in water, block weed growth, and suppress diseases.

The key to success in changing your yard is *planning*. The process doesn't have to be hard, expensive, or overwhelming—you can phase in changes gradually. In Chapters 2 through 6, you'll find lots of ideas to help you plan the types of changes that will work for you, from choosing the right plants to tips on hardscaping and lighting. (If you're already happy with the features and plantings in your yard, you may want to skip these chapters and flip directly to Part Two, where you'll learn how to save time and money by changing your maintenance habits.)

Making a Wish List for Your Yard

Before we delve into *how* to make changes, let's start by investigating specifically *what* you want in your backyard. The whole process will go much more smoothly if you start by thinking seriously about what you want and need from your yard. To make it easy to capture your thoughts, you can record them on "Your Backyard Ideas Checklist" on page 8. You might want to photocopy this checklist so you can use it again as you develop and refine your ideas.

The best place to start is with what you already have in your yard. Think about what works well in your home landscape. Also consider what doesn't work. Your answers may be as simple as "I love our new deck, but mowing around it is a hassle because I always have to come back and trim," or "The shade from the maple tree is wonderful in summer, but the grass doesn't grow very well underneath it."

To help identify things that aren't working for you, think about safety issues first. Uneven ground or poor lighting where people come and go, large trees that have seen better days, or obsolete play sets are all examples of things that probably deserve your attention first.

Next, focus on the things that you'd rather not spend time on. For instance, was the previous owner a fan of hybrid tea roses? Watering and pampering those roses may not be your cup of tea. Perhaps you should dig them out and replace them with plants that are easier to care for. Or, you may be tired of spending time and money replanting a large bed of annuals every year. You could turn it into a perennial or groundcover bed instead. Often, you can get rid of what you don't like and replace it quickly and inexpensively with something that's much more suitable.

As you decide on changes or improvements, be deliberate about protecting the things you really like. For example, the previous owners of our house did a

A quaint garden room—which is big on appeal and low on weekly maintenance—links the main house on this property with the outbuilding.

wonderful job filling the landscape with evergreens, which we greatly enjoy, especially in the winter. A mantle of snow gives them a magical quality, and they provide lots of cover for birds. So even though I've made plans to make some improvements on our property, we'll want to keep those evergreens as we make the changes.

After you've finished analyzing what you like and don't like, ask yourself if there's anything that's conspicuous by its absence from your yard. Shade? A sitting area? Play space for your kids? A storage shed? Privacy? Use the checklist on page 8 to help you identify and rank the things that you want or need. Even if you can't afford something right now or if it's only an imagined future need, go ahead and list it so that you can reserve space for it.

Pick Quick-and-Easy First

Just as it's easiest to pick the low-hanging peaches first because they're well within your reach, it makes sense to start your landscaping changes with the projects that are quick and easy. Some projects may only take an afternoon to finish, yet they'll give you instant rewards. Maybe the benefit is a healthier, better-looking foundation because of fresh mulch you spread, or it could be saving watering time by installing a drip hose. These simple-to-do tasks can give you lasting benefits and build momentum for your next steps.

Some other great places to begin include starting a compost pile, raising the mowing height so that your grass competes better with weeds, or letting shrubs grow to their natural form rather than shearing or shaping them. Go to Part Two to find many more ideas where a simple task or a change in habit can cost you little and earn you time, effectiveness, or enrichment in your own backyard!

Make a Plan

Once you've "picked the low-hanging fruit," identified what works and what doesn't work in your yard, and ranked your needs and wants, you're ready to take the items from your "urgent" column and rank *them* in order of need. Do the same for the "necessary" column, and keep your eye on anything that might be doable in your "desirable" column. With this information in hand, you have some great information to guide your design process. You're ready to start working on your backyard blueprint—a master plan that will incorporate all the changes you want to make. By creating an overall plan for your backyard renovations, you'll see what needs to be done and be better able to figure out a logical order for accomplishing the important things on your list.

Depending on how complex your goals are, you may be able to jump in and take care of one or two items on your list right away. But chances are, you have some big issues to deal with or changes or alterations that may affect other parts of your yard. That's why it's so important to have a plan. In Chapter 2 you'll find helpful information on creating an overall plan for your dream backyard. I'll show you step by step how to create your plan, where to start, how to update it, and how to experiment with various ideas. You'll also find sample backyard makeover plans that you can use for ideas or adapt to your own situation. Let's get started!

YOUR BACKYARD IDEAS CHECKLIST

Use this handy checklist to keep track of your ideas for improving your yard.

For any item that's of interest, check **U** for urgent, **N** for necessary, or **D** for desirable. Anything that might pose a safety hazard should definitely be ranked as urgent, while others that you really need but wouldn't cause anyone harm if they aren't in place can be listed as necessary. For the items you've checked, try to find a few key words to describe your goal for that aspect of your landscape. They will help you remember what you originally intended to do and help you think clearly and specifically about what you want.

BACKYARD CHANGES AND IMPROVEMENTS	U	N	D	YOUR GOALS
LIVING AREAS				
Screened-in porch				
Deck, patio, gazebo				
Cooking/dining				
ENTRY AREAS				
Convenient, well-lit access for you, visitors, and delivery people				
PLAY AREAS				
Open lawn area(s)				
Hard-use area(s) for sports like volleyball				
Swing set				
Fort or treehouse				
UTILITY AREAS				
Wood storage				
Trash and recycling area				
Composting area				
Storage area				
Clothesline				

Backyard Changes and Improvements	U	N	D	Your Goals
Gardening Areas				
Vegetables, fruits, nuts				
Flowers				
Containers				
Vines				
Special interests				
Children's garden				
Greenhouse or potting area				
Amenities				
Swimming pool or hot tub				
Sculpture or other art				
Bird feeding				
Holiday display(s)				
Environmental Concerns				
Shade				
Catching cooling breezes				
Windbreaks				
Noise or glare reduction				
Erosion control on slopes				
Wildlife habitat				
Physical Concerns				
Keep and enhance desirable views				
Screen out undesirable views				
Protect privacy				

CHAPTER 2

Creating a **Backyard Plan** That Keeps on **Giving**

Now that you have a better understanding of your property and what you want to accomplish with it, you're ready to plan some **changes** for your backyard. Planting **scrumptious fruits** and vegetables, creating a cozy sitting area for relaxing, establishing a natural **habitat for birds,** and incorporating **energy savings** into your landscape are all possibilities. When you design your yard with these benefits in mind, you'll find it has a **timeless beauty** that will far outlast any horticultural or design trend. Follow the steps in my design process to create a landscape that is uniquely yours, or adapt ideas in the **sample plans** in this chapter to suit your situation.

Designing Your Dream Backyard

If you're not a designer by nature, the thought of designing your own landscape may be a little intimidating. However, working through the design process is a wonderful way for you to really understand your property and how you can use it to suit your family's needs. And to help keep you on track, my design process flowchart on the opposite page shows how you can break everything down into manageable steps. The information that follows the flowchart will walk you through each step so you're sure to be successful.

Depending on how large your property is, you may have a lot to think about. But by investing some time, thought, and attention to the steps I recommend in this chapter and by reviewing the various sample designs I've provided, you'll be ready to develop plans that will uniquely suit your needs and your specific property. Then, whether you want to carry out your entire design immediately or gradually in phases, you'll have a firm plan to follow so you can move ahead with confidence.

Prioritize Your Goals

When it comes to moving around heavy things like plants, soil, and mulch, it's always a good idea to be clear on what you want to accomplish *before* you dig in. Refer back to "Your Backyard Ideas Checklist" on page 8 that you've already completed. It will help you identify the specific elements—such as trees, shrubs, decks, and walkways—that you want to add, enhance, preserve, or even eliminate from your property.

After you've categorized your needs and wants into three types of projects—urgent, necessary, and desirable—you can further prioritize them by putting any safety-related items from your "urgent" column at the top of the list. Other high priorities

may be projects that will save you time or make your property more enjoyable and even less polluting. For example, if you reduce your lawn area, you'll spend less time mowing each week, which means you'll also be polluting the air less. Or, if you replace an overgrown shrub that demands constant pruning with one that's the right size for its space, you'll be saving yourself the time and trouble of regular pruning to keep it manageable.

Map Out Existing Conditions

Translating your landscape goals into a working plan can be a big job. In fact, this is where some folks like to call in a landscape designer or landscape architect. If you're planning major construc-

Design Process

When you follow these steps to examine your own home ground, you're sure to discover something helpful that you didn't know!

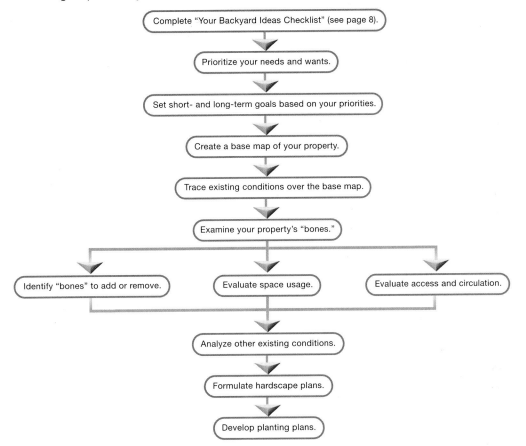

Complete "Your Backyard Ideas Checklist" (see page 8).

Prioritize your needs and wants.

Set short- and long-term goals based on your priorities.

Create a base map of your property.

Trace existing conditions over the base map.

Examine your property's "bones."

Identify "bones" to add or remove.   Evaluate space usage.   Evaluate access and circulation.

Analyze other existing conditions.

Formulate hardscape plans.

Develop planting plans.

tion as part of your landscape plan, that may be a good idea. However, if you merely want to add some trees, shrubs, and planting beds to your yard, you can certainly handle this job yourself. The whole process is really quite manageable, especially when you take it one step at a time. The first step is to gather basic but important information about your property and record it on a drawing called a base map. Your base map will become an at-a-

glance summary of the permanent aspects (or ones that you don't expect to change any time soon) of your property. This map will be useful for years to come since you can repeatedly trace over it as you try out new designs for different areas of your yard. This is one step you won't want to skip!

To make your base map, you'll need graph paper, a ruler, a 50- or 100-foot tape measure, a pencil, and an eraser. It's also helpful to have a clipboard and a friend to help with measuring your property. Later, you'll also need some tracing paper and masking tape.

CREATING YOUR BASE MAP

Start by measuring your property—its dimensions, the location and size of permanent structures as well as the trees and beds, the driveway, sidewalks, paths, fences, and walls. Write down all these measurements on your clipboard; you'll need to translate all these dimensions into a graph paper–size drawing.

If your property is large, you may need to tape multiple sheets of graph paper together so you can fit a drawing of your entire property on one sheet. It's easiest if you work in a scale that's large enough to show detail and to overlay designs later. For small properties (less than $^1/_4$ acre), I recommend a scale of $^1/_8$ or $^1/_4$ inch equals 1 foot; for larger properties, try 1 inch equals 10 or 20 feet.

Plot out your lot lines and the outlines of your buildings and pavements. Then indicate locations of first-floor windows, downspouts and overhangs on buildings, steps, walls, fences, water sources, and utility equipment (see "Locating Underground Utilities" on page 16 for tips). Include any of these types of items that are just over your lot line as well, since your neighbors' trees or fences are visible from your property and can shade part of your yard. Sketch in trees, shrubs, and the edges of beds, noting the species and condition of the plants. Your base map is complete.

RECORDING OTHER DETAILS

Next, reach for that tracing paper and tape it over your base map with masking tape. You're ready to

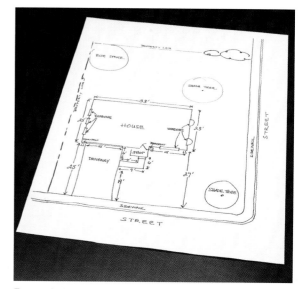

Record all the permanent features of your yard on your base map for easy reference.

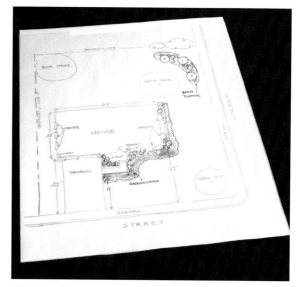

With tracing paper overlays, you can use your base map and inventory information repeatedly for dreaming up and fine-tuning your design ideas.

Jump-Start
Your Base Map

record the next level of detail on your map, which is really an inventory of existing conditions in your yard. You'll want to record important soil and weather features, which I discuss in the next chapter. Referring to the "Growing Conditions Checklist" on page 54, make note of soil and moisture conditions, sun and wind exposure, hills or low spots for your backyard site. An easy way to do this is with highlighter pens. Circle sunny spots in yellow and shady areas in blue. Choose another color to indicate windy or exposed areas.

You'll also want to indicate the following situations that can affect your plant choices:

■ Views into or out of your property and your windows (both the desirable views you want to preserve and the undesirable ones you want to screen)

■ Uses of existing buildings, including those that aren't on your property but that are within view or hearing range

■ Uses of existing yard, including neighboring yards within sight or hearing range

■ Other elements that may affect privacy

■ Pathways for people, pets, bicycles, and other vehicles

■ Storage areas

■ Parking

■ Lighting

■ Easements

■ Pertinent zoning information

Sometimes it's hard to know where to start when you need to make an existing-conditions plan of your property. If you can find the closing papers on your home purchase, you might have the answer right in your files! Your documents may include a property survey that you can enlarge to a workable size on a photocopier and begin tracing important items like lot lines, building and pavement edges, and easements.

Another way to get started is to check and see if your community's land-use planning or zoning department has a Geographic Information System (GIS) in place. If you are lucky enough to have this resource, you can request a computer-plotted drawing of your property. GIS files are developed from digitized aerial photos and include overlays such as building "footprints," pavement edges, trees greater than a certain diameter, utilities, topography, and sometimes soil types. Investigate this option and you may find a ready-made base map for the asking.

If neither of these options is available to you, start at the street, sidewalk, or other straight edge of your property, and measure the shortest distance to one corner of your house. Repeat for the other corner, and you have the start of your house on your map. Once you have your house plotted correctly, you're on your way.

LOCATING UNDERGROUND UTILITIES

"Call before you dig" is a utility company motto, and it's something you *definitely* need to do. When you call, be prepared to provide the following information:

- Address and county where digging will take place
- Nearest cross street to where digging will take place
- Where on the property you expect to dig
- When you expect to dig
- Purpose for digging
- How deeply you expect to dig
- Whether explosives will be used

Never mind that your digging may not take place for some time to come. If you find out now where your underground utilities are, you'll save yourself time and trouble later. After all, you don't want to create an elaborate planting plan just to find out that it would mean digging right where your underground electrical lines are.

Normally, utility employees will pay a visit to your property within 3 days of your call. They'll mark the ground where the underground lines are with spray paint or wire flags, or they may write "clear" or "OK" if there are none. Some utility companies can tell without a visit if none of their equipment is on your property, and they may simply call you to say your property is "clear."

When the time comes to dig, don't hesitate to call again if many months have passed or if you just want confirmation before you dig that footer. Utility companies are usually happy to accommodate you if it means they can prevent expensive service interruption and repairs to their systems.

Finally, jot down your personal likes and dislikes (and those of your family). What works for you and what doesn't? Perhaps you have inherited some plants from previous property owners that you'd like to get rid of. Capture all of this information—either by sketching it or writing notes—on your inventory of existing conditions.

Evaluating the Bone Structure

Landscape designers often say that a yard, garden, or property has great "bones" when the spaces formed by physical features such as buildings, walks, walls, fences, mature trees, and beds are well proportioned and give a comfortable feel to the property. What are the bones like in your yard?

Actually, it's easiest to see what the bones look like when the landscape is dormant and there are no leaves on the trees. Take a look at how the shape and height of trees and buildings define your yard's space. Is the overall structure working well? Are the adjoining uses of space (such as a patio/entertaining area and the kids' play area) compatible and well organized? Are there blank areas where you have no bones, but would like some—perhaps to create a screen?

Keeping the lists from "Your Backyard Ideas Checklist" close at hand, it's time to consider whether there are any space-defining physical features on your property that you want to add or remove. Tape another sheet of tissue paper over your base map and inventory, and make notes about which bones you want to keep and where you might like to add bones. These are important considerations, so let's review them in more detail before you make your final design choices. Be sure to capture your ideas and decisions on your base map overlay!

Working with Existing Trees

In this phase of designing, you need to take an objective look at all the existing trees in your yard. Trees play a key role in defining space, so the trees you plan to keep should be located where you want them and have a safe and useful life expectancy well into the future. While there are no guarantees, there are ways to determine whether a tree is a good candidate for saving or whether you should cut your losses and remove it.

Sometimes a tree's poor condition is obvious, and if it's a threat to people or property, the decision to remove it is clear. If it's on the "back 40" somewhere and its decaying wood is feeding the woodpeckers and providing homes for bluebirds, the decision to keep it may be just as apparent. Sometimes, however, the decision isn't so easy. A tree may look healthy but poses structural problems, or it may be a short-lived, weak-wooded species, offering little justification for keeping it. Sometimes trees are injured by grading that took place far enough in the past so that it's undetectable by looking casually at the ground. Some insults and injuries can take years to kill a tree, but here are some clues to look for:

- Well-formed root flares indicates a tree was planted at the correct height, and if there's no decay, it should be sound at ground level
- A "utility pole" tree trunk that doesn't have root flares indicates the tree was planted too deeply or that it may have been filled in later. The structural

stability of the tree may be questionable. If it's not a tree that your heart is set on keeping, consider removing it or replacing it with a new tree. If you're unsure, get advice from a professional arborist.

- Rotting or damaged root flares indicates the tree probably has suffered from mower or construction damage. Again, the structural stability can be in jeopardy and you may want to remove or replace it.

Root flares, where the base of the trunk tapers out into the roots, that show no sign of decay indicate that a tree was planted at the correct height. If you don't see this type of flare, your tree may have been planted too deeply and is suffering as a result.

WHEN TO CALL
A PRO

WHAT ABOUT WOODLOTS?

Deciding the future of an existing tree may be fairly straightforward, but how do you know what to keep and what to remove on a heavily wooded site?

For basic information and written help, your Cooperative Extension office can be a reliable source; sometimes, however, it's preferable to get in-person advice from an expert. If you prefer to have a professional examine your property and explain your options, ask for referrals from your state's division of forestry, the Society of American Foresters, and the Association of Consulting Foresters of America.

If you're planning to build a new home in a wooded setting, consider getting help from a consulting arborist. Because you have so many trees to evaluate—and once they're cut down they're gone—it makes sense to rely on their experience. It's also a good idea to get written information from your Cooperative Extension Service on tree protection. The International Society of Arboriculture and the American Society of Consulting Arborists can both give you referrals. See "Resources for Backyard Ideas" on page 256 for information.

Planning for Future Bones

While the time to develop specific planting or construction plans is still a few steps away, it's not too soon to anticipate your overall strategy now. Even though you don't need to decide *what* to plant now, if you follow the guidelines below for *how* or *where* to plant a tree or lay a pathway, you'll be able to use space better. You'll also be able to take advantage of opportunities that might be lost later if you don't think about them now.

Avoid locating plants individually in a lawn area. Group them together in a bed instead. Plants grouped together benefit in many ways. They have a larger volume of improved soil and soil moisture than any plant would have on its own. Plants grouped together shade each other and each other's

Group landscape plants together in beds—they'll enjoy greater odds against damage and stress than plants in single planting holes do.

roots, they protect each other from wind, and they raise the humidity around themselves, creating a microclimate that's much more plant-friendly than a lone planting hole. In addition, there is less overall soil compaction and more opportunity for roots to spread out and become well established. Grouped plants tend to mulch each other, and they'll be protected from your mower and weed wacker, too. In short, they form a community.

By grouping plants in beds, you also create a more hospitable habitat for wildlife, and there are benefits for you, too. You'll be reducing the amount of lawn area you have to mow and eliminating multiple mowing obstacles.

Consider the style of new elements. The bones of your landscape design aren't just trees and other tall elements. They also include bed edges and other transitions such as walkways or decks. Each of these items can lend either a formal or informal air to your landscape, depending on their shapes and the materials they're made of. Flowing, curved lines suggest informality, while straight or angled lines represent a more formal design. Edges that curve gently tend to complement the natural shape of landscape plants. As long as the curves aren't too deep or ornate, they'll easily accommodate your lawn mower—and even a bit of neglect—with grace. For instance, a little bit of groundcover or trailing plants that escape over the edge of a curved pathway won't look out of place. On the other hand, you'll quickly notice an untrimmed boxwood edging in a straight, formal hedge.

If you're planning a new bed, walk, fence, or other feature, consider the character or style of what's already in place in your yard and working

For an informal design, give garden beds gently curving lines. Let plants grow in their natural forms rather than pruning heavily, and layer plants so they'll mimic a forest environment.

well. Your personal tastes, the amount of maintenance you want to keep up with, and the visual impact of a formal or informal look are all-important factors in your final decision.

Using Space Wisely

Taking the priority items from "Your Backyard Ideas Checklist" (see page 8) and a fresh piece of tracing paper, begin to identify spaces on your property with

Don't Forget
about *Easements*

If you have an easement on your property (where another person or business has a right of way or is entitled to access to your property), find out how the holder of the easement will need to enter and move about your property during a repair or an emergency. If a utility crew is facing a midnight repair in foul weather, concern for whatever is in the way is not likely to be their top priority.

If easement restrictions do allow you to plant, use only the toughest plants—ones that can come back from the roots if damaged. In other words, don't plant trees in an easement area. Sometimes easements permit fences, but always check the easement restrictions before you install one.

how you want or expect to use them. Options to consider are a play area, if you have children; an outdoor dining and entertaining area; a vegetable garden; and so on. To make the most of your backyard space, try to work out a plan that situates related uses next to one another. For instance, trash and recycling storage should be convenient to the kitchen door or garage and also in a fairly direct (and preferably paved) line to the curb.

Likewise, it makes sense for an outdoor dining area to be close to the kitchen and for play areas to be within view of a convenient window so you can keep an eye on the kids even when you aren't outside with them. A compost pile works best when it's close to the garden *and* within easy reach of the kitchen. If you need work areas for potting, chopping wood, or other chores, plan them so you'll have easy access. For instance, you won't want to haul a truckload of firewood to the back of your property for stacking, only to lug it back to the house to burn.

Think of all the possible ways you'll want to use your property—from play and entertaining to gardening and maintenance. Then, for each intended use, list its relationships with other areas. This task may seem a little tedious but it will help you determine the best plan for your yard. Finally, overlay a new sheet of tracing paper over your base map and existing conditions inventory, and sketch out various possibilities.

Plan for Easy Access

Easy access around your property and from one area to another will let you get much more use—and enjoyment—out of your yard. Think about how you and your family members will need to move about your yard, and don't stop with foot traffic. Also consider how vehicles such as your kids' bikes, your lawn mower, or even a delivery truck can gain access your property. A privacy screen may be just what you need around your outdoor dining area, but make sure it won't block an important access route, or you'll soon have a pathway beaten through your new shrubbery.

Here are some questions to ask yourself about access as you work on your design:

- Is getting from a car on the street or in the driveway to your front door straightforward and safe?
- Can you haul firewood indoors with the least number of obstacles?
- Can you carry garden produce indoors by way of a convenient outdoor spot for cleaning?
- Where will a wheelbarrow or cart need to fit?
- Do you need a route for delivery trucks, such as one delivering mulch or compost?
- Would you rather not walk through wet grass to carry kitchen scraps to the compost pile?

Keep Pathways Simple

Generally, any route where you carry items frequently—deliveries, firewood, groceries, trash, compost—works best when it's as flat and as straight as possible, flush with the ground, and paved. It's best to save meandering paths for the garden where a leisurely stroll is just what you're looking for. Lighting pathways may be helpful, too, especially if you live in an area that's not lit by streetlights.

Make notes about how traffic between related spaces will work best. Before you finalize your plans—or pour a concrete path—see Chapter 6 for tips about planning and installing walks, paths, and steps.

Filling In the Details

Once you have all your ideas, desires, and needs sorted out and planned on a tracing paper overlay, you're finally ready to fill in the details. It's time to map out the garden beds and make a planting plan.

As much as possible, I'd encourage you to think about the character of the area where you live and use it as a model for your planting plans. For instance, is the ground sandy or rocky? Was there once open prairie where you live? Or was your area originally a forest with a canopy, understory, and herbaceous layer? Is there a nearby river, stream, or lake, or do bluebirds frequent open fields? By mirroring what nature originally intended for your area, your plantings are more likely to be successful.

Choose Plants by Function First

As you begin your planting plan and start to look for specific plants to "fill in the blanks," remember to first think about what you want the plants to do for your yard, such as provide shade, form a barrier or screen, or create shelter for songbirds. (For a more complete list of plant functions, see page 46.)

A good way to make sure you look at the tree's or shrub's function rather than just how pretty it is would be to take another piece of tracing paper and draw plant sizes, shapes, and textures that will do the various jobs that you've identified. First identify attributes such as size, shape, character, and evergreen or deciduous. Once you have shapes drawn on your design, then you can begin to choose actual species and cultivars. By approaching plant selection this way, you're more likely to develop a plant list that meets the physical needs of the property, and you will resist the temptation to choose personal favorites when other plants might be more appropriate. In Chapter 3 you'll find plant selection tips to help you select plants that will grow well under your growing conditions and meet your needs.

Keep Design Criteria in Mind, Too

When choosing plants to meet your needs, you'll soon see that some plants suit and others don't. However, you're bound to have more than one good option to choose from. Rather than picking one or two favorites, think about adding more diversity to your landscape with a variety of plants that will work for you. While a huge number of plants can look haphazard or unconnected, you can unite your landscape with repeating colors, textures, and shapes.

FLOWER POWER

Color preference is a very personal thing. Some folks love pastels, while others opt for bright primary hues.

Whatever your personal favorites, you can use color to bring life to your design. For instance, brights, whites, pinks, and grays—whether flowers or foliage—will lighten up a shady spot. To add floral magic to an area like a patio or front entry that you might frequent at dusk, select whites and blues, grays, or lavender. For a bed that might be viewed at a distance, like one at the back of the yard or deep in the front—use hot colors like red, orange, and yellow that tend to advance visually toward the viewer. Save the cool pastels for close-up viewing because their impact will be lost at a distance. If you want to visually shorten a deep bed, put the cooler colors toward the front and hot colors at the rear. If you're aiming for the opposite effect—making a small bed look deeper—simply reverse the strategy.

Evergreen tree or shrub

Deciduous tree

Flowering tree or shrub

Group of broad-leaved shrubs

Perennials

Annuals

Group of evergreen shrubs

When filling in plants on your base map overlay, use these easy-to-draw symbols for different plant types. That way you can see at a glance what type of plant is intended for each spot.

Your landscape will have a more harmonious look and feel when you repeat key colors, textures, and shapes.

FOLIAGE COLOR

When it comes to foliage color, you have almost as many choices as you do with flowers. However, instead of using blue, green, yellow, white, purple, and red foliage all in the same bed, limit your color choices, and use unusual-colored plants as accents. Too many colors can create a jarring rather than soothing effect. If you choose primarily green-foliage plants, you can accent them with some variegated foliage, or perhaps bronze and purple foliage. That doesn't mean you have to repeat the same variegated or bronze plant over and over again, however. You can expand your plant palette into a more diverse group, including two or three different types of plants that can give the same variegated or bronze effect. Because they are similar colors, everything will still tie together quite nicely.

Just keep in mind that you can become carried away and have too many different types of plants, too. Plant diversity can help to reduce pest problems and invite a wider variety of wildlife and beneficial insects onto your property. But repeating a few key plants throughout your design will help it to hang together visually. Strive for the best of both worlds—a nice mix of plants that blend together well.

PLANT SIZE AND TEXTURE

A few other basic design concepts to take into consideration are plant height and texture. Follow nature's cue and plant the tallest plants at the back and the shortest ones in the front, and you'll create layers that let you see everything. This approach applies to all types of plants, from trees and shrubs to perennials and annuals.

You can use color to make an area look smaller or larger, to pull a composition together, or to light up the dusk or the shade.

When it comes to texture, try to vary that, too. Some plants, like hostas and oakleaf hydrangeas, have very broad leaves. Your beds can become weighed down with a heavy look if all the plants you choose have equally bold foliage. Opt for some medium- or fine-textured plants to help lighten things up a bit. Threadleaf coreopsis (*Coreopsis verticillata*), for instance, has fine-textured leaves that can have a light, airy effect in the front of a border or garden. Even among trees, you can vary the foliage texture, from dainty fan-shaped leaves on ginkos to the very broad, dense leaves of maples.

Making It Happen

Depending on how extensive your landscape plans are, you may want to phase them in rather than tackle everything at once. Any safety issues should come first. Next, I find it most satisfying to work on the parts of the yard that will give me the greatest enjoyment, satisfaction, or relief for the least amount of time, effort, and expense. That way, I see results quickly and start to build some momentum. Another approach is to leave the most usable parts of your yard unchanged while working on other areas. If you can make do with the existing foundation planting, for instance, hold off on that while you focus on a play area or new patio.

TASK CHECKLIST

For each project you undertake, use the checklist below to make sure everything stays on track. For instance, if you forget to order a permit, you won't be able to build a deck, which in turn will delay installing the beds you've planned to surround the deck. You can eliminate the things that don't apply to your situation, but generally check the tasks off your to-do list in the order they appear. Your landscaping jobs will proceed smoothly, and you'll avoid unnecessary headaches and hassles.

- Obtain any necessary permits.
- Order your materials.
- Protect trees and transplant any plants that might be in the way.
- Remove unwanted plants or hardscape elements.
- Excavate or grade the area.
- Install utilities.
- Build hardscape items.
- Prepare and plant the beds.
- Plant any trees intended for lawn areas.
- Prepare and plant lawn areas.

Get a Jump on
New Trees

If you're facing a totally treeless yard and you're in need of some shady relief, you may want to get a jump on planting some trees. Even if the trees are for an area that's not first on your to-do list, planting them as early as possible can pay off. As long as they won't be in the way of major construction in the future, planting early will give trees a chance to become established and start growing while you work on the rest of your yard.

If you do go ahead and start off by planting new trees, just be sure to protect them so construction crews or equipment don't damage or kill them. See "Don't Disturb the Trees" on page 26 for steps to take to ensure the health and safety of both new and existing trees. After all, trees can be one of the most costly parts of your new landscape—you won't want to lose them.

Want More Help?

You've been mapping your property thinking about your wants and needs, even eyeing up some great-looking plants. But maybe you're still not quite sure your plan is exactly how you'd imagined. Well, if you'd like a bit more guidance, turn to "Landscaping Makeovers" on page 28. Here you'll find examples, including before and after looks of professionally designed landscapes. Each one describes what the homeowners were staring with and what they wanted to achieve. You'll find a suggestion or two, or even a whole backyard full of ideas that will work for you!

Don't *Disturb* the Trees

If you're making landscape plans that will involve major construction in your yard, think about your established trees before you finalize those plans. Heavy construction equipment can compact the soil around trees, and digging can tear up fragile tree roots. Both of these situations will create stress that most trees just can't take. You'll need to protect your trees as best as possible before construction begins. In addition, knowing a tree's chances for survival before you commit to having a front-end loader on your property may alter your decision about your final landscape plans. Some trees can adapt to the stresses of nearby construction better than others. Take a look at the lists that follow to see if any of the trees you need to protect are exceptionally tolerant—or intolerant—of construction-site stress.

Stress-Tolerant Trees

Silver maple (*Acer saccharinum*)

River birch (*Betula nigra*)

Catalpas (*Catalpa* spp.)

Hackberries (*Celtis* spp.)

Red or white cedars (*Juniperus spp.* or *Thuja spp.*)

Persimmons (*Diospyros* spp.)

Gingko (*Ginkgo biloba*)

Honeylocust (*Gleditsia triacanthos*)

Kentucky coffeetree (*Gymnocladus dioica*)

Sycamores (*Platanus* spp.)

Willows (*Salix* spp.)

Bald cypress (*Taxodium distichum*)

Elms (*Ulmus* spp.)

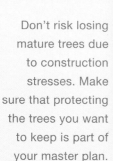

Don't risk losing mature trees due to construction stresses. Make sure that protecting the trees you want to keep is part of your master plan.

Stress-Susceptible Trees

Firs (*Abies* spp.)

Sugar maple (*Acer saccharum*)

Horse chestnut (*Aesculus hippocastanum*)

Paper birch (*Betula papyrifera*)

Flowering dogwood (*Cornus florida*)

Beeches (*Fagus* spp.)

Walnuts (*Juglans* spp.)

Tulip poplar (*Liriodendron tulipfera*)

Spruces (*Picea* spp.)

Pines (*Pinus* spp.)

Sourwood (*Oxydendrum arboreum*)

Hemlocks (*Tsuga* spp.)

Oaks (*Quercus* spp.)

If you're using a contractor for any of your landscape work, make tree protection part of the written contract, including the setup and removal of temporary barriers.

Whatever types of trees you have on your property, you'll need to be firm with contractors that you want physical barriers to protect them from harm while construction is going on. Be sure to get tree protection in writing in your contract. Without a contractual obligation, promises and assurances mean little once work crews show up and things get humming. You can unknowingly lose a valuable tree easily in one morning—although the injury may take several years to kill it.

Standard protection is a construction fence that extends at least to a tree's dripline. Other measures include preconstruction thinning to compensate for some root loss and limbing up to allow construction equipment to pass beneath. Hire a qualified arborist for both of these tasks. Mulching beyond the fencing to reduce soil compaction in root zones (feeder roots can be twice the distance of the trunk to the dripline) and watering to help trees through stress during dry weather are more steps you can take to protect your trees.

Specify ahead of time that you won't allow your contractor to store equipment or supplies under trees or permit employees to park in the shade under your trees. Additionally, if any grade changes are in the plans, make sure they minimize the changes to drainage patterns around the trees that you want to save.

Landscaping **Makeovers**

Now that you've gained some experience in plotting out your property and trying out design ideas, you're well on your way to creating the kind of backyard you've always wanted. If you'd like more help or ideas in formulating your master plan, take a look at the following landscape makeovers.

Revamping a Shady Yard

While this hardiness zone 5 landscape has good "bones," some of the existing plants aren't doing well in an area that has become progressively shadier over the years. Replacing some of the sun-loving plants and reducing the area of turfgrass for easier maintenance are two worthwhile goals for these homeowners.

WHAT WORKS AND WHAT DOESN'T

The large existing trees are in fine condition, and most plants are in scale with the house—few have grown "out of bounds." The landscape bed edges curve gently to accommodate mowing. This house has a nice view, which is open and not threatened by plants growing out of control. The plantings in the side yards are attractive and thriving.

BEFORE

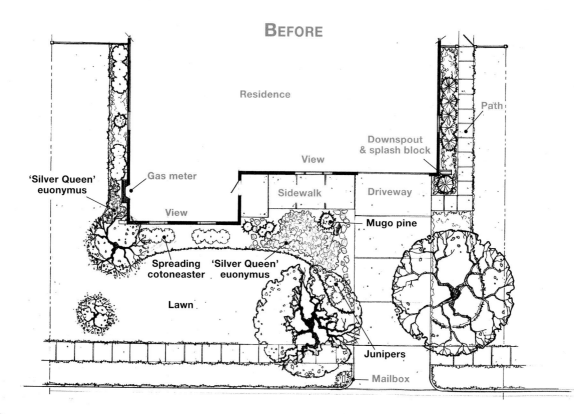

Residence

Path

Downspout & splash block

View

'Silver Queen' euonymus

Gas meter

Sidewalk

Driveway

View

Mugo pine

Spreading cotoneaster

'Silver Queen' euonymus

Lawn

Junipers

Mailbox

Because of its northern exposure and large trees, this front yard is richly shaded. The shade makes it a pleasant place to relax, but it's not the best spot for some of the plants currently living there. The junipers and cotoneasters both prefer full sun. In addition, the mugo pine and the euonymus are highly susceptible to pest problems.

THE NEW PLAN

Though the plant changes aren't extensive in this yard, the new plan will save the homeowner mowing time each week as well as time spent coddling plants that are pest-prone or intolerant of the shade. In the new plan, oakleaf hydrangeas (*Hydrangea quercifolia*) replace the cotoneasters along the front foundation, dwarf English yews (*Taxus baccata*) replace the junipers, and a yellow barrenwort (*Epimedium* × *versicolor* 'Sulphureum') groundcover takes the place of a portion of turfgrass. Spring bulbs planted along with the barrenwort will give a burst of color early in the growing season—before the buds break on the trees and shade the entire area. Periwinkle (*Vinca minor*) replaces some of the pest-prone euonymus in the side yard. Finally, a threadleaf maple (*Acer palmatum dissectum*) will act as a focal point.

AFTER

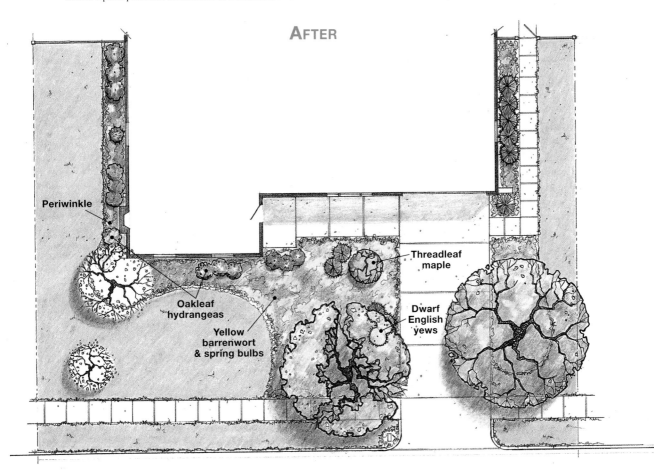

Periwinkle

Threadleaf maple

Oakleaf hydrangeas

Yellow barrenwort & spring bulbs

Dwarf English yews

Starting at Ground Zero with New Construction

The owners of this newly constructed home smartly declined the builder's offer to landscape their hardiness zone 5 property. All the other homes in the neighborhood were getting the full yew treatment. Instead, they opted to do it themselves. These homeowners have identified adding shade as a priority—both for outdoor comfort and to help save home cooling costs. Additionally, they'd like foundation plantings to help unify the house with the property around it.

WHAT WORKS AND WHAT DOESN'T

Since there are no plants on the property, it's hard to say that anything works! Starting with a blank canvas, however, is certainly less work than having to tear out plants you don't like. This house has a wide-open southern exposure that gets lots of sun. While this exposure is good for warming up the house in winter months, the beating sun makes it uncomfortable to sit outside in the summer. Because the soil is sandy loam, it won't retain water very long, so plant choices need to be ones suited to hot, dry conditions unless some shade is put in place fast.

BEFORE

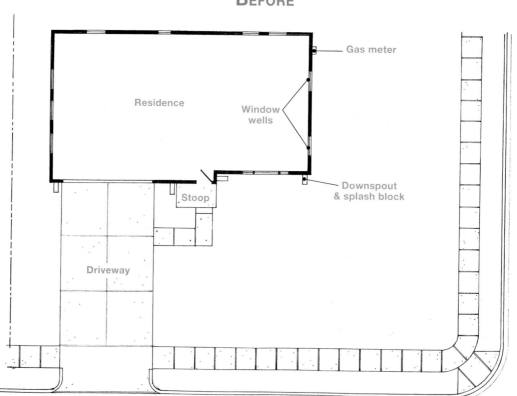

THE NEW PLAN

To create some "quick shade" without sacrificing long-term strength, these homeowners can plant one or more of the following deciduous trees for summer shade: white or green ash (*Fraxinus americana* or *F. pennsylvanica*), ginkgo (*Ginkgo biloba*), and Japanese zelkova (*Zelkova serrata*). Given the intensity of the summer sun—and its impact on cooling costs and on indoor and outdoor comfort—establishing shade trees is an important first step.

Foundation plants will be phase two. Their function is to visually connect the house with the ground, to hide any exposed foundation, to frame the house, and perhaps to accent the entryways. If you're facing this same situation, be sure to choose plants that won't crowd or outgrow the windows. Furthermore, resist the temptation to plant a foundation landscape that looks "finished." Instead, space shrubs and other plants far enough apart to allow for air circulation, room for growth, and maintenance access.

AFTER

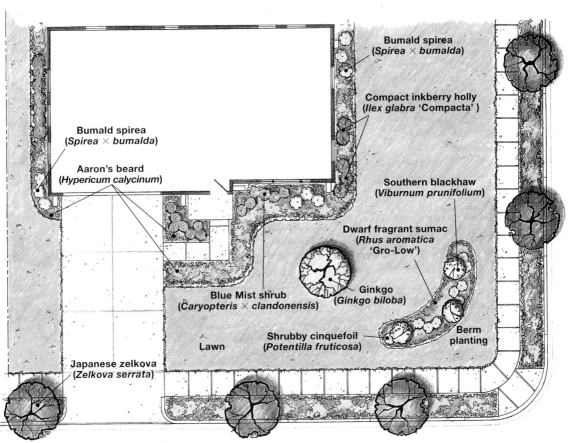

Bumald spirea
(*Spirea* × *bumalda*)

Compact inkberry holly
(*Ilex glabra* 'Compacta')

Bumald spirea
(*Spirea* × *bumalda*)

Aaron's beard
(*Hypericum calycinum*)

Southern blackhaw
(*Viburnum prunifolium*)

Dwarf fragrant sumac
(*Rhus aromatica* 'Gro-Low')

Blue Mist shrub
(*Caryopteris* × *clandonensis*)

Ginkgo
(*Ginkgo biloba*)

Shrubby cinquefoil
(*Potentilla fruticosa*)

Berm planting

Lawn

Japanese zelkova
(*Zelkova serrata*)

Uncluttering a Front Entryway

This hardiness zone 5 yard contains many nice landscape plants, but the overall look is much too busy. The retired property owners have said "enough!" to the demands of this crowded planting. Their goal is to simplify the front yard both in terms of how it looks and in how much time it takes to maintain the space.

WHAT WORKS AND WHAT DOESN'T

Tired of too many plants to care for and a somewhat overgrown and cluttered look, these homeowners want to scale back on their entryway landscaping. They plan to keep only the matching blue hollies on opposite sides of the front door. The owners want a clear view from the front door to the driveway as well as a view from the front window, so any replacement plants need to be shorter than what's in place now.

BEFORE

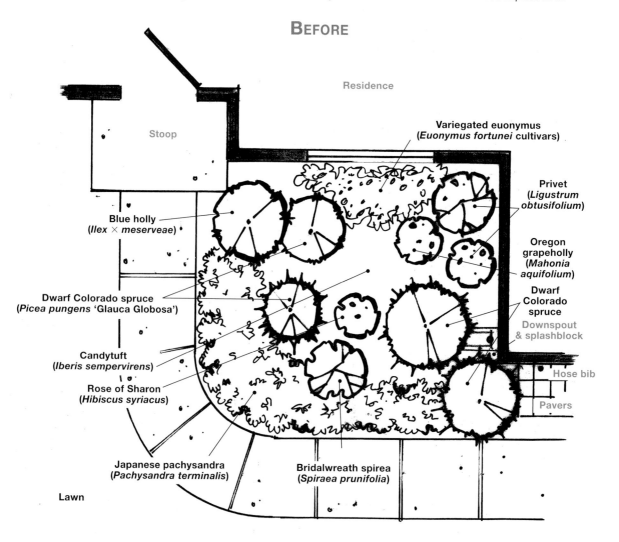

Residence

Stoop

Variegated euonymus
(*Euonymus fortunei* cultivars)

Privet
(*Ligustrum obtusifolium*)

Blue holly
(*Ilex × meserveae*)

Oregon grapeholly
(*Mahonia aquifolium*)

Dwarf Colorado spruce
(*Picea pungens* 'Glauca Globosa')

Dwarf Colorado spruce

Downspout & splashblock

Candytuft
(*Iberis sempervirens*)

Hose bib

Rose of Sharon
(*Hibiscus syriacus*)

Pavers

Japanese pachysandra
(*Pachysandra terminalis*)

Bridalwreath spirea
(*Spiraea prunifolia*)

Lawn

THE NEW PLAN

To simplify the property and add an air of elegance to their entryway, these homeowners decided to create a single focal point. They can choose either a specimen plant or sculpture and surround it with an interesting groundcover. Two good groundcover options are St.-John's-wort (*Hypericum calycinum*) or lilyturfs (*Liriope* spp.). Either way, they'll have a no-mow front yard. For a focal point, a dwarf Hinoki false cypress (*Chamaecyparis obtusa*) cultivar or an attractive, noninvasive ornamental grass or bamboo will do the trick.

AFTER

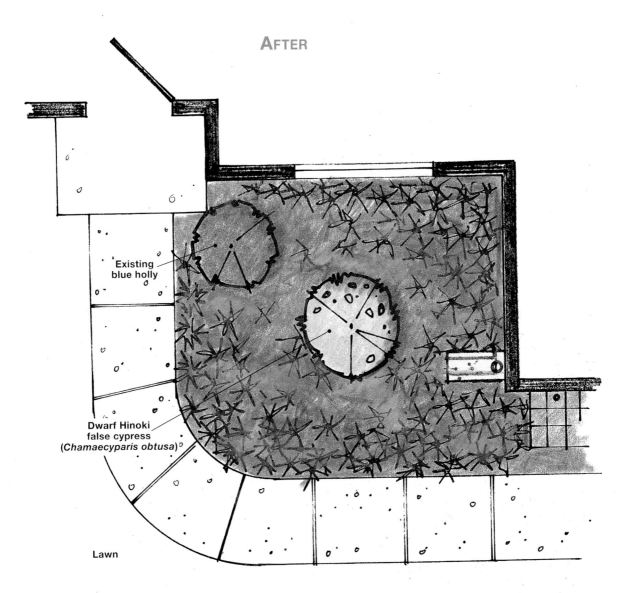

Existing
blue holly

Dwarf Hinoki
false cypress
(*Chamaecyparis obtusa*)

Lawn

Making Way for More Than a Pool

While many homeowners enjoy the benefits of a back-yard pool, landscaping around such a large object has some pitfalls. This family wants more from their hardiness zone 5 backyard than just an occasional swim. A vegetable garden, an attractive year-round landscape, low maintenance, and privacy are all on the wish list.

WHAT WORKS AND WHAT DOESN'T

The structure of this yard is defined by the pool and the required fencing. The beds and planters are work-able, but little attention has been given to edible

gardening or to the expected mature sizes of the pines that are already encroaching on the pool and the bench seating. On the other hand, the yew hedge behind the diving board works nicely as a screen.

A final concern is the foundation bed on the south side of the house. It's shaped with hard angles that make mowing more cumbersome than it has to be.

THE NEW PLAN

Adding raised vegetable beds in the southeast corner where they will be screened nicely by the yew hedge will yield fresh, organic produce throughout the summer. The white pines around the deck and pool

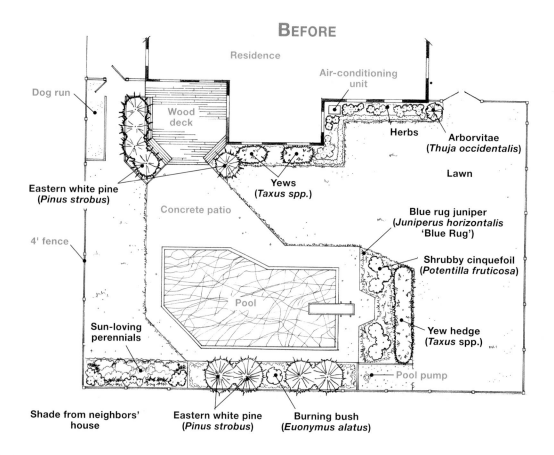

BEFORE

Residence

Air-conditioning unit

Dog run

Wood deck

Herbs

Arborvitae
(*Thuja occidentalis*)

Lawn

Eastern white pine
(*Pinus strobus*)

Yews
(*Taxus spp.*)

Concrete patio

Blue rug juniper
(*Juniperus horizontalis*
'Blue Rug')

Shrubby cinquefoil
(*Potentilla fruticosa*)

4' fence

Pool

Yew hedge
(*Taxus* spp.)

Sun-loving
perennials

Pool pump

Shade from neighbors'
house

Eastern white pine
(*Pinus strobus*)

Burning bush
(*Euonymus alatus*)

will have to go—they'll simply continue to grow and overtake the space. Because the glare of the setting sun off the west side of the deck is so harsh, the white pines will be replaced with evergreens that will serve a similar function but at a smaller mature size. Columnar 'Green Giant' arborvitae (*Thuja plicata* 'Green Giant') is a good option that will grow tall quickly but keep its narrow shape. South of the pool, a dark green and deeply textured dwarf Hinoki false cypress (*Chamaecyparis obtusa*) will make an excellent focal point against the back fence in both summer and winter, since it can be seen from deck as well as from inside the house. (While plant choices can vary, remember to avoid anything spiny, thorny, deciduous, or attractive to stinging insects near a pool!)

Other planned improvements include adding a compost bin in what had previously been dead space, replanting the perennial bed with more shade-tolerant plants, adding a bed for perennials and edibles along the east fence, and reconfiguring the foundation bed on the south side of the house so that mowing can go more smoothly. Mow strips where bed edges meet lawn will make mowing even easier. (See page 137 for ways to construct mow strips.)

AFTER

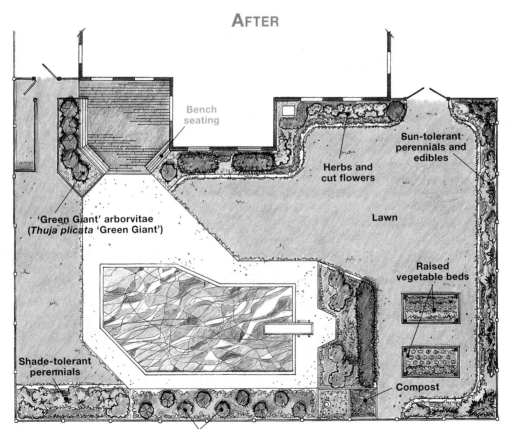

Bench seating

'Green Giant' arborvitae
(*Thuja plicata* 'Green Giant')

Herbs and cut flowers

Sun-tolerant perennials and edibles

Lawn

Raised vegetable beds

Shade-tolerant perennials

Compost

Dwarf Hinoki false cypress
(*Chamaecyparis obtusa* 'Nana Gracilis')

Creating Outdoor Living Space in a Wooded Property

This family choose a 6-acre wooded lot for its home and definitely has an interest in maintaining their hardiness zone 7 property in a natural state. Of course, they do need some cleared areas near the house for play, gardening, and outdoor living. Specifically, the owners would like to plant a foundation bed close to the house and create a courtyard in the back.

Before choosing what to clear and what to keep, it will be wise for the property owner to call a consulting forester to help identify options, goals, and the best management practices for the wooded areas. Top priorities will include keeping the slopes vegetated to prevent erosion, reducing the bramble growth so that the family can enjoy the woods, and protecting wellheads from contamination.

WHAT WORKS AND WHAT DOESN'T

This site features ridge-and-valley topography (in other words, it's hilly) and shallow clay soil with exposed rocks. Pines and brambles cover the south-facing slopes. In order to enjoy the woods, the owners will have to clear out the brambles and re-plant slopes to prevent erosion. With shallow soil and rocky terrain, planting won't be easy going.

Sweetgums, southern oak species, and mountain laurels all grow on the north slopes at the front of the house, making a secluded property, but also a shady front yard. When it comes to choosing plants for this area and the backyard, the homeowners will need to keep the northern and southern exposures in mind. Clay soil and an abundance of deer are two more critical factors that will affect plant choices.

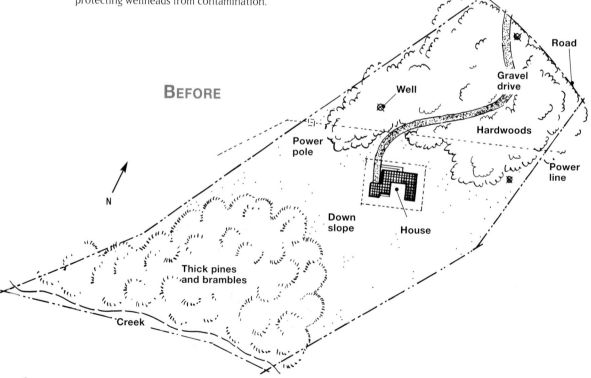

BEFORE

THE NEW PLAN

In the south-facing courtyard, dining and play are the main activities. By planting low-growing shrubs and perennials in this area, the parents can easily keep an eye on the courtyard (and their children) from the windows and patio doors.

Shade and shelter for the courtyard are critical, and trees such as sugar hackberry (*Celtis laevigata*), green ash (*Fraxinus pennsylvanica*), and sweetgum (*Liquidambar* spp.) are options for fast growth and long-term strength. Until the trees begin giving shade, a generous-size umbrella over the table—or a festive canopy—will give some relief. Even though this area will one day be shady, it's a good idea to start off with sun-tolerant plants. As the trees begin to shade the space, more shade-tolerant choices can replace the sun lovers.

In the shady front bed, wildflowers and ferns are a natural choice in this woodsy setting. Shade-loving perennials and groundcovers will also work nicely. Either way, it's important to dig in some organic matter to improve the compacted clay!

AFTER

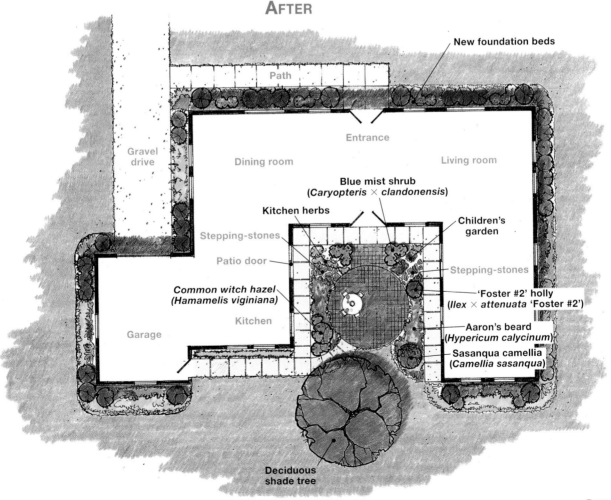

New foundation beds

Path

Entrance

Gravel drive

Dining room

Living room

Blue mist shrub
(*Caryopteris* × *clandonensis*)

Kitchen herbs

Children's garden

Stepping-stones

Patio door

Stepping-stones

Common witch hazel
(*Hamamelis viginiana*)

'Foster #2' holly
(*Ilex* × *attenuata* 'Foster #2')

Kitchen

Aaron's beard
(*Hypericum calycinum*)

Garage

Sasanqua camellia
(*Camellia sasanqua*)

Deciduous shade tree

Landscape Solutions for Problem Areas

Lots of homeowners are faced with less than ideal situations that they need to landscape over or around. Whether you have a constantly wet, low area or loud street noise to contend with, you can turn your problem spot into an asset. And if your "problem" is a small yard, I've got two possible solutions for you. You can either turn a tiny yard into a contained oasis or broaden your horizons—literally—by borrowing some of your neighbors' view.

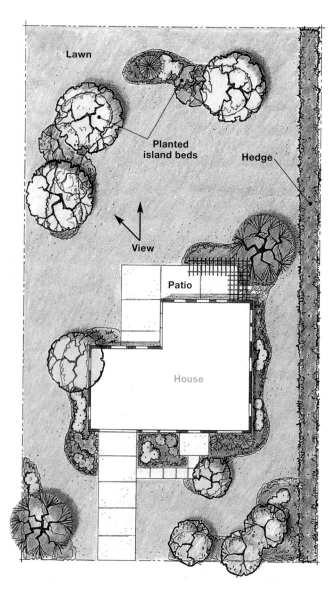

Lawn

Planted
island beds

Hedge

View

Patio

House

"Borrowing" Space from Your Neighbors

If your backyard is small, resist the temptation to regiment your lot line with a fence, hedge, or row of trees. While it creates privacy, what you're really doing is outlining and calling attention to the exact shape of your small lot.

Instead, try this design trick for the appearance of more space: Create one or more long flowing beds *inside* the lot line, and plant it naturalistically. Let the size and scale of your property help you determine the bed's size and distance from the lot line. For instance, if your property is only 30 feet wide, you won't want your bed to be 16 feet wide, or you'll just consume the entire backyard.

In the bed, plant trees that will eventually get large enough so that you'll be able to see beneath them and establish a groundcover or low shrub layer, as well. Your eye will be drawn to the planting, which will act as a focal point in your backyard. But since there's no fence or hedge acting as a barrier, you'll see past your plantings to take in the surrounding "borrowed" scenery. This bigger view will give you the effect of spaciousness, provided your neighbors have a backyard that's as attractive as yours.

Getting the Most from a Small Urban Lot

If your small property isn't surrounded by especially pretty views, which is sometimes the case in a tightly compacted urban setting, here's another way to deal with a small backyard.

This property includes a historic home on one narrow lot. The adjoining lot line and home to the south are just a few feet away, and most of that limited space is dedicated to paved walkway. Since that's not a particularly enticing view, this homeowner decided to create a more confined, private courtyard. The first thing you may notice about this property is that the owner smartly designed it with no lawn—there's just not enough space for it! Instead, the owner planted English ivy (*Hedera helix*) beneath the street trees and chose pavers surrounded by planting beds for the enclosed back courtyard. The pavers provide space for outdoor seating and entertaining without the fuss of having to move furniture to mow.

Plant selections for this shady site include Siberian carpet cypress (*Microbiota decussata*) on the east end of the courtyard to add an evergreen element for year-round enjoyment outside as well as from the kitchen window. The arrowwood viburnums (*Viburnum dentatum*) provide spring flowers, fall color, and tasty fruits for birds. In the sunnier spots, plants like purple coneflower (*Echinacea purpurea*) and threadleaf coreopsis (*Coreopsis verticillata*) also add color as well as nectar, seeds, and fruits for birds and butterflies, making this narrow property a haven for outdoor reading, relaxing, and watching nature.

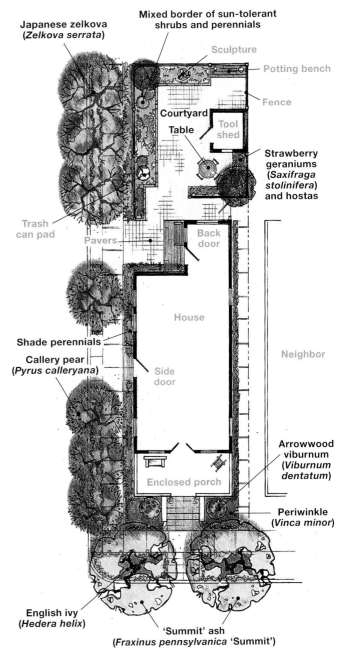

Japanese zelkova (*Zelkova serrata*)

Mixed border of sun-tolerant shrubs and perennials

Sculpture

Potting bench

Fence

Courtyard Table

Tool shed

Strawberry geraniums (*Saxifraga stolinifera*) and hostas

Trash can pad

Pavers

Back door

Shade perennials

Callery pear (*Pyrus calleryana*)

Side door

House

Neighbor

Arrowwood viburnum (*Viburnum dentatum*)

Enclosed porch

Periwinkle (*Vinca minor*)

English ivy (*Hedera helix*)

'Summit' ash (*Fraxinus pennsylvanica* 'Summit')

Transforming Rectangular into Informal

If you have a rectangular lot, planting along the lot lines can make your yard look rigid and formal. If you prefer a more informal, fluid style, it may seem like you're trying to put a round peg in a square hole, but don't worry. It can be done! What you lose in usable space, you can gain in wildlife habitat, cooling shade, runoff absorption (and less watering on your part), and even privacy. The trick is to establish a small oval- or kidney-shaped lawn, below. This will give you curved edges that you can plant around. Some planting areas will be deeper than others, as the curved outline of your lawn area ebbs and flows.

One mistake that homeowners are apt to make is overdoing the lawn area. It really needs to be just large enough for a pleasing visual effect and for play. That way, you'll have deep enough beds all around where you can surround the lawn with perennials, shrubs, trees, or edibles—whatever works for you. In the back corners, where the planting areas are especially deep, you can create a bird-feeding station, a secluded composting corner, a secret garden for yourself, or a special play area for your children.

Far from being "lost," the lawn space you give up will give back what some of our urban and suburban environments tend to take away: a bit of wildness. This is a great example of how your new backyard can give back!

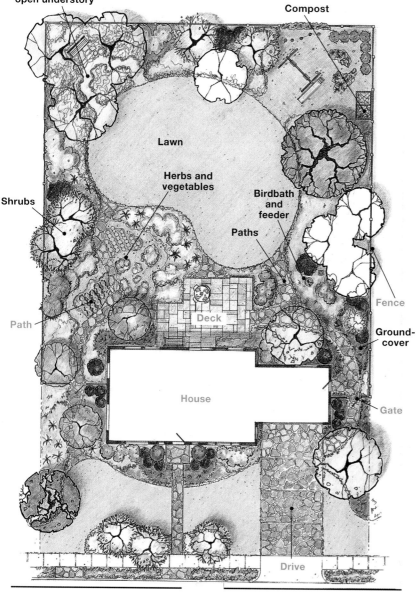

Trees, shrubs, open understory

Compost

Lawn

Herbs and vegetables

Shrubs

Birdbath and feeder

Paths

Path

Deck

Fence

Ground-cover

House

Gate

Drive

Replacing Weak Turf

Homeowners often knock themselves out trying to grow grass beneath a tree, which presents the double jeopardy of deep shade and competing surface roots. You may have limited success thinning the tree and removing lower limbs for more sunlight. However, the best and most sustainable approach is to replace the grass with a shade-tolerant groundcover.

Because you're likely to have limited planting space due to those vexing surface roots, choose a groundcover that can spread easily. You won't have room to plant lots of plants, so you'll need one that will cover lots of ground on its own. Barrenworts (*Epimedium* spp.), English ivy (*Hedera helix*), or lily-turfs (*Liriope* spp.) may work well, but check to make sure they're hardy in your growing zone and suitable for your particular conditions. Moss might be another option but only if your soil is acidic and compacted. For a burst of color each spring, slip in some compatible bulbs such as snowdrops (*Galanthus* spp.), miniature daffodils like 'Peeping Tom' (*Narcissus cyclamineus* 'Peeping Tom'), or Siberian squill (*Scilla siberica*). These early spring-flowering bulbs will be up and blooming before the tree leafs out.

Even if you weren't very successful at growing grass under the tree, there's probably still enough of it that you'll need to get rid of it before planting the groundcover. Shape your new groundcover bed so that the lawn mower can move freely. Then kill the grass within the bed boundaries by layering cardboard, black plastic, or newspaper over it, weighed down with rocks to hold it in place. It should take about 6 weeks to smother the grass and then you can plant your groundcover.

Tilling or even digging with a spade around tree roots isn't feasible, so do your best to tuck the plants into any available space using a trowel. Add a handful of compost or topsoil in each planting spot to give the roots something to grow in. Whatever you do, *don't* add soil over the tree's roots. Extra soil can smother the roots, which will eventually kill the tree.

Liriope adds color and interesting texture below a tree, and it's much easier to grow in this spot than turfgrass.

Making the Most of a Low, Wet Area

If you have a spot in your yard that's low and frequently or always wet, you may be looking at it as a problem area. That's certainly understandable if it's planted in turfgrass! In areas like this, grass will grow more quickly than in drier places, yet it will be harder to mow because the wet clippings will clog the mower and the tires will sink into the ground.

Provided that your low, wet area isn't right outside your door or part of a functioning drainage way, the solution is to treat it as a source of pleasure on your property rather than to try to grow grass. You can lure songbirds and butterflies with seed- or nectar-producing plants and invite frogs and other amphibians with cover. Your low, wet area will come alive with color, character, and movement.

Plant choices for wet conditions range from annuals and perennials to trees and shrubs. When selecting plants, remember to keep the other growing conditions in mind, too. For instance, is your wet area sunny or shady? Is it wet all year, or just sometimes? What's the soil pH, and is the soil sandy, loam, or clay? Some plant possibilities include wild ageratum (*Ageratum houstonianum*), Jack-in-the-pulpit (*Arisaema triphyllum*), swamp milkweed (*Asclepias incarnata*), sedges (*Carex* spp.), Joe-Pye weeds (*Eupatorium* spp.), swamp sunflower (*Helianthus angustifolius*), skunk cabbages (*Lysichiton* spp.), arrowheads (*Sagittaria* spp.), cattails (*Typha* spp.), and ironweeds (*Vernonia* spp.). If your wet area is large enough to accommodate shrubs, have fun with alders (*Alnus* spp.), sweetshrub (*Calycanthus floridus*), white fringe tree (*Chionanthus virginicus*), red- or yellow-twig dogwoods (*Cornus* spp.), winterberry holly (*Ilex verticillata*), spicebush (*Lindera benzoin*), or swamp azalea (*Rhododendron viscosum*). Some trees like soppy soil, too. Trees to consider include red maple (*Acer rubrum*), river birch (*Betula nigra*), persimmons (*Diospyros* spp.), larches (*Larix* spp.), sweetgums (*Liquidambar* spp.), magnolias (*Magnolia* spp.), black gum (*Nyssa sylvatica*), pin oak (*Quercus palustris*), and bald-cypress (*Taxodium distichum*).

A pretty garden in a low wet area offers lots of benefits and eliminates the hassle of trying to mow soggy turf.

Reducing Unwanted Noise, Glare, and Wind

Whether your goal is creating privacy, reducing noise or glare, or cutting down on excess wind, a berm can be the solution. Berms build height and provide interest in what might otherwise be a flat landscape. And for problem situations, they make effective barriers that can be much nicer to look at than a fence. The secret to using a berm is smart construction.

First, be sure you have the space you need for the height you want. For every foot in height, allow at least 4 feet in spread on either side (often called a 4-to-1 slope). A steeper slope tends to make a berm look dinky and out-of-scale, although you can use a 3-to-1 slope if the space is really tight.

Second, you need to compact the soil on your berm as you put layers of soil (every 4 to 6 inches) in place. Skipping this important step means that plants may settle too deeply as the soil settles naturally. A berm under 2 feet tall can settle on its own for several months if you'd rather not roll it. If you prefer to let it settle naturally, cover your berm with mulch, weighed-down newspapers, or cardboard, or cover it with a porous landscape fabric that will let rainwater through. This will prevent weeds from popping up and keep the soil from washing away.

Berms are usually most effective when planted heavily. After all, in addition to looking nice, their main function is to block sound, views, or wind. To do that, the plants should be close together but with spacing that allows for growth. For year-round coverage, consider wind- and drought-tolerant evergreens that are appropriate for your climate. Flowering and fruiting shrubs like viburnums (*Viburnum* spp.) and deciduous hollies (*Ilex* spp.) will add interest and invite wildlife. Also remember how stunning fall color can look against a backdrop of evergreens. For this effect, in addition to viburnums, think about adding amur maples (*Acer tataricum* subsp. *ginnaea*) or sumacs (*Rhus* spp.) to the mix.

If you're going to plant some or all of your berm with turfgrass, be sure to build it with that 4-to-1 slope to keep the mowing safe and easy. While a bermed slope may look innocent in dry, sunny weather, a bit of dew can make it treacherous for someone mowing.

A planted berm not only protects your property from strong winds and other harsh conditions, but it also improves your scenery.

CHAPTER 3

Choosing the Right Landscape Plants for Your Yard

What makes a **tree or shrub** right for your yard? How it looks obviously comes to mind. But beyond beauty, you should consider its **mature size,** its shape, its preferred growing conditions, how much **maintenance** it will require—and more—before you buy a plant and take it home. In this chapter you'll learn about all the things you need to be aware of before you **visit the nursery** or fall in love with a perfect specimen pictured in a catalog. You'll also find a **handy checklist** and a quick and easy flowchart to help you narrow your choices and make decisions about **which plants are best** for your situation.

Getting Started: **Understanding** What **Plants** Can Do for **Your Yard**

While there are lots of technical considerations for choosing plants, such as heat tolerance, soil pH, and so on, you first need to know what you're trying to accomplish. Perhaps you want a tree to shade your deck, or shrubs that will screen the unsightly view of your neighbor's trash cans, or a planting that will create a habitat for wild birds. In broad terms, you can use plants to define the physical space of your yard as well as to create artistic effects and a richer natural environment.

Once you learn about all the ways to use plants—everything from providing shade to directing breezes toward your patio—you can focus on your specific wishes for your yard and choose plants that can match those purposes. From there, you'll need to can narrow your list by eliminating plants that don't meet the basic conditions of your climate or of a particular spot in your yard. But to start, let's explore all the exciting ways you can use landscape plants to make your yard perfect for you and your family.

Using Plants to Reach Your Landscape Goals

Thinking about goals may seem a little intimidating, but you're already planning to make a change to your landscape for one reason or another. The more specific you are about what you want a plant to do, it's more likely that you'll be happy with the result. Below you'll find a number of ways you can use plants—some you're familiar with and some you may have never considered. Read through them to help you clarify exactly what you want for your backyard.

When you're thinking about what you want from a plant, be sure to take into consideration both how it looks (aesthetics) and what it can do for your yard (function). While functions can include shading for energy savings, stabilizing a steep bank, or creating privacy, the way a plant looks is important, too. So don't overlook bloom time, fall color, size, shape, and other physical characteristics. If you have a sentimental favorite that you'd like to include in your yard, put it to the test. See how it measures up to the purpose you want it to serve in your yard before you go ahead and plant it.

USING PLANTS TO CREATE A VISUAL FRAMEWORK

Focal point. Plants used as focal points need to be distinctive—they function almost as artwork or sculpture in your yard. A focal point is a plant that everyone will notice because it takes center stage.

You can't go wrong when you choose plants that match your growing conditions, available space, and family's needs. The result will be a beautiful, functional, and easy-care landscape.

Because they are so special, plants that make good candidates for a focal point usually don't function well in a mass planting. It's best to set off a single specimen in a small grouping of other plants. A nice example is Japanese cutleaf maple (*Acer palmatum* var. *dissectum*)—it has a striking form and beautiful leaves, and you can choose from a variety of foliage colors to suit your needs.

Accent. Plants that highlight a feature of your house or a focal point plant are called accent plants. You can use them to set off the entrance of your house, for instance, where they flank the entryway to welcome guests. Another way to use accent plants is to select plants with interesting color or different textures to enhance your landscape. Don't overdo it, though. Accent plants are distinctive—if you use too many of them, they'll no longer have any prominence.

Frame. You can use plants to frame your house or a focal point. Plants that are at least one-third taller than what they're framing work best, as well as those that don't tend to call too much attention to themselves. Think of them as supporting players, not the star.

Background. Background plants provide a total backdrop for other more colorful landscape features. Evergreens, such as 'Emerald' arborvitae (*Thuja occidentlais* 'Emerald'), are often used this way, since they can fill in the background with year-round color.

A spot in your landscape that you see quite frequently, such as the view from your deck, may be the perfect spot for a focal point plant, such as this Japanese cutleaf maple whose reddish foliage grows among the greenery.

Unifier. When repeated through the space, unifiers pull the composition together visually. Evergreens make great unifiers, as do plants that bloom for long periods, like abelia (*Abelia × grandiflora*) or potentilla (*Potentilla* spp.).

Mass planting. If you have a large property with an area that you'll be viewing from a distance, consider a mass planting. A group of several plants of one species can beautifully express features from a distance in ways that a single plant could not. For very large spaces, a massing of river birches or bald cypresses makes a wonderful impact. Shrubs like winterberry holly (*Ilex verticillata*), chokeberry (*Aronia* spp.), and fragrant sumac (*Rhus aromatica*) are also effective plants for massing.

Screen or buffer. You can use a group of plants to totally or partially obstruct a view. Tall, narrow

You can use plants to close off part of a large open space to create an intimate outdoor sitting room.

arborvitaes can fit this bill, but a border of mixed shrubs can make a more colorful, interesting screen if you have a wide enough space for planting.

Foundation. Foundation plantings visually connect the house with the ground and hide the foundation. Pay careful attention to mature sizes so you won't run the risk of plants that grow too large for the space and overwhelm the house. Depending on your window height and other details, plants such as Gro-Low sumac (*Rhus aromatica* 'Gro-Low'), dwarf inkberry holly (*Ilex glabra* 'Compacta'), or dwarf boxwood (*Buxus* spp.) are good bets.

USING PLANTS TO DEFINE SPACES

Traffic flow. Adults and kids alike, whether in cars, on bicycles, or on foot, need to know where to go and what's off limits. You can use plants to give directional signals as subtle or strong as you like. Just remember, when you use plants to act as barriers to certain areas, depending on the plant choices, they can also block your view.

Outdoor "room." Evergreens planted close together can create the privacy, security, and comfort of a secluded outdoor space or "room."

Control views. You can place plants strategically to direct the eye to desirable sights. You can also use plants to intentionally block a desirable view until you move your way through the landscape. Using plants in this subtle way is a rewarding design feat.

Groundcover. The most common plant for areas that get regular wear and tear is turfgrass. For areas that don't get heavy traffic, you have many additional choices, most of which require much less maintenance than grass. (See "Groundcovers" on page 82 for ideas.)

USING PLANTS TO IMPROVE YOUR ENVIRONMENT

Shade. Shade trees can make a property more comfortable indoors and out and help reduce your cooling costs.

Windbreak. In cold climates with open terrain, well-positioned evergreens can form windbreaks that can help reduce heating costs and add comfort.

Breezes. Sometimes all it takes to cool things off is to get the prevailing breezes to windows or porches. Cool breezes usually come from a different direction than the ones you want to block. You can use plants to direct and scoop that air toward desirable places. (See "Wind Scoops and Funnels" on page 108 for more details.)

Noise reduction. Dense landscape plants such as evergreens that are full all the way to the ground year-round can help to deaden traffic noise or other undesirable sounds.

Glare reduction. Protect the enjoyment of your property—both indoors and out—by using trees and shrubs to block the glare of paving, automobiles, and off-site lighting.

Air filter. Trees remove carbon from the air by taking up carbon dioxide, making air fit for us to breathe. In addition, the leaves help trap air pollution particles.

Erosion control. Plants can hold soil in place along a slope and prevent silt from building up in a creek, stream, or pond on your property and downstream.

Natural habitat. Plants, insects, and people all benefit when you restore or create a natural habitat. Native plants are one ingredient, but you don't have to limit your choices to plants that are native to your area. Simply arranging plants natu-

Evergreen trees and shrubs planted on a berm can help block street noise and activity.

ralistically—with shrubs and perennials planted under a tree canopy—can give the appearance of a more natural setting.

USING PLANTS FOR AESTHETICS

Keep this category in mind, but don't use it as your only selection criteria. No matter how beautiful a plant may be, its good looks can't make up for a landscape that doesn't function well day to day. That weeping cherry you plant may be simply stunning for a few weeks each spring, but if it outgrows its space, you'll spend the other 49 weeks of the year regretting your choice. Explore each of the categories below, but use them in conjunction with the other reasons for planting to ensure a perfect fit in your landscape.

Seasonal change. From spring blooms to fall leaves, choose how the color changes and other seasonal characteristics of a plant will blend with or accent your home and your other plants.

Wildlife. If your family would like to enjoy more of nature, select plants that birds can use for shelter, as well as those that provide food such as seeds or berries.

Color. Don't just think green! Foliage comes in many shades of green from yellow-green to deep blue-green. Plus you'll find plants with variegated foliage, red, purple, or bronze foliage, silver foliage, and more. Interesting bark colors and textures will add drama and interest to your landscape even in winter when most leaves are gone.

Movement. Whether it's an ornamental grass tossing in the wind or the drumming of rain on large-leaved plants like ligularias (*Ligulaira* spp.), movement adds a soothing aspect to your garden.

Fragrance. From foliage or flowers, fragrance can perfume a patio you use in the evening, as with moonflower (*Impomea alba*), or it can enhance an entire season, as with winter honeysuckle (*Lonicera fragrantissima* spp.).

Texture. Soft, hairy, crinkly, spiny—plants can offer such a variety of textures, both up-close and at a distance. A variety of textures will add interest to your landscape, but as with other features, choose some for repeating.

Refining Your **Plant List**

People often ask me, "How do you choose what tree or shrub to plant? There are so many choices!" Indeed there are. For instance, the Ohio Nursery and Landscape Association reports that there are nearly 2,000 types of woody landscape plants and 400 selections of perennials grown in that state alone. But finding the right plant for a specific part of your landscape doesn't need to be a hit-or-miss proposition. Once you know what you want and need from your landscape, all it takes to identify the perfect plants for your yard is a little bit of investigative work. First, you'll need to identify the specific growing conditions where you'll be planting. Then you can look for plants that offer what you want and that will thrive in the growing conditions in your yard.

To make narrowing down the choices easier, I've created a "Plant Selection Flowchart" on the opposite page. As you can see, you start by identifying your landscape needs. But even if you know you want an accent plant, there are still so many choices that you'll have to refine your list to make sure the final choice is right. Follow the steps in the flowchart to pare away plants that won't survive in your hardiness or heat zone, ones that won't thrive in the acid or alkaline soil you might have, or ones that simply require too much maintenance. Voilà! The plants remaining on your list should all be great choices for your yard.

Completing the Plant Selection Questions

Using the "Plant Selection Flowchart" can certainly make the job of narrowing down your choices easier. But it's only helpful if you can easily answer the questions on the chart. To help you accurately answer the questions it poses, read through the following descriptions. Once you have a better understanding of each of the issues you need to address, you'll be able to create a short plant list that's right on target.

Plant Selection Flowchart

Use the shorthand of this flowchart to help you choose the landscape plants best suited to your needs, available space, and growing conditions. You can also use it to evaluate a plant's odds for success if you've got a specific one in mind.

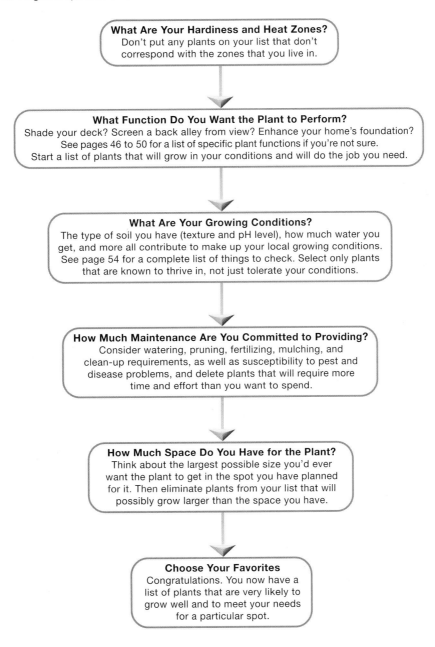

What Are Your Hardiness and Heat Zones?
Don't put any plants on your list that don't correspond with the zones that you live in.

What Function Do You Want the Plant to Perform?
Shade your deck? Screen a back alley from view? Enhance your home's foundation?
See pages 46 to 50 for a list of specific plant functions if you're not sure.
Start a list of plants that will grow in your conditions and will do the job you need.

What Are Your Growing Conditions?
The type of soil you have (texture and pH level), how much water you get, and more all contribute to make up your local growing conditions. See page 54 for a complete list of things to check. Select only plants that are known to thrive in, not just tolerate your conditions.

How Much Maintenance Are You Committed to Providing?
Consider watering, pruning, fertilizing, mulching, and clean-up requirements, as well as susceptibility to pest and disease problems, and delete plants that will require more time and effort than you want to spend.

How Much Space Do You Have for the Plant?
Think about the largest possible size you'd ever want the plant to get in the spot you have planned for it. Then eliminate plants from your list that will possibly grow larger than the space you have.

Choose Your Favorites
Congratulations. You now have a list of plants that are very likely to grow well and to meet your needs for a particular spot.

Understanding Microclimates

A microclimate is the climate of a small distinct area or space. The temperature, presence or lack of wind, amount of sun, and other varied conditions can cause an area to be one or more zones warmer or cooler than its surrounding area. For instance, a bed along a south-facing brick wall that soaks up the sun, warms early in spring, stays warm later in the fall, and bakes through the summer is very likely to be a full zone warmer than the rest of the yard.

Many things can affect the climate on your property. A garden shed that protects your yard from westerly winds, for example, or a creek that helps moderate the air temperatures can both tame your climate. By paying attention to microclimates, you may be able to include some plants that wouldn't normally grow in your hardiness zone. Northern gardeners might even be able to enjoy the company of a sentimental favorite, like a camellia. If you live in the Midwest, astonish your friends with pansies blooming through winter. Whether you use a bit of caution or creative zeal, a spot with an unusual microclimate is a place where you can garden with a spirit of experimentation.

It's easier to use the plant selector with the help of a good plant reference. Look for a reference book that lists plants by functions such as hedges, shade, or specimens. (See "Resources for Backyard Ideas" on page 256 for some suggestions.) Then you can start by listing all of the landscape plants for your hardiness and heat zone that can fit the bill. To get started, turn to Chapter 4 for a look at some reliable plants that have worked well for me.

Hardiness and Heat Zones

Not all plants can survive in all climates. Some prefer tropical-like heat while others can survive outdoors all winter long in subzero temperatures. To select plants that will survive in your climate, use the USDA Plant Hardiness Zone Map (see page 276), which is based on average annual low temperatures. You simply find your hardiness zone on the map, and then select plants that are hardy in the zone in which you live.

The AHS Heat Zone Map (see page 275), on the other hand, was developed by the American Horticultural Society. It looks at the average number of days that a region experiences temperatures above 86°F. Don't be surprised to find that you'll have two different zone numbers: one for hardiness and one for heat tolerance. The heat zone information is particularly helpful to southern gardeners who don't have to worry so much about whether or not a plant can survive freezing temperatures, but whether it will thrive in heat over long periods.

In general, if you buy only plants that fit your heat and hardiness zones, you'll avoid predictable hassles, such as regular watering of plants that require more moisture than your area gets, or extra winter care to protect a tree or shrub from freezing temperatures and drying winds. While adventurous gardeners sometimes successfully grow plants outside of these guidelines, it's best to save a marginal plant choice for a special sheltered spot where it won't require extra care.

Growing Conditions

While the hardiness of a plant is important, the specific growing conditions where you intend to plant a tree, shrub, or perennial are just as important. By that, I mean the soil conditions (its pH level, soil texture, and drainage), how much sun and shade the area gets, how windy it can become, and so on. You'll find an explanation of what to look for regarding specific growing conditions below. In addition, you can use the handy "Growing Conditions Checklist" on page 54 to evaluate and record the specific conditions where you'll be planting.

SOIL CONDITIONS

If you haven't had your soil tested recently, take a sample and send it to your state Cooperative Extension Service or local farm co-op for analysis. For a nominal fee, you can purchase a soil test kit that contains a bag with directions for taking and mailing the sample. Once the soil is tested, you'll receive results that show the pH level, fertility, and texture, as well as recommendations for soil management. I find county soil maps to be helpful, too, as they show the locations and characteristics of local soils. They're available at little or no cost from your county's Natural Resources Conservation Service (NRCS, formerly the Soil Conservation Service). Some communities even provide this information via the Internet.

For your plant list, it's wise to choose only plants that are compatible with your soil conditions. You can try to modify your soil, but it's a constant struggle to maintain it. A good plant reference book often provides lists of plants adapted to specific soils, which makes it easy to narrow down the choices.

DRAINAGE

Constant or frequent standing water is a make-or-break condition for many landscape plants. The good news is that there are perfectly great plants that actually *prefer* standing water. See "Making the Most of a Low, Wet Area" on page 42 for some suggestions of plants that grow best with wet feet. If you have wet areas, simply choose plants suited to that condition. Also, be sure you know the location of your septic field, if you have one, because maintenance on the septic field is inevitable! Unless you're game for ripping out your plants when the septic system needs repair, avoid planting over it.

SUN AND SHADE PATTERNS

Sun and shade patterns won't be constant on your property because day length changes through the year as does the angle of the sun. Deciduous trees can change the amount of sun and shade an area gets, too, as they grow and drop leaves. Take notice of how sunlight and shade move about your yard throughout the day at various times of the year, and jot down notes on your growing conditions checklist. Then eliminate any plants that aren't recommended for the amount of sun or shade on the exact spot where you want to plant.

Also pay attention to overhangs from buildings that can create "rain shadows." These spots can either bake in the sun or never see daylight, depending on which direction they face. Additionally, rainwater pouring over gutters in a heavy rain makes inhospitable conditions for plants. This type of space is off-limits for planting unless you specifically select plants that can withstand your extreme growing conditions, whether it's dry shade, baking sun, drought, or deluge.

GROWING CONDITIONS CHECKLIST

Photocopy this checklist to use for each area in your landscape where you intend to add plants. Then check off conditions that apply to a particular site. You'll be able to tell at a glance the exact planting conditions and select plants that are most likely to be top performers for that spot.

EXPOSURE

- [ ] North-facing
- [ ] South-facing
- [ ] East-facing
- [ ] West-facing

LOCATION

- [ ] Hilltop
- [ ] Hillside or slope
- [ ] Low spot
- [ ] Flat

PREVAILING WINDS FROM

- [ ] East
- [ ] West
- [ ] North
- [ ] South

WIND PROTECTION

- [ ] From building, fence, or other
- [ ] None

SOIL pH LEVEL

- [ ] _____

SOIL MOISTURE

- [ ] Standing water
- [ ] Wet
- [ ] Evenly moist
- [ ] Moderate
- [ ] Dry
- [ ] Extremely dry

SOIL TEXTURE

- [ ] Sandy
- [ ] Clay
- [ ] Loamy
- [ ] Humusy
- [ ] Rocky

SUN

- [ ] Morning
- [ ] Afternoon

SHADE

- [ ] Morning
- [ ] Afternoon
- [ ] Dappled shade
- [ ] Deep shade

OTHER CONDITIONS

- [ ] Auto exhaust
- [ ] Traffic
- [ ] Power lines
- [ ] Underground utilities
- [ ] Pedestrians
- [ ] Children playing
- [ ] Animals
- [ ] Ice-melting materials
- [ ] Vandalism
- [ ] Pool chemicals
- [ ] Damage from wildlife, such as deer
- [ ] Septic field

WIND PATTERNS

Is your planting site windswept, sheltered, or somewhere in between? For a windy or moderate spot, eliminate any plant from your list that requires shelter, such as Hinoki false cypress (*Chamaecyprus obtusa*) or aucuba (*Aucuba japonica* spp.). If your planting area is sheltered, just be sure to recognize any space limitations of the area.

PEOPLE FACTORS

Don't underestimate how people—your family members and others—can affect growing conditions. Wear-and-tear patterns of auto traffic, foot traffic, and children playing can all wreak havoc on plants in their way, so factor these activities into your landscape decisions. In addition, not all plants can stand up to salty conditions caused by snow- and ice-melting compounds or constant exposure to car exhaust. Make sure the plants you choose for roadside or sidewalk area plantings are up to the task. Litter is another consideration. Some plants like barberries (*Berberis* spp.) and cotoneasters (*Cotoneaster* spp.) collect it, so you might want to avoid them, too.

WILDLIFE FACTORS

If your area has a history of damage from deer, rabbits, or other animals, advice from your state's USDA Wildlife Services office will be helpful in shaping your plant list. See "Resources for Backyard Ideas" on page 256.

Maintenance Needs

One of the reasons it's so important to make the right plant choices is that you can minimize the amount of work or pampering you'll have to do. After all, the goal is to enjoy your landscape improvements—not

When space is tight, as in this courtyard, be sure to pay careful attention to a plant's mature size before planting.

become a slave to them! When you choose plants that are suited to their surroundings, they'll be able to thrive under the given conditions naturally. Watering, pruning, pest control, fertilizing, mulching, and cleanup work will become occasional tasks rather than daily or weekly chores.

WATERING

Assume that for the first summer or two, you'll need to water the plant to get it established. If you prefer to stop regular watering after that (and you can), then don't consider planting anything that requires more moisture than your ground or rainfall can provide.

Use Sprinkler Systems Wisely

The best kind of watering is a good soak to the root zone rather than wetted foliage. If you have a system that uses overhead sprinklers, avoid any plants that are susceptible to fungal diseases. Otherwise, leaf spots, blights, and other fungus problems are sure to develop with the constant wetting that even a well-managed sprinkler system causes. The best bet is to choose plants that can thrive with the amount of moisture your climate gets. That way, you can just leave the system off or use it only for emergencies.

PRUNING

To avoid unnecessary pruning or ultimately having to remove an overgrown plant, make sure you choose a plant that won't grow larger than the space you have planned for it. Physical barriers such as fences and walls are easy to identify as space limits. Look for less obvious barriers, too, such as overhead utility wires, sidewalks, and patios. Also think about where you might have invisible barriers, such as drainage fields and underground utilities. Resist the temptation to plant anything that—no matter how long it takes—will eventually outgrow its space, run afoul of utilities, or obstruct a desired view such as into the front door and out of your kitchen window. It's always surprising how soon tomorrow comes!

Plants with neat, compact, dwarf, or slow-growing characteristics are excellent options for limited spaces. You'll need to do occasional renewal pruning on most shrubs to remove a few of the oldest branches at ground level, but avoid plants that need constant shearing or shaping. When it comes to trees, think about future maintenance now, too. If you plant a tree in the lawn or near a sidewalk, will you want to remove lower limbs in future years for clearance? Or can you live with a variety that will naturally brush the ground? Finally, avoid trees with a tendency to produce weak wood or unstable structural characteristics,

Some trees like beeches (*Fagus* spp.), lindens (*Titia* spp.), and pin oaks (*Quercus palustris*) have branches that naturally sweep the ground as these pin oaks do. If you have the room to accommodate them, they'll not only look great but also help you reduce mowing, mulching, and pruning.

"Not in *My* Lifetime!"

such as 'Bradford' pear (*Pyrus calleryana* 'Bradford') and silver maple (*Acer saccharinum* spp.), and you'll be eliminating pruning headaches and ultimately tree removal.

PEST AND DISEASE CONTROL

You can also shorten your plant list by eliminating plants that are certain to attract pests or that are susceptible to diseases. Instead, focus on plants that have demonstrated resistance to insect and disease troubles in your region. (Your local Cooperative Extension office can often provide lists based on research done in your state.) You might be tempted to make a rare exception for a plant that you just can't live without, but plan on some extra work and be ruthless regarding all your other selection criteria. If you give in on pest problems, pruning needs, and water requirements, your choice will soon be a plant you can't *wait* to live without.

MULCHING AND FERTILIZING

You can easily reduce mulching and fertilizing chores by grouping plants in beds or masses that include low-growing shrubs and groundcovers that will eventually fill the bed. Once they grow together, they'll conceal leaves and other litter dropped by the plants above them. As long as the trees or shrubs have small leaves that won't smother the groundcover (in other words, sycamores aren't a good choice!), you can leave fallen leaves in place

As gardeners, we find it so tempting to plant for a fairly instant effect that we sometimes don't think about the long-term consequences. When it comes to trees, taking the future into consideration before we plant really is a must. After all, these plants can grow to more than 100 feet and live way beyond our lifetimes.

Many hazardous trees exist today because someone a generation ago, when considering a tree that might someday grow into nearby power lines or house eaves, said, "Not in *my* lifetime!" Let your trees be a blessing to future generations, rather than an unnecessary danger, headache, or expense. Make a choice based on the mature size because the future needs all the safe, healthy trees it can get.

where they'll break down and feed the groundcover and other plants in the bed. Of course you'll be mulching—and weeding—while the groundcover gets established, but the investment will pay off when the bed fills in. See Chapter II for additional tips on making shorter, easier work of that mulching job.

HUNGRY GROUNDCOVERS, TASTY TREES

With a savvy combination of small-leaved trees and coarse-textured groundcovers, you may be able to avoid some fall cleanup and build organic matter into your soil as well. The trick is to use a groundcover that has the ability to "swallow" the leaves in combination with a tree with small leaves. Some groundcovers that work well for this purpose include English ivy (*Hedera*

Choosing Annuals

Just as with any other type of plant, if you like to make colorful annuals part of your landscape, you'll want to get the greatest visual impact while keeping maintenance to a minimum. Your selection of annuals obviously isn't as critical as it is for long-lived plants. The investment isn't huge, and you won't have long-term worries or maintenance with annuals. However, you'll still want to get a big impact from the annuals you choose, so look for long-blooming varieties, and consider these additional angles for stunning, undemanding plants.

Growing Conditions

Even though annuals will be replaced every year, choose annuals that will thrive under the conditions of your chosen spot. You especially won't want to waste time coddling annuals. Just as with other plants, some annuals grow better in full sun, while some prefer shade. Some like constantly moist conditions, while others have no problem baking in full sun all day. Make a short list of appropriate flowers before you open the seed catalog or head for the garden center. Your Cooperative Extension office is an excellent source for this plant information.

Viewing Distance

For a bed that you'll view from more than a stone's throw away, consider hot colors—reds, oranges, hot pinks, and yellows. They'll show up better because they appear to advance toward you as you view them. For a garden that you will enjoy up-close, such as alongside a patio, cooler colors such as soft pinks, lavenders, and blues make nice choices.

Desired Height

Annuals don't have to stay down around your ankles! Add some dramatic eye-level appeal with spider flower (*Cleome hassleriana*), plume poppy (*Macleaya cordata*), castor bean (*Ricinus communis*), Mexican bush sage (*Salvia leucantha*), or Mexican sunflower (*Tithonia rotundifolia*).

Night Viewing

Will the flowerbed you're planning have evening company? Blues, yellows, whites, silvers, and grays all show up well under dusky conditions. Choose plants with flowers or foliage of these colors and you'll be planting enchantment. Also opt for plants that release fragrance at night, such as moonflower (*Ipomea alba*) or nicotiana (*Nicotiana alata*). Even when it's too dark to see them, you can still enjoy their beautiful aromas.

helix), St.-John's-wort (*Hypericum calycinum*) where it's evergreen, and Japanese spurge (*Pachysandra terminalis*). Small-leaved trees for this situation include juneberries (*Amelanchier* spp.), honey locust (*Gleditsia triacanthus*), and Chinese scholar tree (*Styphnolobium japonicum*).

LITTER

Peeling bark from sycamores, seed capsules from sweetgums, and even pinecones may call for constant cleanup. If your property is large or rural, this may not be a worry because the size and nature of the setting may make the plant-litter issue delightfully irrelevant. If you live in town, however, safety issues may arise with rotting crabapples attracting wasps or sweetgum balls cluttering sidewalks and driveways. You can avoid repeated weekend cleanups by choosing plants that produce minimal litter.

What's Left on Your List?

If you've edited your plant list ruthlessly as you answered all the questions on the plant selector chart, you probably have only a handful of plants left on your list. If you still need to pare down, double check watering needs, maintenance demands, mature size, and soil and sun requirements. Scratch off any plants that you just don't like (if they've gotten this far), and you should have an awesome list of plants that will be sure to perform well in your situation.

Landscape Plants
at a **Glance**

Once you've identified where you **want to plant**—and what purpose you have in mind for that planting—you can use this handy **plant directory** to select the right plants for the job. From **trees** and shrubs to groundcovers and **vines,** to perennial and annual **flowers,** you'll find dozens of top-notch plant picks in this chapter. Each entry is packed with information to help you narrow down your **choices** to plants that are best suited to your growing conditions and your needs.

Kris's **Top** Plant **Picks**

With hundreds of plants to choose from, narrowing your list down to one or two choices can seem daunting. You may feel like you have to do so much research, you'll *never* actually get around to planting. To help you move more quickly to the final stage of selecting the right plants, I made my own list of great landscape plants, which I've whittled down to just 10 or so of each plant type: trees, shrubs, groundcovers, vines, perennials, and annuals.

To make it onto my list, plants have to be generally resistant to pests and diseases, create minimal litter to clean up, and have tough constitutions so you won't have to spend time coddling them. Another important factor is that many (but not all) of them have compact growth, which will help reduce maintenance and let the plants grow naturally without pruning or transplanting even on small properties.

Most of the plants on my list are suitable for a wide geographic range of North America (spanning USDA Plant Hardiness Zones 3 through 9) and a variety of conditions including sun; shade; wet, dry, and poor soils; dry climates; and damp climates. I favor plants native to North America and especially those that possess a wonderful capacity to "give back," whether it be offering food and cover for wildlife or enriching our environment with cooling shade, soil erosion prevention, or improved air quality.

Of course, my choices won't cover every angle for every location. You may find a plant listed here that's simply a bad choice for your area. And there are surely plants that are wonderful for your climate and situation that I haven't picked. So use this chapter as a guide, but don't be limited by it or afraid to explore beyond my recommendations. Pair my list with information from local resources such as your Cooperative Extension office, public gardens, arboreta, as well as other gardeners, and you'll be on your way to discovering some great plants that can enrich your home landscape.

Fiveleaf akebia

Astilbe

Black haw

Sweet autumn clematis

Japanese zelkova

Mexican sunflower

Bald cypress

Morning glory

Amur maple

AMUR MAPLE

Amur maples make a big splash in mass and provide good company in a small space.

ACER TATARICUM SUBSP. GINNALA

This tough, attractive little maple bears fragrant but inconspicuous flowers in early spring, but it's the reds and oranges of its leaves in the fall that make it a standout. Choose a single trunk or the clump variety.

Uses: Focal point for small-scale area; massing; screen

Size: 15 to 20 feet tall and about as wide

USDA Plant Hardiness Zones: 3 to 7

AHS Heat Zones: 7 to 1

Preferred Site: Full sun to partial shade; even moisture with good drainage

Other Planting Options: Amur maple will grow in a wide range of soil types and pH levels. It can also grow well in partial shade but may not produce striking fall color in that location.

Growing Guidelines: Prune as necessary to develop the tree's form to your liking—open and up off the ground, or low and shrubby.

Pest and Disease Prevention: No serious pest or disease problems

Special Tips: Fall color isn't consistent throughout the species, so choose this plant at a local nursery in the fall, when you can be sure you're getting one with superb fall color.

Related Plants: 'Flame' is a cultivar that produces red fruit and fiery red fall foliage.

RIVER BIRCH

River birch is a fine native tree suitable for large-scale sites, especially wet ones!

BETULA NIGRA

Peeling bark in shades of pink make river birches appealing trees in all seasons. It's a relatively quick grower that can reach 30 to 40 feet in just 20 years. River birches can be found with a single trunk or in clump form with multiple trunks. Leaves turn yellow in fall.

Uses: Massing in marshy area has a subtly striking effect; single focal point at close range; food plant for several species of North American butterflies

Size: Up to 60 feet tall and almost as wide

USDA Plant Hardiness Zones: 4 to 8

AHS Heat Zones: 7 to 2

Preferred Site: Full sun; moist to swampy soil

Other Planting Options: River birch can withstand periodic flooding, standing water, and a pH level of 6.5 or lower.

Growing Guidelines: Prune as necessary to develop the tree's form to your liking: You can remove the lower limbs or let them naturally sweep the ground.

Pest and Disease Prevention: No serious pest or disease problems

Special Tips: River birches look very innocent in the nursery, causing people to plant them right next to their house, often at the corner of a foundation planting. Knowing their mature size will make you think twice before you plant one there!

Related Plants: The river birch cultivar 'Heritage' has nearly white bark and is a good substitute for paper birch (*B. papyrifera*), which is pest prone.

WHITE FRINGE TREE

CHIONANTHUS VIRGINICUS

Plant this focal-point tree where you can enjoy its white flowers, which are both attractive and fragrant. White fringe tree blooms in midspring, and the leaves turn yellow in fall. Female trees develop purplish blue grapelike fruit in the fall that are appealing to birds. The habit of this small tree can vary, but it's normally low-branched and shrubby.

Uses: Focal point for a small-scale area; massing; food source for birds

Size: Up to 30 feet tall and about as wide

USDA Plant Hardiness Zones: 5 to 8

AHS Heat Zones: 9 to 1

Preferred Site: Full sun with moist, well-drained humusy soil

Other Planting Options: White fringe tree can adapt to a wide range of soil pH levels.

Growing Guidelines: You can either prune lower branches to develop a more open, treelike appearance or let the plant grow low and more shrubby.

Pest and Disease Prevention: No serious pest or disease problems

Special Tips: May also be sold in nurseries or catalogs as grancy gray-beard or old-man's beard

White fringe tree is a beauty in spring and has many other fine qualities.

KOUSA DOGWOOD

CORNUS KOUSA

Kousa dogwood is both handsome and superior to flowering dogwood (*C. florida*) because it's more resistant to diseases and the white flowers, which are profuse in late spring to early summer, hold well. On older trees, the bark peels to reveal patches of tan and cream. Kousa dogwood bears berrylike fruit that turn from hard green to spongy pink as autumn approaches, and the leaves turn reddish in fall.

Uses: Focal point for a small-scale situation; on a large property, kousa dogwood can be stunning planted in a mass.

Size: Up to 20 feet tall and about as wide

USDA Plant Hardiness Zones: 5 to 8

AHS Heat Zones: 8 to 3

Preferred Site: Full sun to partial shade; humusy soil with even moisture and good drainage, protected from wind

Other Planting Options: Kousa dogwood can tolerate sun and drought much better than flowering dogwood (*C. florida*).

Growing Guidelines: This tree tends to be low-branched. Prune away low branches if you want to be able to walk beneath it.

Pest and Disease Prevention: No serious pests or disease problems; resistance to dogwood anthracnose makes it a better choice than flowering dogwood in most areas. Also, it's rarely attractive to deer.

Special Tips: Sometimes found under the common names of Japanese dogwood or Korean dogwood

Related Plants: 'Milky Way' is known for its abundant flowers.

Kousa dogwood tolerates harsher conditions—sun, drought, pollution—than the native flowering dogwood, making it a better choice for many situations.

GINKGO

GINKGO BILOBA

Don't let the pretty fan-shaped leaves fool you. The fine texture of the ginkgo's leaves belie its toughness. A ginkgo is massive at maturity, so choose its site wisely. Leaves are bright green and turn a spectacular bright yellow in the fall.

Little else matches the majesty of a mature ginkgo in the fall.

Uses: Shade, focal point, or street tree in a large-scale setting

Size: 80 feet tall or more; the spread depends on the cultivar

USDA Plant Hardiness Zones: 4 to 7

AHS Heat Zones: 9 to 3

Preferred Site: Full sun, deep soil, good drainage, plenty of space

Other Planting Options: Ginkgos can withstand air pollution, heat, drought, and a wide range of soil pH levels, which is why they're so popular as street trees.

Growing Guidelines: Prune young trees for future structural stability by removing dead, crossing, or rubbing branches any-time you see them, as well as gradually re-moving limbs to create an open scaffold structure.

Pest and Disease Prevention: No serious pest or disease problems

Special Tips: Female ginkgos produce a foul-smelling, messy fruit. Female trees are rare in the North American nursery trade because avoiding the stink and mess of the fruit is a top priority with most buyers.

Related Plants: Consider 'Autumn Gold' for full form and good fall color; 'Princeton Sentry' has a columnar form, which makes it a good choice for tight spaces. Both are male cultivars.

KENTUCKY COFFEETREE

GYMNOCLADUS DIOICA

Kentucky coffeetree is a large, open tree for a large-scale situation. Its compound leaves give a fine-textured, tropical appearance during the growing season, and after the leaves drop, the tree looks stark and stubby in winter. Female trees bear leathery pods that are interesting to look at but a mess to clean up when they drop.

Shady in summer and stark in winter, Kentucky coffeetree is durable and interesting in the landscape.

Uses: Shade tree

Size: Height to 80 feet; spread normally narrower than height

USDA Plant Hardiness Zones: 4 to 7

AHS Heat Zones: 9 to 2

Preferred Site: Full sun and deep soil with good drainage on a large site; with the annual drop of leaves and seedpods, this isn't a tree for a small property.

Other Planting Options: This is one tough tree that can withstand drought, and pollution, as well as a wide range of pH levels.

Growing Guidelines: Prune only for form and future structural stability as needed. (See Ginkgo entry for details.)

Pest and Disease Prevention: No serious pest or disease problems

Special Tips: The common name of this tree came from the early colonial use of its seeds for a coffee bean substitute, a practice that was curtailed when imported coffee became widely available. The roasting of the beans is thought to have destroyed the harmful alkaloid called cystin, which is contained in the leaves, pods, and seeds. This alkaloid has been known to poison cattle, so don't plant this tree where it could pose a risk to livestock.

ARISTOCRAT PEAR

PYRUS CALLERYANA 'ARISTOCRAT'

Like the popular cultivar 'Bradford', the 'Aristocrat' callery pear has a neat, upright, pyramidal form, but 'Aristocrat' is a much sturdier tree because its branches form wider crotches that aren't prone to splitting. White flowers—considered strong- or foul-smelling by some folks—appear in early spring, normally before the leaves emerge. Fall color appears late, in reds, oranges, and yellows, depending on the weather. It bears small (½-inch), brownish fruit that are inconspicuous and require little cleanup.

With its neat form and tidy habit, 'Aristocrat' pear is perfect for a smaller site. Its leaves are among the last to turn color and drop in the fall. The fruit hang on well into winter and, as they ripen on the tree, are often eaten by birds.

Uses: Small shade tree; street tree; focal point; food source for some birds, such as robins, which eat the fruit.

Size: Height to 40 feet; spread proportionally narrower than height

USDA Plant Hardiness Zones: 5 to 8

AHS Heat Zones: 8 to 2

Preferred Site: Full sun with good drainage

Other Planting Options: 'Aristocrat' pear can adapt to a wide range of soil pH levels, drought, and pollution.

Growing Guidelines: Prune for structure by removing branches that form narrow crotch angles.

Pest and Disease Prevention: Though callery pears are generally resistant to pests and diseases, they can contract fireblight, depending upon the spring weather conditions. To prevent this problem, prune for good air circulation (at anytime but spring) and remove leaf litter in the fall. Protect young trees from deer. (See "Controlling Animal Pests" on page 216.)

Special Tips: The early flowering of 'Aristocrat' pear can sometimes make it vulnerable to a spring freeze, which means no flowers for that year. Additionally, a summer drought followed by fall rains may bring on sporadic fall flowering, a curiosity that's not harmful to the tree.

Related Plants: 'Cleveland Select', also called 'Chanticleer', is a comparable cultivar.

BLACK HAW

VIBURNUM PRUNIFOLIUM

When you don't have room for a lot of trees, you want to be sure the ones you do plant will make a big impact. Black haw is a proven performer that offers year-long appeal, making it a good choice for small properties.

If you're looking for a small tree, you can hardly go wrong with the native black haw. This round-headed tree bears white flowers in midspring, with or after the leaves. In the fall, leaves turn to shades of purple or red (color varies from plant to plant) and are accompanied by blue-black fruit that birds love. Black haws are available with a single trunk or in multiple-trunk clump form.

Uses: Naturalizing; focal point; food source for birds; the genus *Viburnum* is one of several that are food plants for the Henry's elfin and spring azure butterflies.

Size: 18 to 20 feet tall and almost as wide

USDA Plant Hardiness Zones: 3 to 8

AHS Heat Zones: 9 to 1

Preferred Site: Sun or shade; well-drained soil

Other Planting Options: Black haw adapts to a wide range of soil pH levels and can withstand drought.

Growing Guidelines: You can either let your tree grow low and shrubby, or prune it (gradually) to remove the lower limbs and create a more open tree form.

Pest and Disease Prevention: No serious pest or disease problems

Special Tips: This small tree has year-round appeal and many great qualities, including adaptability, toughness, and low maintenance.

Related Plants: Southern or rusty black haw (*V. rufidulum*) is less hardy than black haw (Zones 5 to 9) but is similar in size and shape. Its buds are covered with short, rusty brown hairs that are the source of its common name.

BALD CYPRESS

TAXODIUM DISTICHUM

There are few better trees for a pond edge than bald cypress.

When young, common bald cypress has a pyramidal shape, but it grows more irregular and interesting-looking with age. Yellow-green needlelike leaves appear in early spring, but don't be fooled. This needle-bearing tree will change color to russet brown and drop its foliage in the fall. Round, 1-inch cones turning from green to brown appear late in the growing season. Older trees in wet sites often form interesting-looking buttress roots and protruding "knees" at the soil or water level.

Uses: Shade tree; focal point; naturalizing on a larger site

Size: About 70 feet tall in the landscape; taller in the wild; width is proportionately narrower than height.

USDA Plant Hardiness Zones: 5 to 9

AHS Heat Zones: 12 to 5

Preferred Site: Full sun; even soil moisture; away from reflected heat

Other Planting Options: Common bald cypress can easily withstand saturated soil as well as occasional drought and wind.

Growing Guidelines: Prune only to manage the ultimate height of the lowest limbs and to remove dead wood.

Pest and Disease Prevention: Avoid spider mite infestations by planting common bald cypress away from the reflected heat of pavement and cars. Galls may occasionally form, but they're rather inconspicuous and aren't life-threatening.

Special Tips: In the wild, this native tree grows almost exclusively on swampy ground. However, in the landscape, it has become a proven performer on moderate soils. Of course, it's not a good choice if you live in an area that is susceptible to drought.

Related Plants: 'Prairie Sentinel' has a narrow, columnar shape.

JAPANESE ZELKOVA

ZELKOVA SERRATA

While it's not quite an elm, Japanese zelkova has a similar, large, vase shape with serrated leaves that turn yellow-orange to russet in autumn. After the leaves drop, you can still enjoy this tree's pretty shape as well as the interesting mottled bark that develops on older trees.

Uses: Street tree; shade tree; focal point

Size: 50 to 80 feet tall, with a spread about as wide

USDA Plant Hardiness Zones: 5 to 8

AHS Heat Zones: 9 to 5

Preferred Site: Full sun with even moisture and good drainage

Other Planting Options: Japanese zelkova can tolerate a wide range of soil pH levels, drought once it's established, and pollution and other urban conditions.

Growing Guidelines: Little pruning is necessary unless it's to promote future structural stability or to open the crown of a mature tree for improved air movement. See Chapter 10 for more information.

Pest and Disease Prevention: No serious pest or disease problems.

Japanese zelkova has shown good resistance to both elm leaf beetle and elm bark beetle, as well as Dutch elm disease problems that have plagued its relative, the American elm. Young zelkovas, however, can suffer from freeze injury in sudden or severe winter weather, so be sure to follow the hardiness zone recommendations and don't plant this tree in an unprotected, wind-swept site.

Special Tips: You might also find this plant sold under the common name sawleaf zelkova.

Related Plants: Consider the cultivars 'Halka' or 'Green Vase' for quick growth and graceful form. 'Village Green' is also a fast grower, but it has a stiffer, more upright shape.

Some folks consider Japanese zelkova to be a substitute for the endangered American elm, but it has much to offer on its own merits.

GLOSSY ABELIA

ABELIA × GRANDIFLORA

Loosely arching, semievergreen branches bear fragrant pink or white tubular flowers. Glossy abelia blooms in late spring and sporadically through summer, providing a long season of flowers and fragrance. Glossy abelia is the hardiest of all the abelias. Its leaves may last all winter in the South, but in colder climates, leaves will turn bronze or fall off.

Glossy abelia's compact but informal character makes it useful in many settings. Blooming lightly through the hot summer months, glossy abelia provides interest during times when most other trees and shrubs are through blooming.

Uses: Low hedge; foundation planting; shrub or mixed border; large-scale groundcover; also a nectar source for some butterflies

Size: 4 to 6 feet tall and about as wide

USDA Plant Hardiness Zones: 5 to 8

AHS Heat Zones: 9 to 1

Preferred Site: Full sun to partial shade; well-drained, acid soil; protected from northerly wind

Other Planting Options: Glossy abelia prefers acid soil but will tolerate pH levels approaching neutral.

Growing Guidelines: Prune at ground level (whether removing older branches for rejuvenation or dead wood from winter damage) to promote flowering and natural character.

Pest and Disease Prevention: No serious pest or disease problems

Special Tips: In northern areas, abelia's size is often limited by winterkill to the ground or snow line. However, rapid growth from the roots quickly overcomes the loss and promotes free flowering.

Related Plants: 'Sherwood' is a low-growing cultivar, to about 3 feet.

DWARF HINOKI FALSE CYPRESS

CHAMAECYPARIS OBTUSA 'NANA GRACILIS'

Deep green, compactly tufted evergreen foliage gives this shrub a textured appearance. The plant itself is compact and grows in a somewhat pyramidal shape. Because it starts out small and is a slow grower, it's great for small sites, but make sure you plant it in a protected spot so harsh winter winds won't damage its foliage.

Deep green color and compact growth make dwarf Hinoki false cypress a good choice if you want to grow an evergreen in a small space.

Uses: Focal point; foundation planting; shrub or mixed border

Size: Height to about 8 feet

USDA Plant Hardiness Zones: 5 to 8

AHS Heat Zones: 8 to 1

Preferred Site: Moist, loamy, well-drained soil in full sun to part shade, protected from winter wind

Other Planting Options: Damp, humid conditions

Growing Guidelines: Given the right site, this plant needs little care aside from occasional pruning.

Pest and Disease Prevention: No serious pest or disease problems

Related Plants: The straight species, *Chamaecyparis obtusa*, is every bit as handsome as this cultivar. However, it grows to a mature height of 50 to 100 feet, so it requires much more room.

SUMMERSWEET

CLETHRA ALNIFOLIA

Summersweet has a mounded, suckering habit and is an excellent choice for damp to soggy sites. It sports dark green foliage that contrasts perfectly with its fragrant, creamy white, upright flower spikes that bloom in summer. Leaves may turn yellow or orange in fall.

Uses: Naturalizing; massing; nectar for butterflies

Size: 5 to 8 feet tall and about as wide

USDA Plant Hardiness Zones: 5 to 9

AHS Heat Zones: 9 to 1

Preferred Site: Moist, acid soil; full sun to partial shade

Other Planting Options: Wet soil; shade; seaside conditions

Growing Guidelines: When matched well with its site, this native shrub needs little care.

Pest and Disease Prevention: Grow summersweet only in moist or wet conditions to prevent spider-mite infestations.

Related Plants: 'Hummingbird' is a free-flowering, compact cultivar that grows to about 3 feet tall. *Clethra alnifolia* var. *rosea* has pinkish flowers, while a related species, *C. barbinervis*, from Japan, has attractive bark, hanging flower clusters, and an affinity for drier soils. If you don't have consistently moist conditions, this species may be for you.

You can hardly go wrong planting summersweet beside still or running fresh water. Summersweet lures butterflies with its nectar.

JAPANESE KERRIA

KERRIA JAPONICA

Noted for its bright yellow flowers that bloom in spring and sporadically through the summer, Japanese kerria is a nice flowering shrub option for shady sites. Its arching green branches hold their color through the year, providing winter interest. The branches form a loose mound and they can grow to form a thicket. Foliage has a crisp look and sometimes turns yellow before dropping in autumn.

Uses: Focal point; massing; border

Size: Height to about 5 feet, and eventually about as wide

USDA Plant Hardiness Zones: 5 to 9

AHS Heat Zones: 9 to 1

Preferred Site: Partial to full shade, with evenly moist, humusy, well-drained soil

Other Planting Options: Japanese kerria will grow in a wide range of soil pH levels. It can also be planted in full sun as long as it's in a site protected from wind.

Growing Guidelines: Prune to remove dead or old stems at ground level.

Pest and Disease Prevention: No serious pest or disease problems; rarely attractive to deer

Special Tips: While full shade isn't required, flowers may bleach out in full sun, so Japanese kerria is best planted where it will get at least afternoon shade.

Related Plants: 'Pleniflora' has abundant, larger, double flowers that hold well.

Japanese kerria provides a beautiful understory for mature trees where its bright yellow flowers lighten up the shade.

DWARF INKBERRY

ILEX GLABRA '*COMPACTA*'

Don't look for bright red holly berries on this plant. This native, upright evergreen shrub is grown primarily for its glossy dark green foliage, and it blends well in a natural setting. It bears inconspicuous flowers and small black berries that develop by fall.

Dwarf inkberry's compact growth makes it a desirable landscape plant for smaller sites.

Uses: Naturalizing; foundation planting; hedges; fruit provides food for birds; the genus *Ilex* is one of several food sources for Henry's elfin butterfly.

Size: About 5 feet tall and about as wide

USDA Plant Hardiness Zones: 5 to 9

AHS Heat Zones: 9 to 5

Preferred Site: Full sun, with evenly moist, acid soil

Other Planting Options: Inkberry holly can take some shade and wet soils. It can withstand seaside conditions and deicing salts.

Growing Guidelines: Extremely cold temperatures may cause winter burn on inkberry foliage in the northern areas of its range. If this happens, prune heavily to remove the damage and to promote new growth. Inkberry spreads by suckers; remove them to contain its spread. But this plant is a real bed filler, so if its wide spread is undesirable, it's easiest to choose another plant.

Pest and Disease Prevention: No serious pest or disease problems; rarely attractive to deer

Special Tips: In swamps on the eastern coastal plain, the species is often found growing in great thickets, so if you have a wet area, this plant is a good choice.

Related Plants: The straight species has similar characteristics but can approach 10 feet in height.

OAKLEAF HYDRANGEA

HYDRANGEA QUERCIFOLIA

A beauty in any season, oakleaf hydrangea bears white flowers in summer that fade to pink then papery brown by fall. The oakleaf-shaped foliage turns orange and red to burgundy in fall, while the cinnamon brown bark peels with age. Oakleaf hydrangea is mounded and dense on a sunnier site and open and rangy in deep shade.

Few shrubs can brighten the summer shade of a woodland garden like oakleaf hydrangea.

Uses: Naturalizing; borders; focal point

Size: Up to 6 feet tall throughout most of its range; shorter and fuller in the North where winter conditions can limit its height; taller and sometimes more open in the South

USDA Plant Hardiness Zones: 5 to 9

AHS Heat Zones: 9 to 3

Preferred Site: Evenly moist soil with good drainage, partial shade

Other Planting Options: Oakleaf hydrangea can grow in full sun (as long as the soil is kept consistently moist) to full shade. It also performs quite well in a wide range of soil pH levels.

Growing Guidelines: Winter conditions in the northern reaches of its range will cause this plant to die back either partially or completely some years, resprouting from the roots. Just remove any winter-killed wood in spring and enjoy the vigorous regrowth. Flowers should return the following year.

Pest and Disease Prevention: No serious pests or diseases, although this plant does appeal to deer and rabbits. You may want to put up a physical barrier (see "Controlling Animal Pests" on page 216) at least until the plant outgrows rabbit browsing height.

Special Tips: Flowers hang on the plant and dry intact. Cut them to use for dried flower arrangements and wreaths.

Related Plants: 'Snowflake' produces long, large, weighty double flowers with subtle color shadings.

COMPACT HEAVENLY BAMBOO

NANDINA DOMESTICA 'HARBOR DWARF'

Compact heavenly bamboo is one small plant that packs a big punch—season after season. The upright canes form a dense mound and bear fine-textured, evergreen leaflets that sprout bronze red then change to green in the summer and reddish purple in fall. In the spring, pink buds open into white flower clusters that are followed by attractive, bright red berries in the fall.

Uses: Groundcover; foundation planting; massing; focal point

Size: Height to 3 feet and as wide with age

USDA Plant Hardiness Zones: 6 to 9

AHS Heat Zones: 12 to 4

Preferred Site: Moist, well-drained soil in sun, shade, or any combination

Other Planting Options: Compact heavenly bamboo will grow in a wide range of soil conditions and exposures.

Growing Guidelines: Remove a few of the oldest canes each year to promote vigorous growth of new canes. The plant will fill in nicely and bear flowers and berries more abundantly.

Pest and Disease Prevention: No serious pest or disease problems

Special Tips: Compact heavenly bamboo spreads by underground rhizomes. While its spread isn't rampant like running bamboo, you should remove any you don't want to contain its spread.

Related Plants: The species grows to about 8 feet tall and has many of the same attractive features, except that it can become leggy. You can remedy that by renewal pruning (cutting out old canes). Many nandina cultivars feature compact growth, interesting variations in foliage color, and white or yellow fruit. 'Moon Bay' is a compact variety with bright red winter foliage. 'Yellow Fruited' has yellow berries. 'Alba' sports off-white berries but grows 4 to 6 feet tall.

'Harbor Dwarf' nandina or heavenly bamboo is admired for its fine texture, compact form, and impressive seasonal interest year-round.

DWARF FRAGRANT SUMAC

RHUS AROMATICA 'GRO-LOW'

This low-growing shrub offers attractive foliage that stays green through the hottest of summers and turns vibrant red-orange in fall. It fills in beds quickly, helping to "connect" groups of trees and other taller shrubs. Dwarf fragrant sumac also boasts yellow spring flowers, but it's the fragrant bark and foliage that gives this plant its name.

An unstinting performer under many conditions, dwarf fragrant sumac forms a pretty yet effective barrier that will protect tree trunks and root zones from cars, mowers, and other hazards.

Uses: Groundcover; low hedge; barrier; fruit provides food for birds.

Size: 2 to 3 feet tall and equally as wide

USDA Plant Hardiness Zones: 4 to 9

AHS Heat Zones: 9 to 3

Preferred Site: Baking in the sun

Other Planting Options: Dwarf fragrant sumac can stand up to drought once it is established and will grow in a wide range of soil pH levels. It can also tolerate reflected heat from pavement and piled-up snow from plowing or shoveling.

Growing Guidelines: Though this plant needs little or no pruning, it easily tolerates heavy pruning for renewal or repair of snowplow damage.

Pest and Disease Prevention: Generally free of pests and diseases

Special Tips: Although dwarf fragrant sumac is related to poison sumac, this species has none of the poisonous properties.

Related Plants: The species can grow to 6 to 8 feet tall, but it is sometimes mislabeled as 'Gro-Low' in nurseries, so double-check before buying.

RUGOSA ROSE

ROSA RUGOSA

With so many rose cultivars on the market, it can be hard to choose just one rose to plant. But this species rose is naturally hardy as well as disease- and pest-resistant, making it an excellent option. It forms a mounded shrub and bears red, pink, or white flowers in spring. In fall, colorful orange-red fruit called hips appear, and the crinkled green foliage turns to a glowing orange. The stout canes are prickly with spines.

Don't let the beauty and aroma of roses fool you; rugosa rose is one tough plant.

Uses: Hedge; focal point; hips provide food for birds and a vitamin C—rich fruit for making jelly

Size: Height 4 to 6 feet tall and about as wide

USDA Plant Hardiness Zones: 2 to 9

AHS Heat Zones: 9 to 1

Preferred Site: Full sun, well-drained soil

Other Planting Options: Rugosa rose is well adapted to windy conditions, including the salty/windy combination of seaside areas. It will also grow in a wide range of soil textures and pH levels.

Growing Guidelines: Cut back a few of the oldest canes to the ground in winter to promote new growth and flowering.

Pest and Disease Prevention: Unlike many rose hybrids, rugosa rose is remarkably trouble-free, but remove leaf litter in fall as added insurance against black spot. Deer can be a nuisance, however, so if they're a problem where you live, you might want to consider another plant.

Special Tips: Don't deadhead the spent flowers or you'll miss out on the striking fall rose hips that add color and attract all sorts of birds to your garden.

Related Plants: There are literally hundreds of rose cultivars and hybrids available. Check with your local Cooperative Extension office for selections that are resistant to pests and diseases under your growing conditions. While this species rose has natural disease resistance, so do some cultivars.

'EMERALD' ARBORVITAE

THUJA OCCIDENTALIS 'EMERALD' OR 'SMARAGD'

This compact (just 10 to 15 feet tall), conical evergreen with emerald green foliage answers the call for an arborvitae that doesn't take over the yard. It's attractive enough to use as a focal point, especially since its lush green color holds well all winter long.

Uses: Screen; hedge; focal point; arborvitae is one of two food plants for the juniper hairstreak butterfly.

Size: Up to 15 feet tall and narrow—to about 3 feet wide

USDA Plant Hardiness Zones: 3 to 7

AHS Heat Zones: 7 to 1

Preferred Site: Full sun and well-drained soil, protected from sweeping winds

Other Planting Options: This plant can withstand a wide range of soil conditions, including heat and drought, once it is established.

Growing Guidelines: Prune only to remove the occasional stray branch; there's no need to shape this shrub.

Pest and Disease Prevention: To prevent spider-mite infestation, don't plant

'Emerald' arborvitae near the reflected heat of pavement, buildings, or cars. If bagworms should appear, remove them, referring to "Controlling Common Landscape Pests" on page 210 for details. Arborvitae are also appealing to deer, so think twice before planting them if deer are a problem in your area.

Special Tips: If you're growing 'Emerald' arborvitae in a windy site, stake it until the plant is well established.

Related Plants: 'Holmstrup' is another compact cultivar. It grows to a maximum height of about 10 feet and has good color retention throughout the winter. 'Techny', which grows to 15 feet, has a strong pyramidal form and also holds its color well.

Improved arborvitae cultivars such as 'Emerald' offer new choices to homeowners who are understandably wary of evergreens that grow too big for their landscapes.

FIVELEAF AKEBIA

AKEBIA QUINATA

Fiveleaf akebia is a vigorous, clockwise-twining perennial vine that's grown primarily for its foliage. It produces a lush cover of compound leaves, and its small purplish flowers in spring and scarce 2- to 4-inch pods in fall are normally hidden by the foliage. This tough plant is quick to establish.

Clean, green leaves unaffected by insects or other adversities make fiveleaf akebia a desirable plant for a tough site.

Uses: Fast cover for a fence, arbor, or pergola

Size: Up to 20 feet tall is common, but fiveleaf akebia can grow up to 40 feet or more depending on the support. It often grows too large for a typical garden trellis.

USDA Plant Hardiness Zones: 5 to 9

AHS Heat Zones: 9 to 3

Preferred Site: Grows equally well in sun or partial shade, in evenly moist soil

Other Planting Options: Fiveleaf akebia can withstand heat, drought, flooding, and hard pruning.

Growing Guidelines: Akebia needs small-diameter support such as a chain-link fence or a sturdy trellis on which to wind and grow. Fiveleaf akebia regrows readily when cut to the ground, making maintenance tasks easier. It's best to prune in the dormant season, but this tough vine can recover from pruning almost anytime.

Pest and Disease Prevention: No serious pest or disease problems

Special Tips: *Warning:* Fast, aggressive growth can make this vine an invasive nuisance in some areas and a welcome survivor in others, so check with local sources such as your Cooperative Extension office before you plant it.

Related Plants: 'Alba' features white flowers and fruit, while 'Rosea' offers lavender or light purple flowers rather than the intense purple of the species.

CAROLINA JESSAMINE

GELSEMIUM SEMPERVIRENS

While it's not hardy beyond Zone 7, this twining vine with fragrant yellow flowers is a landscape staple in areas the South. Carolina jessamine, the state flower of South Carolina, blooms in spring against glossy dark evergreen leaves.

You can find Carolina jessamine growing just about everywhere in warm-climate areas because of its beauty and durability.

Uses: Cover for a trellis, fence, arbor, pergola, as well as lampposts or mailbox posts

Size: Up to 20 feet tall

USDA Plant Hardiness Zones: 7 to 9

AHS Heat Zones: 9 to 4

Preferred Site: Full sun to light shade in humusy, well-drained soil

Other Planting Options: Carolina jessamine can adapt to a wide range of conditions and will readily grow in clay soil.

Growing Guidelines: Prune after flowering to promote flowering the next year.

Pest and Disease Prevention: No serious pest or disease problems

Special Tips: *Warning:* All parts of Carolina jessamine are poisonous when eaten. Don't plant it where children would have access to it.

Related Plants: 'Pride of Augusta' is a double-flowered cultivar.

HYACINTH BEAN

LABLAB PURPUREUS

If you like purple, this plant is for you! This dense, annual twining vine grows quickly to make a full screen that's quite interesting to look at, with its bright, purplish pink, pealike flowers, and zany purple seedpods. The purplish green leaves are supported by purple petioles and stems.

Hyacinth beans, with their purple stems, bright purplish pink flowers, and deep purple pods can lend a whimsical element to your landscape.

Uses: Cover for trellis, fence, or poles; hyacinth bean grows densely to the ground, making a good screen; seeds and pods are edible but only when cooked.

Size: 15 or 20 feet tall

AHS Heat Zones: 12 to 1

Preferred Site: Full sun on a well-drained soil

Other Planting Options: Wide range of soil types and conditions, including heat and humidity

Growing Guidelines: Hyacinth bean is easy to grow from seed, but its need for a long growing season may prompt you to start seeds indoors about 6 weeks before the predicted last frost in your area for earlier blossoms.

Pest and Disease Prevention: No serious pest or disease problems

Special Tips: Hyacinth bean is regularly found growing in Asian vegetable gardens, but to make the pods and beans edible, you must cook them to remove tanins and other natural toxins. *Warning:* If you have small children, you might want to hold off on planting hyacinth beans because those pretty purple beans may be tempting to pick and taste.

BLACK-EYED SUSAN VINE

THUNBERGIA ALATA

The medium green foliage of this annual twining vine sets off the bright, hot colors of its flowers. Flowers may be yellow, orange, or white—with purple or black centers. They bloom from midsummer until frost, slowing a bit during hot periods, and picking up again when the weather cools.

Fine-textured and cheery, black-eyed Susan vine combines well with other hot colors, while the white cultivar, 'Alba', combines well with caladiums and impatiens in shady settings.

Uses: Cover for trellis or fence; hanging baskets or window boxes; an effective screen

Size: About 6 feet tall

AHS Heat Zones: 12 to 1

Preferred Site: Full sun to partial shade in a moist, humusy, well-drained soil

Other Planting Options: Black-eyed Susan vine will adapt to most soil types and conditions.

Growing Guidelines: Sow seeds indoors about 4 to 6 weeks before the predicted last frost. This vine is sensitive to frost, so gradually acclimate seedlings to outdoor conditions as the danger of frost passes.

Pest and Disease Prevention: No serious pest or disease problems

Special Tips: To get the best flowering, plant black-eyed Susan vine away from hot afternoon sun.

Related Plants: White black-eyed Susan vine (*Thunbergia alata* 'Alba') is one of the few annual vines that blooms in full shade.

Sweet Autumn Clematis

The exuberant blooms of sweet autumn clematis are a pleasant harbinger of fall in many gardens.

CLEMATIS TERNIFLORA

This vigorous twining vine becomes covered with fragrant white flowers from August through October. When the flower show is finished, it's followed by silver-gray feathery seedheads that often reflect light and color.

Uses: Cover for a pergola, fence, or arbor; normally too exuberant for a typical garden trellis; nectar source for some butterfly species

Size: About 8 feet tall

USDA Plant Hardiness Zones: 4 to 9

AHS Heat Zones: 9 to 1

Preferred Site: Full sun to partial shade on well-drained soil

Other Planting Options: Sweet autumn clematis will grow in a wide range of soils and other conditions. It regrows readily when cut to the ground for support maintenance or other purposes.

Growing Conditions: Sweet autumn clematis is susceptible to winterkill in the North, but it regrows readily from the roots and blooms the following growing season.

Pest and Disease Prevention: No serious pest or disease problems—except for deer

Special Tips: Fast, aggressive growth can make this vine a nuisance in some areas and a welcome survivor in others, so do some checking about its growth in your area before you plant it.

Related Plants: There are many other clematis species and cultivars to choose from which generally have larger but less numerous flowers and less vigorous habits. You'll find they also aren't as adaptable to such a wide range of growing conditions as sweet autumn clematis.

English Ivy

English ivy softens hard edges and lends a handsome presence.

HEDERA HELIX

English ivy is an evergreen vine with handsome three-lobed leaves and attractive vein patterns. It is used both as a groundcover and as a climbing vine. It climbs using aerial rootlets, which can actually damage brick or other house sidings, so be wary of where you plant it.

Uses: Groundcover; a cover for walls

Size: 45 feet or taller, depending on the climate and support

USDA Plant Hardiness Zones: 5 to 11

AHS Heat Zones: 12 to 1

Preferred Site: Partial to full shade, well-drained, humusy soil; even moisture; a sheltered site; good air circulation. In colder areas, protect English ivy from wind and from winter sun that can dry the foliage.

Other Planting Options: English ivy can adapt to a wide range of soil pH levels.

Growing Guidelines: You may need to prune frequently to keep this plant tidy and in bounds. Find out how English ivy behaves in your area before choosing to plant it.

Pest and Disease Prevention: Good air circulation and leaf cleanup can help to prevent bacterial leaf spot and fungal diseases. Avoid reflected heat, which can encourage spider mites. Deer enjoy this plant, so choose another vine or groundcover if deer are a problem in your area.

Special Tips: *Warning*—English ivy can be an invasive nuisance in some areas and welcome survivor in others. Check with your local Cooperative Extension office before planting. Though English ivy can be charming on brick, beware that those aerial rootlets can be damaging to mortar. Though it can shade a building—saving cooling costs—it can also trap damaging moisture. It looks dramatic growing on tree trunks, but it can eventually shade and outcompete the leaves in the crown. Based on your needs, grow English ivy solely as a groundcover or on a garden wall.

Related Plants: Extra-hardy cultivars such as 'Baltica' and 'Thorndale' have been selected for colder climates. Cultivars such as the fine-textured 'Needlepoint' and the variegated 'Gold Heart' can be grown in warmer areas and as potted or topiary plants.

BOSTON IVY

PARTHENOCISSUS TRICUSPIDATA

Boston ivy's striking fall foliage and fruit against the texture of a wall make a charming combination. This large-scale vine features green, three-lobed leaves that turn to variations of orange, scarlet, and burgundy in the fall. Clusters of blue-black fruit sporting a waxy coating appear in fall and become obvious after the leaves drop. Boston ivy climbs using tendrils with sticky discs.

Boston ivy can shade a building beautifully, but there are trade-offs.

Uses: Cover for walls or fences; berries provide food for birds.

Size: About 50 feet—or taller

USDA Plant Hardiness Zones: 4 to 8

AHS Heat Zones: 8 to 1

Preferred Site: Full sun to full shade, in a humusy, well-drained soil

Other Planting Options: This tough plant can withstand a wide range of soil types as well as seaside conditions, wind, and urban challenges like pollution.

Growing Guidelines: If you grow this vine on a building, you may need to prune it to remove it from windows.

Pest and Disease Prevention: Though rarely deadly on this tough plant, Japanese beetles, leaf spots, or scale insects can sometimes cause damage. Avoid overfertilizing, as succulent growth can attract otherwise uninterested pests. Boston ivy is a favorite of deer.

Special Tips: Though Boston ivy looks charming on a building and can lower cooling costs with its shade, it can also trap damaging moisture and leave behind a sooty residue or mold stains when you remove it. You may also need to prune it to remove this vine from windows. Weigh the pros and cons based on your climate and your needs. It can also become weedy in some areas, as birds distribute the seeds.

Related Plants: Virginia creeper (*P. quinquefolia*) has many of the same characteristics, though its compound leaf of five leaflets gives it a coarser texture.

CYPRESS VINE

IPOMOEA QUAMOCLIT

Don't let the delicate, fine-textured foliage fool you—cypress vine is a tough performer. This annual twining vine has wispy leaves and small funnel-form flowers—red, orange, or white—that bloom from midsummer until frost.

The light and airy look of cypress vine gives it an unusual presence in the summer garden.

Uses: Cover for fence, trellis, poles, or compost bin; nectar source for hummingbirds and butterflies

Size: 10 to 20 feet tall

AHS Heat Zones: 12 to 1

Preferred Site: Full sun to light shade in moist, well-drained soil

Other Planting Options: Cypress vine will grow in a wide range of soil types and conditions, including heat, drought, and humidity.

Growing Guidelines: This plant is easy to grow from seed indoors or outside, and it freely self-sows. The best type of support for this climber is a fine-textured wire fence or compost bin, narrow pole, or string.

Pest and Disease Prevention: No serious pest or disease problems; rarely attractive to deer

Special Tips: Cypress vine's self-sowing ways can make it a nuisance in some areas and a welcome survivor in others. Check with your local Cooperative Extension office before you plant it.

Related Plants: Cardinal climber (*Ipomoea × multifida*) has similar feathery foliage but broader leaves. And its 2-inch flowers are larger than those of cypress vine.

MORNING GLORY

IPOMOEA PURPUREA

Morning glory is an easy-to-grow, twining annual vine with heart-shaped leaves. Its colorful funnel-form flowers bloom from midsummer through frost. As its name implies, it blooms mostly in the morning or during cloudy conditions. Morning glory tends to take a break during the hottest days of summer and resume blooming when the weather cools. Depending on the cultivar you choose, flower colors can be white, pink, blue, or variegated.

Morning glories have few lateral branches, so plant several plants about 18 inches apart for good coverage.

Uses: Cover for fence, trellis, post, or compost bin; food plant for some North American butterfly species

Size: About 15 feet tall

AHS Heat Zones: 12 to 1

Preferred Site: Full sun and well-drained soil

Other Planting Options: Morning glory grows successfully in a wide range of soil types and conditions and it's drought-tolerant.

Growing Guidelines: Morning glory is easy to grow from seed either indoors or outside (soak the seeds for 24 hours first), and it's freely self-sowing. It needs a fine-textured support like a wire fence or compost bin, or a narrow pole or post for climbing. For reliable flowering, don't overfertilize it.

Pest and Disease Prevention: Avoid overfertilization, as succulent growth can attract otherwise uninterested pests. In areas where deer are a problem, site morning glories close to the house or in another area—such as near the dog run—where deer might hesitate to visit.

Special Tips: Morning glory's self-sowing ways can make it a nuisance in some areas and a welcome survivor in others. Check with your local Cooperative Extension office before you plant it.

Related Plants: Moonflower (*I. alba*) has large fragrant white flowers that bloom at night and also into the morning if conditions are overcast. They're magical, especially in an evening garden, but apparently tasty to deer. If deer aren't a problem in your area, try planting morning glory and moonflower together on the same support for a show of flowers in the morning and evening.

'ELEGANS' PORCELAIN VINE

AMPELOPSIS BREVIPEDUNCULATA 'ELEGANS'

Porcelain vine or porcelain berry is a vigorous-growing member of the grape family. 'Elegans' is a less aggressive cultivar that offers pretty variegated three-lobed leaves and colorful berries—yellow, violet, turquoise, and blue—in the fall. Porcelain vine climbs with tendrils.

'Elegans' porcelain vine can cover a support quickly, where it will charm you with its dazzling berries and variegated foliage.

Uses: Cover for a pergola, fence, or arbor; it normally grows too large for a typical garden trellis; berries provide food for birds

Size: About 15 feet tall is common.

USDA Plant Hardiness Zones: 5 to 8

AHS Heat Zones: 8 to 3

Preferred Site: Full sun to light shade in evenly moist, well-drained soil; a limited root zone is said to promote berry production, so try planting it in a confined area where the roots won't have unlimited space to spread.

Other Planting Options: Porcelain vine can adapt to a wide range of soil conditions and easily withstands hard pruning. It regrows readily when cut to the ground for support maintenance or other purposes.

Growing Guidelines: This plant climbs with tendrils—it needs wire, woody plant stems, or a similar structure to climb on; otherwise, you'll need to tie it. Promote blooms and fruit on new growth with hard pruning each spring. Also, 'Elegans' will sometimes revert to green leaves. Prune any green growth to prevent unwanted problems associated with the species.

Pest and Disease Prevention: If Japanese beetles are troublesome in your area, consider another vine.

Special Tips: *Warning*—Fast, aggressive growth can make the species an invasive nuisance in some areas and a welcome survivor in others, so do some checking before you plant. The 'Elegans' cultivar isn't nearly as aggressive. Porcelain vine self-sows readily, so keep your eye out for unwanted seedlings.

Related Plants: *A. brevipedunculata* var. *maximowiczii* has deeply lobed leaves and a vigorous, invasive habit.

PERIWINKLE

VINCA MINOR

Also called creeping myrtle, this spreading plant features pointed, evergreen leaves and violet-colored flowers in spring. Periwinkle forms a handsome carpet in shady areas with its glossy, dark green foliage. It also combines nicely with spring bulbs.

Planted beneath trees, periwinkle unifies the landscape and has a solid presence.

Size: About 8 inches tall; spread is limited only by growing conditions.

USDA Plant Hardiness Zones: 5 to 9

AHS Heat Zones: 9 to 1

Preferred Site: Full to partial shade, and moist, humusy, well-drained soil. Good air circulation can prevent fungal diseases.

Other Planting Options: Periwinkle can adapt to a wide range of soil pH levels, and it can even withstand exposure to sun in cooler climates.

Growing Guidelines: Cut back young plants to promote branching and fullness. Top-dress yearly with compost.

Pest and Disease Prevention: Avoid overfertilizing, which promotes fungal diseases such as phomopsis, which can wipe out a planting under the right (or wrong!) conditions. Rarely attractive to deer.

Special Tips: Periwinkle spreads by creeping along the ground and rooting along the stems. It spreads quickly once established, so plant it where you aren't concerned about its spread or use a barrier or edging to contain it.

Related Plants: 'Alba' and 'Gertrude Jekyll' have white flowers. Big periwinkle (*V. major*) sports bright blue flowers and large waxy leaves. 'Variegata' has cream-colored margins and is popular as an annual accent plant for pots and hanging baskets north of USDA Plant Hardiness Zone 7.

VARIEGATED BISHOP'S WEED

AEGOPODIUM PODAGRARIA 'VARIEGATUM'

The bright green and creamy white leaves of variegated bishop's weed are quite pretty and add a bright spot to a shady area; it will do equally well in sun. But watch out—this plant is very invasive unless you plant it in a contained space! White, flat-topped flower clusters bloom in early summer, and the leaves retain their color until they die back in the fall.

Bishop's weed is one of those tough groundcovers that tolerates dry shade, in addition to other harsh conditions, but be sure to protect the rest of your yard from its invasiveness.

Uses: Groundcover or filler for beds that are contained on all sides by permanent edges, such as a bed between the house and a sidewalk

Size: About 12 inches tall; flowers reach about 15 inches tall. This plant will spread almost indefinitely.

USDA Plant Hardiness Zones: 4 to 9

AHS Heat Zones: 9 to 3

Preferred Site: Sun or shade in practically any soil; restrict root growth, if invasiveness is a concern, by planting where there is a paved or hard edge. Plastic or steel edging will give only a temporary and ultimately false sense of security where this plant's wandering ways are concerned.

Other Planting Options: Variegated bishop weed's wide tolerance and durability make it a good choice for difficult sites where little else will grow.

Growing Guidelines: If the foliage becomes sun-scorched, damaged by leaf blight, or trampled by the dog, just cut it back and it will regrow. For larger plantings, use a lawn mower set to cut high to trim back damaged foliage.

Pest and Disease Prevention: No serious pest or disease problems

Special Tips: *Warning*—Fast, aggressive growth can make variegated bishop's weed an invasive nuisance in some situations and a welcome survivor in others. Check with your local Cooperative Extension office before you decide to plant it.

Related Plants: The species has medium green leaves, bears white flowers, reaches about 12 to 24 inches in height, and tends to be even more aggressive than 'Variegata'.

YELLOW BARRENWORT

EPIMEDIUM × VERSICOLOR 'SULPHUREUM'

This mounded-habit groundcover bears small, leathery, heart-shaped leaflets that emerge in spring. Thin, wiry stems support small yellow flowers, making the flowers look as if they're floating in air. Foliage may go bronze in fall or winter in colder areas, remaining green in milder regions.

Uses: Groundcover under trees; filler in woodland garden

Size: Approximately 10 inches tall and about as wide

USDA Plant Hardiness Zones: 5 to 9

AHS Heat Zones: 9 to 3

Preferred Site: Full to partial shade in humusy, evenly moist, well-drained soil

Other Planting Options: Yellow barrenwort can withstand shade as well as competition from tree roots, making it a good option for growing under trees.

Growing Guidelines: Barrenwort is somewhat slow to spread, but once it's established, it becomes full and reliable. If the foliage turns bronze or becomes tattered over the winter, cut it back before growth begins in the spring and you'll soon have a flush of new growth.

Pest and Disease Prevention: No serious pest or disease problems; rarely attractive to deer

Special Tips: Epimediums combine well with trees and with spring-blooming bulbs because they cover fading foliage and fill in bare spots. Sometimes slow to establish and spread, epimediums can require patience but are remarkably rewarding as they mature.

Related Plants: Other useful epimediums include red barrenwort (*E. × rubrum*), *E. pinnatum*, and longspur epimedium (*E. grandiflorum*). American barrenwort (*Vancouveria hexandra*) is a great choice for cooler, damper areas of USDA Plant Hardiness Zones 5 to 7 and is impressive in woodland gardens.

Yellow barrenwort or epimedium has a distinctive and delicate yellow flower that will add a burst of color to a shady spot in your landscape.

SWEET WOODRUFF

GALIUM ODORATUM

Small, fresh-looking green leaves formed in whorls create a fine-textured carpet that dies back in fall. Small, four-petaled white flowers bloom above the foliage in spring. Sweet woodruff combines beautifully with spring ephemerals such as geranium, celandine poppy, or Virginia bluebells, hiding fading foliage and filling in bare spots. When dried or crushed, the leaves release a sweet fragrance.

The fine texture and visual freshness of sweet woodruff's leaves make it a welcome addition to a shady garden.

Uses: Groundcover for under trees

Size: 8 to 12 inches tall and twice as wide

USDA Plant Hardiness Zones: 5 to 8

AHS Heat Zones: 8 to 5

Preferred Site: Full to partial shade with evenly moist, humusy, well-drained soil

Other Planting Options: Deep shade

Growing Guidelines: Cut back established plants and add compost each year before new growth begins in the spring.

Pest and Disease Prevention: No serious pest or disease problems

Special Tips: Although sweet woodruff combines well with North American native plants and is often used with pleasing results in woodland gardens, it's not a native plant like many people think. Its old-world origins classify this handsome groundcover as an exotic.

Related Plants: Yellow bedstraw (*G. verum*) is a weedy and well-known relative of sweet woodruff. It's unwelcome in most gardens, so don't confuse the two species.

ST.-JOHN'S-WORT, AARON'S BEARD

HYPERICUM CALYCINUM

Shiny blue-green leaves highlight the bright yellow flowers that bloom through the summer. The many stamens give the flowers a powder-puff appearance. Evergreen in the warmer areas of its range, St.-John's-wort turns burgundy or brown during the winter in colder regions.

Looking cool and composed on even the hottest of days, St.-John's-wort produces cheery yellow blooms through the summer.

Uses: Tough groundcover for dry slopes and sunny, exposed spots

Size: 15 inches tall and about 2 feet wide

USDA Plant Hardiness Zones: 5 to 9

AHS Heat Zones: 9 to 4

Preferred Site: Full sun to partial shade with well-drained, evenly moist soil

Other Planting Options: St.-John's-wort can also sustain drought and baking heat.

Growing Guidelines: If you live in a colder climate where the foliage turns color or burns in the winter, cut plants back to about 3 inches tall before growth begins in spring.

Pest and Disease Prevention: No serious pest or disease problems

Special Tips: St.-John's-wort is used as an herbal treatment for depression. In some cases, ingesting this herb can cause harmful photosensitization (sensitivity to light) in people and some animals. Don't plant it around grazing animals.

MONDO GRASS

OPHIOPOGON JAPONICUS

Mondo grass, which is also called monkey grass, has dark green, narrow, evergreen grasslike leaves. This is primarily a southern and coastal groundcover, as it's only hardy to Zone 7. Mondo grass is grown primarily for its foliage; its white flowers and pea-size blue fruit are often hidden by the foliage.

Fine-textured mondo grass combines well with trees and can pull together a planting when it's repeated in several spots throughout the landscape.

Uses: Groundcover; edging

Size: About 12 inches tall

USDA Plant Hardiness Zones: 6 to 11

AHS Heat Zones: 12 to 1

Preferred Site: Partial shade; moist, well-drained soil

Other Planting Options: Mondo grass can grow successfully in full sun to full shade and in a broad range of soil conditions. It does well in seaside conditions and grows among roots and shade from trees, too.

Growing Guidelines: If the foliage becomes tattered or tired, cut it back before the plants begin spring growth. For large plantings, do this with a lawn mower set at the highest cutting level.

Pest and Disease Prevention: Slugs can be damaging. See page 211 for control methods.

Special Tips: Contrasts nicely with hardscape elements like benches or walls

Related Plants: Creeping lilyturf (*Liriope spicata*) and big blue lilyturf (*L. muscari*) offer a similar look but are hardy farther north (see page 86). Dwarf mondo, (*O. japonicus* 'Nanus') grows to a clipped-looking 3 inches tall.

SIBERIAN CARPET CYPRESS

MICROBIOTA DECUSSATA

Known by a variety of names including Russian arborvitae and Siberian carpet grass, Siberian carpet cypress looks much like a juniper, with arching, scaly, feathery green foliage. Unlike creeping juniper, however, this low plant doesn't lie flat on the ground, so it gives a little more structure to the landscape. It also prefers somewhat shadier sites than juniper. Its foliage can turn purplish bronze in fall or winter, and it bears tiny cones.

Siberian carpet cypress looks similar to a juniper, so it makes a good juniper substitute in shady sites such as under mature trees.

Uses: Groundcover for shade or sun; bank stabilization

Size: About 15 inches tall; spreads to 5 feet

USDA Plant Hardiness Zones: 2 to 7

AHS Heat Zones: 7 to 1

Preferred Site: Shade or partial shade, with a well-drained, evenly moist and slightly acid soil

Other Planting Options: Siberian carpet cypress can grow in sun, and it can withstand drought and pH levels approaching neutral.

Growing Guidelines: Needs little care

Pest and Disease Prevention: No serious pest or disease problems

Special Tips: Siberian carpet cypress looks especially nice grown in groupings.

CREEPING LILYTURF

LIRIOPE SPICATA

A creeping groundcover that spreads by stolons, creeping lilyturf or liriope is a striking plant that forms a thick, medium-textured grassy carpet. Its dark green, grasslike leaves come up in spring and are evergreen in warmer climates, but the leaves will turn brown and tattered during northern winters. Spikes bearing lavender flowers shoot up in mid- to late summer—a time when many other flowering plants are fizzling out due to the heat. The flowers are followed by black berries.

Creeping lilyturf makes a reliable, attractive groundcover that combines well with trees and looks especially nice bordering a brick wall or pathway.

Uses: Rock garden; edging; appealing groundcover for many situations, except very steep slopes which would make annual mowing problematic

Size: About 12 inches tall

USDA Plant Hardiness Zones: 6 to 11

AHS Heat Zones: 12 to 1

Preferred Site: Sun or shade; well-drained, evenly moist soil

Other Planting Options: Lilyturf can grow in a broad range of soil conditions, such as in the shade and roots of trees, in drought, and in seaside conditions.

Growing Guidelines: Cut back plants in spring, before growth begins, to remove tattered, discolored foliage and to promote thicker growth. On large patches of lilyturf, it's easiest to do this with a lawn mower set at its highest cutting level.

Pest and Disease Prevention: No serious pest or disease problems

Special Tips: Lilyturf's foliage contrasts beautifully with brick or stone walls.

Related Plants: Cultivars include 'Variegata', which is nicely variegated and somewhat less vigorous than the species. Big blue lilyturf (*L. muscari*), a clump-forming rather than creeping species, sports a wider leaf blade and is slightly taller. It's hardy in USDA Plant Hardiness Zones 6 to 10. 'Monroe's White' is an *L. muscari* cultivar that bears white flowers.

CREEPING JUNIPER

JUNIPERUS HORIZONTALIS

Spreading and layered evergreen branches bear scaly or needlelike blue-green leaves that may turn purplish in winter. Waxy, blue fruit forms late in the growing season, if at all. Creeping juniper is a good option to replace turf on steep slopes because it fills in nicely and requires very little maintenance.

Uses: Groundcover for steep slopes

Size: Height and spread both vary depending on the cultivar. Maximum height is less than 2 feet tall, while the spread can vary up to 8 feet.

USDA Plant Hardiness Zones: 3 to 9

AHS Heat Zones: 9 to 1

Preferred Site: Full sun with well-drained, sandy soil and good air circulation to prevent phomopsis twig blight

Other Planting Options: Creeping juniper will adapt to a wide range of soil

Creeping juniper is in its element hugging the ground on a sunny, south-facing slope.

conditions including shallow, rocky soils. It also tolerates extreme drought, baking heat, seaside conditions, and wind.

Growing Guidelines: If pruning for size control is necessary, use thinning cuts to preserve the plant's natural character, rather than simply cutting back the branch tips. (See page 221 for more details on pruning.)

Pest and Disease Prevention: Should phomopsis twig blight appear with its brown, dead foliage following a wet spring, prune and destroy affected branches. Bagworms can sometimes attack creeping juniper. Remove the bags in winter before the caterpillars have a chance to do damage. See "Controlling Common Landscape Pests" on page 210 for details.

Special Tips: Juniper is one of several food plants for the juniper hairstreak butterfly.

Related Plants: There are many cultivars of creeping juniper. Two popular ones are 'Bar Harbor', which has grayish foliage that turns purplish in winter, and 'Blue Rug', which has blue-green foliage.

JAPANESE PACHYSANDRA

PACHYSANDRA TERMINALIS

If you have a shady edge in a landscape bed, the dark green, glossy-toothed leaves of Japanese pachysandra is a good option. The foliage grows in whorls, and in spring, clusters of white flowers bloom above the leaves. Japanese pachysandra is evergreen, which is one reason for its popularity over the native but deciduous Allegheny pachysandra.

Japanese pachysandra is a reliable groundcover for shady situations, making it one of the most popular choices available at nurseries and garden centers.

Uses: Groundcover in shady areas, including on slopes or banks and under both evergreen or deciduous trees

Size: About 8 inches tall; the spread is limited only by soil, light, and moisture conditions.

USDA Plant Hardiness Zones: 4 to 8

AHS Heat Zones: 8 to 1

Preferred Site: Full to partial shade in moist, slightly acid, fertile soil that is well drained.

Other Planting Options: Japanese pachysandra can even withstand deep shade.

Growing Guidelines: Plants may yellow if they get too much sun or insufficient nutrients. Top-dress them each spring with compost to prevent nutrient deficiencies. Trim or mow plantings every few years to renew growth.

Pest and Disease Prevention: No serious pest or disease problems; rarely attractive to deer; good air circulation will go a long way toward preventing fungal diseases.

Special Tips: Pachysandra grows by rhizomes (underground runners), but it's not as hard to contain as many other groundcovers that spread in this manner.

Related Plants: Allegheny spurge (*P. procumbens*), our native North American pachysandra, is quite pretty and features leaves mottled with white. It's not used as commonly as Japanese pachysandra, however, because it's deciduous through much of its range.

PERENNIALS

LADY'S-MANTLE

ALCHEMILLA MOLLIS

Velvety, pleated pale green leaves capture beads of morning dew for a sparkling effect. This self-sower blooms with small, greenish yellow flowers that create airy clusters above and within the foliage beginning in late spring or early summer.

The mounded clumps of neatly pleated foliage and foamy chartreuse flowers of lady's-mantle almost seem to glow in the shade or the dusk.

Uses: Front of beds or borders; groundcover; also a nice addition to a cottage-style garden.

Size: About 8 inches tall (with flowers a few inches taller) by about 2 feet wide

USDA Plant Hardiness Zones: 4 to 7

AHS Heat Zones: 7 to 1

Preferred Site: Full sun to partial shade with evenly moist, humusy soil in a cool, moist environment; where summer temperatures are hot, afternoon shade is a must.

Other Planting Options: Lady's-mantle can grow in a wide range of soil and climatic conditions, provided it's given steady moisture and shade.

Growing Guidelines: Keep this plant mulched to preserve soil moisture. Remove tattered leaves as necessary and cut back the entire plant before growth begins in spring. Divide clumps in spring or fall.

Pest and Disease Prevention: Fungal diseases can become troublesome when the foliage stays wet for long periods. Water early in the day so that any wet foliage may dry, and try to water the soil, not the foliage. This plant is rarely attractive to deer.

Special Tips: Use the unusual yellow flower color to brighten shade or a spot you like to frequent at dusk—the chartreuse flowers seem to glow in the dark. The flowers are also useful and attractive in fresh or dried arrangements.

Related Plants: There are other species of lady's-mantle, including *A. alpina* (mountain lady's-mantle) and *A. conjuncta,* but none is as readily available as *A. mollis.*

ASTILBE

ASTILBE × ARENDSII

Astilbes are known for their showy flower plumes of white, lavender, pink, or red that bloom in early summer. The foliage of these clump-forming perennials is fine-textured and fernlike.

Astilbe can unify a shady area when planted in drifts. It also combines well with other shade-tolerant plants such as bergenia, bleeding hearts, and hostas.

Uses: Shade garden; border, streamside, or lakeside planting; cut flowers; nectar source for some butterflies

Size: Normally about 12 to 24 inches tall, but larger cultivars can approach 4 feet; about as wide as it is tall

USDA Plant Hardiness Zones: 4 to 9

AHS Heat Zones: 9 to 1

Preferred Site: Full to partial shade in an evenly moist, well-drained, humusy soil; good air circulation and an absence of reflected heat sources such as pavement, cars, and buildings are also important site considerations.

Other Planting Options: Astilbe can withstand some sun in cooler areas, as long as it's given a steady water supply.

Growing Guidelines: Cut back the old foliage in spring before growth begins. Top-dress annually with compost or a balanced organic fertilizer, as astilbe is a heavy feeder. Divide clumps in spring or fall about every 3 or 4 years or if the crowns push out of the soil.

Pest and Disease Prevention: Prevent spider mites by avoiding reflected heat, which attracts them. Good air circulation helps to prevent root rot. Plants are rarely attractive to deer.

Special Tips: Astilbes make lovely cut flowers. Cut when the flowers are just half-open; their airy, plume shape adds dimension and texture to a vase or arrangement.

Related Plants: 'Deutschland' is a cultivar that blooms early with white flowers and grows to about 2 feet. While 'Sprite' blooms late with pink flowers and lacy foliage, it reaches a 12- to 18-inch height. 'Fanal' is an early bloomer with red flowers, dark bronze foliage, and a 2-foot height. 'Bressingham Beauty' approaches a stately height of 3 feet, with late pink flowers.

PERENNIAL FOUNTAIN GRASS

PENNISETUM ALOPECUROIDES

The graceful, arching mound of narrow blades combined with the flowers that are followed by attractive seedheads make perennial fountain grass an appealing part of your garden through the summer months. Depending on the cultivar, seedheads can range from tan to almost black. The dried foliage makes a nice winter feature, but the seedheads will have shattered by then.

Uses: Planted in mass; solitary accent in a bed, border, or pot; seedheads make a nice addition to flower arrangements.

Size: About 3 feet tall and at least as wide

USDA Plant Hardiness Zones: 6 to 9

AHS Heat Zones: 9 to 6

Preferred Site: Full sun to partial shade in fertile, moist, well-drained soil

Other Planting Options: Perennial fountain grass also tolerates seaside conditions and makes an attractive container plant.

Growing Guidelines: Remove seedheads before they shatter if perennial fountain grass tends to seed itself in your area (check with your local Cooperative Extension office). Cut back the entire plant before growth begins in the spring. Divide clumps in spring if the plant centers begin to weaken.

Pest and Disease Prevention: No serious pest or disease problems

Special Tips: Perennial fountain grass combines beautifully with Russian sage and daisy-type flowers such as purple coneflower and black-eyed Susan.

Related Plants: 'Hameln' has a compact form and dark tan seedheads. 'Little Bunny' grows only to about 1 foot and makes a charming groundcover. 'Moudry' has dramatic dark brown seedheads.

Perennial fountain grass gives movement to the landscape with every breeze and provides wonderful contrast in form and texture to other leaf and plant shapes.

Showy Stonecrop

Showy stonecrop is a succulent plant that can bake in the sun all summer long and still look fresh.

SEDUM SPECTABILE

Dozens of tiny individual flowers make up large flower clusters that can reach 3 to 6 inches across. These nearly flat-topped clusters cover the top of the plant's mounded form in late summer to fall. Choose from red, pink, or white flowers. Showy stonecrop is a tough performer but is not invasive.

Uses: Beds, borders, rock gardens, and areas where little else will grow; nectar source for butterflies; cut flowers used either fresh or dried

Size: 2 feet tall and about as wide

USDA Plant Hardiness Zones: 4 to 9

AHS Heat Zones: 9 to 1

Preferred Site: Full sun and well-drained soil

Other Planting Options: Showy stonecrop can take heat and drought, as well as a wide range of soil types.

Growing Guidelines: Cut back before growth begins in spring. Divide plants in spring if they're overgrown and fall open.

Pest and Disease Prevention: No serious pest or disease problems.

Special Tips: While many succulent plants can't take much moisture, showy stonecrop can withstand a rainy climate and even partial shade. Just note that the plant may flop over if it doesn't get enough sun or good drainage.

Related Plants: *Sedum* 'Autumn Joy' is an outstanding hybrid that tends to hold together through the fall, providing some winter interest in the garden. Many other cultivars are available, with flower colors ranging from white and yellow to pink, lavender, and dark red.

Wild Geranium

The high shade of a moist open woodland or grove is a natural setting for wild geranium.

GERANIUM MACULATUM

Native to the Appalachian Mountains, wild geranium or spotted cranesbill forms loose mounds of deeply segmented leaves. Purplish pink flowers bloom in late spring for about 2 weeks. The plant's foliage turns red to orange in fall before dying back.

Uses: Woodland garden or shady border; naturalizing

Size: 1 to 2 feet tall

USDA Plant Hardiness Zones: 4 to 8

AHS Heat Zones: 8 to 1

Preferred Site: High shade and a rich, moist, well-drained soil

Other Planting Options: Wild geranium can grow in a wide range of soil types, from sandy soil to silt to clay.

Growing Guidelines: Cut back in fall or in spring before new growth begins. Add shredded leaves or compost in spring and in fall, but avoid overfertilizing as it promotes weak, floppy growth. If conditions are dry for more that a week or two during the growing season, the plants disappear into dormancy. Divide clumps in spring or fall as necessary.

Pest and Disease Prevention: No serious pest or disease problems

Special Tips: Combines well with wild bleeding heart (*Dicentra formosa*), cardinal flower (*Lobelia cardinalis*), Virginia bluebells (*Mertensia pulmonarioides*), and ferns.

Related Plants: Related hardy geranium species, such as *G. endressii* with bright pink flowers or *G. sanguineum* with deep magenta flowers make equally nice substitutions for wild geranium.

THREADLEAF COREOPSIS

COREOPSIS VERTICILLATA

It's easy to see why this low-care perennial is among the favorites at garden centers everywhere. Its fine-textured, airy foliage forms a dense, erect, rounded habit with no pruning or staking required. Pair that with yellow flowers that bloom all through the summer, and you have a standout for any garden.

Uses: Broad sweeps; front of a border; nectar source for butterflies

Size: About 3 feet tall, depending on the cultivar, and about as wide

USDA Plant Hardiness Zones: 4 to 9

AHS Heat Zones: 9 to 1

Preferred Site: Full sun to partial shade in moist, well-drained soil

Other Planting Options: Threadleaf coreopsis is drought-resistant.

Growing Guidelines: Cut back in fall or in spring before growth begins. You can deadhead for stronger prolonged bloom, cut back after blooming for a late-season rebloom, or do nothing and enjoy moderate, ongoing bloom throughout the summer. Divide clumps in spring or fall as plants begin to show signs of weakening in the center.

Pest and Disease Prevention: No serious pest or disease problems

Special Tips: Coreopsis combines well with spring-blooming bulbs by concealing the fading bulb foliage and filling in bare spots. The yellow flowers also mix well other primary-colored summer-bloomers such as blue Russian sage and red crocosmia.

Related Plants: 'Moonbeam' is a compact 18 to 24 inches tall with luminous pale yellow flowers. 'Zagreb' features bright yellow flowers with a stiffer, more upright habit and a height up to 18 inches.

The glowing pale yellow of coreopsis 'Moonbeam' combines beautifully with other colors in the summer garden.

OXEYE DAISY

LEUCANTHEMUM VULGARE

Oxeye daisy blooms from late spring through early summer, bearing 2-inch-wide flowers in the typical yellow center–white petals color scheme. The toothed foliage is dark green, which really helps to show off the creamy white blooms. Plants are clump-forming in the garden.

At home along the roadside, in a meadow, or in the garden, oxeye daisy is tough and durable and combines beautifully with other early bloomers.

Uses: Border, bed, or naturalizing; good in combination with other early-season bloomers; nectar source for some butterflies; also makes good cut flowers

Size: 1 to 2 feet tall, depending on the growing conditions

USDA Plant Hardiness Zones: 3 to 8

AHS Heat Zones: 8 to 1

Preferred Site: Full sun; evenly moist soil

Other Planting Options: Oxeye daisy is a tough competitor, adapting to a wide range of soil conditions, heat, drought.

Growing Guidelines: Grow this plant "hard" (with little, if any, fertilizer or compost) to keep growth compact and sturdy. Divide clumps in early fall or early spring. Deadhead flowers for longer bloom.

Pest and Disease Prevention: No serious pest or disease problems, except deer

Special Tips: Avoid high fertility as it will produce tall, floppy plants that will require staking.

Related Plants: 'May Queen' is a free-flowering, long-blooming cultivar. Shasta daisy (*Leucanthemum × superbum*) is short-lived, with larger flowers that bloom through the summer.

BOLTONIA

BOLTONIA ASTEROIDES

The mounded gray-green foliage of boltonia is willowlike and beautiful in its own right. When it's covered with 1-inch daisylike flowers from late summer through fall, it's like getting a bonus!

Boltonia 'Snowbank' is charming and tough, blooming in the late season.

Uses: Border, bed, or naturalizing; combine with other late-season bloomers.

Size: 4 to 6 feet tall and about 4 feet wide

USDA Plant Hardiness Zones: 4 to 9

AHS Heat Zones: 9 to 1

Preferred Site: Full sun to light shade in moist, well-drained, humusy soil

Other Planting Options: Boltonia is drought-resistant and can succeed in a wide range of soil types.

Growing Guidelines: Cut boltonia back in fall after it blooms or in early spring before growth begins. Divide clumps in spring. While other boltonia cultivars may need staking, 'Snowbank' grown in the sun rarely does.

Pest and Disease Prevention: No serious pest or disease problems

Special Tips: While boltonia is drought-resistant, drier soil produces smaller plants.

Related Plants: 'Pink Beauty' produces soft pink flowers, and 'Snowbank' bears bright white flowers. Both are compact varieties. The species can grow to 6 feet.

RUSSIAN SAGE

PEROVSKIA ATRIPLICIFOLIA

This plant is upright and shrubby, with fine-textured gray-green foliage and purplish blue flowers that bloom mid- to late summer. It's tall enough to use in the back of a border but airy enough to plant in front of other bolder foliage plants, too. Russian sage is aromatic, and the dried foliage can make a nice winter feature.

Combine Russian sage with other plants that can't take hot sun, such as sedums, yarrows, and dwarf fragrant sumac.

Uses: Beds and borders

Size: 4 feet tall and about as wide

USDA Plant Hardiness Zones: 6 to 9

AHS Heat Zones: 9 to 6

Preferred Site: Full sun, well-drained soil

Other Planting Options: Russian sage is tough enough to withstand drought and baking heat.

Growing Guidelines: Cut Russian sage back to within several inches of the ground in spring before new growth begins. Division is seldom necessary.

Pest and Disease Prevention: No serious pest or disease problems; rarely attractive to deer

Special Tips: If you live in a cooler climate, don't be surprised if this plant dies back to the ground in winter. It will resprout from the roots in spring.

Related Plants: 'Blue Spire' has violet-blue flowers, finely dissected leaves, and an upright habit.

SIBERIAN IRIS

IRIS SIBERICA

Graceful and upright, this plant has narrow, swordlike leaves and elegant flowers of violet, blue, or white that bloom in late spring or early summer. A clump of Siberian iris lends a simple yet elegant air to any garden.

Use the vertical lines of Siberian iris to complement other more rounded or mounded plants in your landscape.

Uses: At water's edge; beds or borders; also makes great cut flowers

Size: About 3 feet tall

USDA Plant Hardiness Zones: 3 to 9

AHS Heat Zones: 9 to 1

Preferred Site: Full sun to partial shade in moist, rich, well-drained, and slightly acid soil

Other Planting Options: Siberian iris is drought-resistant and can adapt to a wide range of soil conditions.

Growing Guidelines: Cut growth back in fall or in spring before new growth begins. Divide clumps in spring as needed.

Pest and Disease Prevention: No serious pest or disease problems. Siberian iris is fairly free of the pests such as iris borer and soft rot, which trouble other iris species.

Special Tips: While Siberian iris prefers adequate moisture, it is drought-resistant. Plants that grow in drier conditions tend to be shorter, however.

Related Plants: 'Caesar's Brother' has dark blue flowers and grows to 36 inches. 'Little White' grows only to 18 inches and features white flowers. Many other cultivars in a range of colors are also available.

ANNUALS

MADAGASCAR PERIWINKLE

CATHARANTHUS ROSEUS

For easy care and heat tolerance, annual periwinkle has few rivals.

Pinwheel flowers measuring about 1 ½ inches across bloom against glossy, clean, dark green foliage from late spring until frost. Flower colors include white and shades of purples, pinks, and magenta. You can also choose from upright, creeping, and cascading cultivars to suit your planting spot.

Uses: Beds, planters, and hanging baskets

Size: Typically 10 to 15 inches tall

Preferred Site: Full sun to partial shade in moist, well-drained soil

Other Planting Options: Madagascar periwinkle can tolerate heat and tough urban conditions.

Growing Guidelines: Once established, water as needed

Pest and Disease Prevention: No serious pest or disease problems

Special Tips: Also called annual vinca; repeat colors or mixtures to pull together a garden composition, combining Madagascar periwinkle with ornamental grasses and bold-textured plants for height and color.

Related Plants: 'Polka Dot' creeps and cascades over planters and hanging baskets. The 'Pretty' series is compact and free-flowering; the 'Cooler' series has round, overlapping petals.

COCKSCOMB

CELOSIA ARGENTEA

'Apricot Brandy' provides a soft shade that combines well with yellows and blues.

It's easy to see how this plant got its common name! Its bright flowers, borne on erect stems, resemble rooster combs. You'll find many cultivars offering various heights, habits, and colors, but most bloom from late spring through frost.

Uses: Beds, planters, cut flowers for fresh or dried use; one of several food plants for the common sootywing butterfly

Size: 6 to 24 inches tall, depending on the cultivar

Preferred Site: Full sun and well-drained soil

Other Planting Options: Cockscomb is a tough plant, able to stand up to drought, heat, and urban conditions.

Growing Guidelines: Once established, water as needed. For sturdy growth, don't overfertilize.

Pest and Disease Prevention: No serious pest or disease problems

Special Tips: Cockscomb's self-sowing ways can make it a nuisance in some areas and a welcome survivor in others. Check with your local Cooperative Extension office before you plant it.

Related Plants: 'Apricot Brandy' has vibrant apricot-orange color and reaches a height of about 15 inches. The 'Century' series features hot colors like vivid red, rose-pink, and yellow and tall plants with plumelike rather than ruffled flowers.

MEALY-CUP SAGE

SALVIA FARINACEA

Use this upright plant anywhere in your gardens or planters where you want strong vertical lines and a soft, muted color. It has medium green leaves, and its blue, purple, or gray-white floral spikes will bloom from late spring through frost.

Uses: Beds and borders; planters; cut flowers for fresh or dried use

Size: 18 to 24 inches tall

Preferred Site: Full sun with moist, well-drained soil

Other Planting Options: Mealy-cup sage withstands heat, drought, and humidity.

Growing Guidelines: Grow "hard" (don't overfertilize) for sturdy growth and reliable flowering.

Pest and Disease Prevention: No serious pest or disease problems

Special Tips: Perennial in USDA Zone 8 and higher but treated as an annual in other zones. Mealy-cup sage may self-sow but generally not to the point of being weedy.

Related Plants: 'Blue Bedder' reaches 2 feet in height, 'Victoria' comes in medium blue or white flowers, and 'White Porcelain' is an 18-inch-tall white variety.

The neutral blues and grays of mealy-cup sage help to ease color combinations in a composition. Use its muted shades anywhere you need a resting place for the eye in your design.

MEXICAN SUNFLOWER

TITHONIA ROTUNDIFOLIA

In addition to its eye-level appeal, Mexican sunflower feeds butterflies with its colorful flowers and goldfinches with its seedheads. The taller cultivars can add height to a garden quickly, with sturdy stems, coarse green foliage, and gaily colored orange flowers in summer. A shorter cultivar is available for smaller scale plantings.

Uses: Back of a border; temporary screen; cut flowers

Size: 2 to 6 feet tall, depending on the cultivar; 3 to 4 feet wide

Preferred Site: Full sun and good drainage

Other Planting Options: Mexican sunflower is excellent at withstanding drought as well as heat and humidity, but wet conditions are not an option.

Growing Guidelines: Mexican sunflower is easily grown from seed. Don't overfertilize it, or plants will grow extra large but have weak stems.

Pest and Disease Prevention: No serious pest or disease problems; rarely attractive to deer

Special Tips: The intense orange flower color can liven up summer bouquets. To use as a cut flower, sear the ends of the stems before placing the flowers in a vase of warm water.

Related Plants: 'Torch' is a culivar with orange-scarlet flowers. 'Fiesta Del Sol' is a fairly compact culivar, maturing at 2 to 3 feet tall, which makes it a better choice for small gardens.

The quick height attained by Mexican sunflower provides wonderful opportunities for vibrant color at eye-level. Who said annuals had to be down around your ankles?

GLOBE AMARANTH

GOMPHRENA GLOBOSA

Cloverlike flowers of red, purple, rose, white, or orange bloom from early summer until frost on dense, upright, rounded plants. Globe amaranth is often grown for cutting and drying, but it makes a nice edging plant and grows nicely in containers, too.

Tough, compact, and colorful, globe amaranth can spend all day in the sun and still look great.

Uses: Beds and borders; cut flowers for fresh arrangements; dried flowers

Size: 8 to 24 inches tall

Preferred Site: Full sun with well-drained soil

Other Planting Options: Globe amaranth can stand up to heat, drought, and windy conditions.

Growing Guidelines: Grow "hard" (don't overfertilize) for sturdy growth.

Pest and Disease Prevention: No serious pest or disease problems

Special Tips: Dried flowers hold their color well; just cut stems before blooms open fully and hang them upside them down to dry.

Related Plants: 'Strawberry Fields' has true red flowers and is a great companion for white annual vinca. The 'Buddy' series has compact 9-inch plants with purple or white flowers.

IMPATIENS

IMPATIENS WALLERIANA

Impatiens are one of the most popular annuals grown in the United States, and it's easy to see why. These compact plants form neat mounds with rounded, pointed leaves. They bloom continuously from late spring through frost in every flower color except true blue.

Nothing thrives in the shade quite like impatiens.

Uses: Beds, borders, and edgings; planters and hanging baskets; nectar source for butterflies

Size: 6 to 18 inches tall and as wide, depending on the cultivar

Preferred Site: Partial to full shade with a rich, well-drained soil

Other Planting Options: Impatiens will grow in a wide range of soil types and can even withstand some sun as long as the soil is consistently moist.

Growing Guidelines: Impatiens are pretty low maintenance, but if they get leggy by midsummer, you can pinch them back for bushier growth and renewed flow-

ering. If you plant them in containers, you may have to water daily to meet their needs.

Pest and Disease Prevention: See page 211 for tips on discouraging slugs, which like the same conditions as impatiens. Impatiens are also appealing to deer.

Special Tips: Use white or violet shades to light up the shade or the dusk.

Related Plants: 'Accent' series offers a wide range of individual colors as well as a mix; flowers are large and bloom early. The New Guinea hybrids have a larger (2 feet tall) and coarser appearance and grow in full sun. 'Macarena' is a New Guinea cultivar with orange flowers.

'Medallion' Blackfoot Daisy

Leucanthemum paludosum 'Medallion'

The perky flowers and foliage of 'Medallion' blackfoot daisy (sometimes still sold as melampodium) stay that way through heat, drought, and humidity. The plants are mounded with oval, grayish green leaves and numerous 1-inch yellow, daisylike flowers. You can count on blooms from late spring through frost.

Uses: Beds, borders, planters

Size: 8 to 15 inches tall and about as wide

Best Site: Full, baking sun, and well-drained soil

Other Planting Options: 'Medallion' blackfoot daisy is a tough plant that can stand up to a wide range of soil types and conditions as well as heat, humidity, and drought.

Growing Guidelines: Grow "hard" (don't overfertilize) for sturdy growth and reliable flowering.

Pest and Disease Prevention: No serious pest or disease problems

Special Tips: *Warning*—This plant's self-sowing ways can make it an invasive nuisance in some areas and a welcome survivor in others, so check with your local Cooperative Extension office to find out before you decide to plant it.

Related Plants: 'Million Gold' is another cultivar you might like to try, although it's not as readily available as 'Medallion'.

Combine blackfoot daisy with Russian sage and showy stonecrop for a dynamic heat-tolerant combination.

Four-O'Clock

Mirabilis jalapa

Unrefined but exuberant and colorful, four-o'clocks have been garden favorites for generations. Plants form a bushy, shrublike—sometimes sprawling—jumble, with deep green leaves and trumpetlike, fragrant flowers that open in late afternoon.

Uses: Borders; cottage garden; evening garden; as a placeholder for shrubs to be planted later

Size: 18 to 36 inches tall

Preferred Site: Full sun or partial shade with moist, well-drained soil

Other Planting Options: Once established, four-o'clocks will tolerate heat, humidity, drought, urban challenges, and a wide range of soil types and conditions.

Growing Guidelines: Four-o'clocks are easy to grow from seed. In the South, they will overwinter; in the North, you can ei-

ther dig up the tubers and replant them in the spring, or simply start again with new seeds or transplants.

Pest and Disease Prevention: Japanese beetles can cause damage, so avoid using this plant if you live in an area where these beetles are common.

Special Tips: *Warning*—The seeds are poisonous, so be careful if your small children are helping you plant them.

Related Plants: 'Tea Time' is a relatively compact 24 to 30 inches tall with pink, yellow, white, and red blooms.

During the growing season four-o'clocks can assume a shrublike stature, bloom profusely, and perfume your whole yard.

YELLOW COSMOS

COSMOS SULPHUREUS

Upright stems bear deeply cut leaves and double flowers in orange, yellow, or red that reach 2 to 3 inches across. Yellow cosmos blooms freely from early summer until frost, although the plants may give out in hot climates. Not to worry—they self-sow and create more plants, so your season of bloom won't be affected.

In a butterfly garden, yellow cosmos combines beautifully with verbena, marigold, and lantana.

Uses: Beds and borders; naturalizing; cut flowers; significant nectar source for butterflies

Size: 12 to 36 inches tall, depending on the cultivar

Preferred Site: Full sun in well-drained, not-too-rich soil

Other Planting Options: Yellow cosmos adapts to a wide range of soil conditions and can withstand drought.

Growing Guidelines: Although plants are available in flats where summer annuals are sold, you can have great results by direct-seeding the plants where you want them. Grow "hard" (don't overfertilize) for sturdy growth and reliable flowering. Cosmos are easily damaged by late spring or early fall frosts.

Pest and Disease Prevention: Japanese beetles can be damaging, so you might want to avoid cosmos if you live in an area where these beetles are common.

Special Tips: Cosmos's self-sowing ways can make it a nuisance in some areas and a welcome survivor in others. Check with your local Cooperative Extension office before you plant it.

Related Plants: 'Bright Lights' mixes yellows and oranges for a colorful effect. 'Cosmic Orange' is a compact 12 inches. Common cosmos (*C. bipinnatus*) has finely dissected leaves and large billowy flowers, which are typically white, pink, and shades of purple. Common cosmos can reach 36 inches and also self-sows readily.

Spider Flower

CLEOME HASSLERIANA

Spiky petals and stamens give this popular annual its name. Spider flowers have fine-textured foliage, but they grow tall and sturdy enough to hold their own growing among shrubs and perennials. Flowers are usually either rose-purple or white. Plants have a pungent, musky odor, so you may want to think twice before using them in a cut arrangement.

Spider flower's fine texture and large presence make it distinctive when it's combined with other plants.

Uses: Beds and borders; temporary screen since they grow tall quickly; cut flowers

Size: Up to 5 feet tall, with a spread of 2 to 3 feet

Preferred Site: Full sun to partial shade in evenly moist, well-drained soil

Other Planting Options: Spider flower can take the heat as well as the hostilities of urban environments.

Growing Guidelines: Once established, water as needed. Grow "hard" (don't overfertilize) for sturdy growth. Otherwise, plants may need staking, which isn't easy to do because they develop sharp spines by midseason. If you prefer shorter, stout plants, pinch them back when they are young.

Pest and Disease Prevention: No serious pests or diseases

Special Tips: Spider flower's self-sowing ways can make it a nuisance in some areas and a welcome survivor in others. Check with your local Cooperative Extension office to find out.

Related Plants: Any cultivars in the 'Queen' series are excellent choices.

CHAPTER 5

Saving Energy
with **Ease**

Unless your home was **designed** to be particularly energy-efficient, you could probably use a little help from your landscape to make your house **easier and less expensive** to heat in the winter and cool in the summer. Surprisingly, some of the most **effective** energy-saving landscape strategies require little in the way of effort and expense. All you need is **a good eye** for energy-saving opportunities. The **right plants** in just the **right spots** can make your landscape one that's beautiful and easy to maintain, as well as one that **makes your home** more **energy-efficient** What more could you ask for?

Put **Nature** on **Your Side**

Being warm-blooded creatures, we humans tend to be most comfortable when our environment is around that perfect 70°F temperature. Too much humidity or temperatures that are 20°F hotter or cooler, and we head for the thermostat to regulate our comfort. Both heating and cooling can be expensive, plus they eat up a lot of our natural resources. So it just makes sense to use nature to help control the negative effects of weather.

The climate where you live isn't the only factor that determines how cool or hot your property is. The amount and direction of wind, the amount of sun, and the lay of the land (hills, valleys, flat terrain) are all major players in shaping your comfort. These features all work together to create climates that range from hospitable to downright hostile. Often, it's our own manipulation of the environment that makes for less than ideal conditions. Building, excavating, paving, and clearing land all have an impact on the climates we live in. To reverse some of those negative effects, simply enlist nature to help. You might need cooling shade or perhaps a protective wind block. Either way, you can use landscape plants and benefit from their natural ability to moderate the weather conditions on your property.

Saving Energy-Saving Money

Whether you're planning a major renovation to your property or you simply want to enhance part of your yard, you can use the ideas in this chapter to ensure that the changes you make are more than cosmetic. They can also be ones that improve your bottom line by helping you save heating and cooling costs. From big, earth-moving productions like building a berm or siting a new house to smaller, do-it-yourself projects like planting a fast-growing vine to cover a trellis for some shady relief in the summer, you'll find lots of ideas to make your landscape naturally beautiful *and* worth every penny you spend on it.

Making the Most of Microclimates

If you're building a new home, identify areas where you can use existing conditions as opportunities to keep indoor and outdoor spaces cooler in the summer and warmer in the winter. For example, if your property has protected areas, consider situating entrances in these directions. You'll be less likely to let in blasts of cold breezes in winter or hot, humid air in the summer. Cooler, windier spots are more likely to need winter protection, so fewer doorways and windows facing in this direction is a good idea. In a warm climate, cool air pooling at

The shade of a healthy tree can not only cool your home but also help to reduce the "heat island" effect—a hot situation that occurs when buildings and paving absorb sunlight.

the bottom of a slope might be just the thing to help keep your house cool. If you're building in a cooler climate, however, such a low-lying spot might get frost more frequently.

If your property has existing shade, see that it won't obstruct winter sun where you need it to warm up and light up indoor spaces. A better idea is to use the shade to protect the air-conditioning unit (if that's in the plans) or an outdoor-seating area.

In the backyard, warm protected spots are ideal for lounging or outdoor reading during transitional fall or spring weather. They're also great for growing plants that might be otherwise marginally hardy in your area. Areas that stay cool and breezy might be inhospitable in winter but pleasant for outdoor activities in hot weather. Keep these ideas in mind whether you're working with new construction or planning some revisions to your old home place.

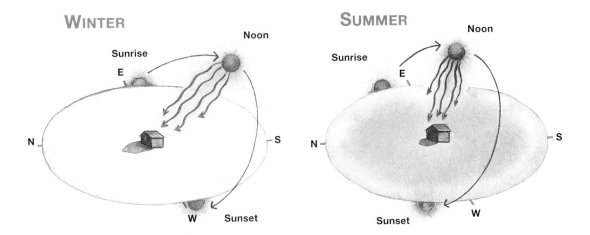

As you observe the conditions of your property, being aware of how the sun moves—through the day and through the seasons—can help you to make the most of beneficial microclimates and also avoid vexing mistakes.

The **Gift** of **Shade**

Shade is one of the most pleasant and effective ways to control cooling costs. Hot summer sun entering the house can raise indoor temperatures, damage or fade fabrics and furnishings, and cause glare. You're likely to have outdoor spots where harsh, beating sun can be just as problematic. Paved areas located in the blazing sun not only reflect glare where it's not wanted, but they also continue to radiate heat long after the sun sets. Sun beating down on an air-conditioning unit can reduce its efficiency and increase its operating cost measurably. Heat and glare can make outdoor living downright hostile, too.

If your family prefers to head for air-conditioned comfort over the muggy outdoors, you can reverse the situation by adding some comforting shade to your property. Even new construction that's initially bare of trees can be fully clothed before long. Simply pick your priority areas and start planting! Try these ideas to reduce the problems or discomfort from too much sun.

- Keep sun-reflecting elements like pavement to a minimum. While you probably need the sidewalk in front of your house, you can limit paved walkways around your property or replace a concrete slab with a wooden deck.
- Use trees and shrubs to protect your house, pavement, air-conditioning unit, and outdoor living areas from too much sun. (See "Shading Your Air-Conditioning Unit" on the opposite page for ideas.)
- Install an arbor, pergola, canopy, or trellis in an area that needs some shade but where a tree wouldn't suit. (See "Energy-Saving Structures" on page 109.)

Strategic Shade

There's nothing like shade to make a space more welcoming and humane and nothing like its economy for inexpensive cooling. A mature tree provides both shade and evaporation—a combination that can remove as much heat as several air conditioners! The first places to consider shading include

- Hard surfaces like driveways and patios that can reflect heat onto your house
- Window and roof areas of your house, using deciduous trees for summer shade
- Air-conditioning units for greater efficiency and cost savings from 10 to 50 percent
- Eastern or western exposures to prevent glare in your home from the low angles of the sun
- The upwind side of your home where shade can cool your breezes

Well-placed shade can reduce the air temperature as well as cooling costs, making a space more inviting and economical.

Shading Your *Air-Conditioning* Unit

If you have central air-conditioning, one of those big green or tan units most likely is taking up space somewhere along the foundation of your house. Quite often, homeowners landscape on either side of them, leaving the unit exposed. Rather than treat this metal unit as just another shrub in line with all the other foundation plants, you could landscape around it. Not only will you be hiding the air conditioner from sight, but you'll also be keeping it cooler. When it's cooler, it will take less energy—and money—for it to cool your house.

Believe it or not, shading an air-conditioning unit can reduce your cooling costs by up to 50 percent! If more homeowners did this, we could greatly reduce peak demand and power plant emissions during summer heat waves. But even if you're the only one on your block to take advantage of this trick, you can still reap the benefits.

Air-conditioning units are normally installed quite close to the house, so shade from a tree may not be an option. Instead, you can plant evergreen or deciduous shrubs. To avoid future size battles with your shrubs, choose plants that will reach a maximum height of 6 to 8 feet and that have compact growth. And when you plant, be sure not to block air flow from the unit. You'll need to allow enough room for the maximum size your plant will become, as well as clearance space as indicated by the air-conditioner manufacturer. Evergreens will keep your unit hidden from view year-round. Some good choices are certain dwarf false cypresses (*Chamaecyparis* spp.),

smaller yews (*Taxus* spp.) or junipers (*Juniperus* spp.), compact heavenly bamboo (*Nandina domestica*), and the more compact arborvitaes (*Thuja occidentalis*) like 'Smaragd' or 'Techny'. Deciduous shrubs can also do the job because the unit really only needs to be shaded during the summer months. Depending on your growing conditions, you may want to plant butterfly bush (*Buddleia davidii*), sweetshrub (*Calycanthus floridus*), winterberry holly (*Ilex verticillata*), star magnolia (*Magnolia stellata*), elderberry (*Sambucus canadensis*), or certain spireas (*Spiraea* spp.).

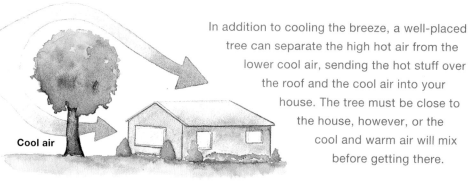

Warm air

Cool air

In addition to cooling the breeze, a well-placed tree can separate the high hot air from the lower cool air, sending the hot stuff over the roof and the cool air into your house. The tree must be close to the house, however, or the cool and warm air will mix before getting there.

Get the Most from Your Shade Trees

Before you plant a shade tree, which is a long-term commitment, decide just how much shade you want it to create. For your patio or deck area, dappled or light shade will cool things down, yet still let through some sunlight. You probably want more dense shade around your air-conditioning unit. After all, the air conditioner doesn't need sunlight for any reason. The lists below can help you decide what to plant.

Lighter Shade

Birches (*Betula* spp.)

Kentucky coffeetree (*Gymnocladus dioica*)

Black locust (*Robinia pseudoacado*)

Moderate Shade

Catalpas (*Catalpa* spp.)

Hickories (*Carya* spp.)

Ashes (*Fraxinus* spp.)

Ginkgo (*Ginkgo biloba*)

Walnuts (*Juglans* spp.)

Goldenrain tree (*Koelreuteria paniculata*)

Pears (*Pyrus* spp.)

Crabapples (*Malus* spp.)

Cottonwoods (*Populus* spp.)

Elms (*Ulmus* spp.)

Heavier Shade

Maples (*Acer* spp.)

Beeches (*Fagus* spp.)

Sycamores (*Platanus* spp.)

Oaks (*Quercus* spp.)

Watching the Winds

Wind can be either a bane or a blessing. Depending on the climate in which you live and the season, air movement can vary from cooling summer breezes to harsh winter winds that rattle your windows and sap heat from your home. You can plan your landscape to take advantage of the benefits breezes provide or to protect your property from the downsides of wind. But first you have to know which direction the winds are likely to be coming from.

When cold winter winds blow, where do they hit your property? Are hot, dry summer winds an issue? Do you have cool breezes that you want to reroute toward your house? Combining this information with specifics on windbreaks, wind scoops, fences, and protective hedges will help you make the best of air movement on your property.

Warmer Ways with Windbreaks

If you live in an area that tends to suffer from harsh, windy winters, putting up a windbreak can give your home some much needed protection. Windbreaks work by using friction and drag to reduce some of the wind's energy, by deflecting winds upward, and by breaking a smooth, straight-line force into turbulence.

Homes in more temperate sites can also benefit from a windbreak that will keep things calm on occasional windy days. And even a modest windbreak in urban areas can reduce home heating costs by 3 to 4 percent. In rural areas, the annual cost savings can run from 10 to 17 percent and sometimes as high as 40 percent!

If you're in the market for a windbreak, here are a few guidelines that will help make it most effective.

Plant perpendicularly. Plant windbreaks perpendicular to the prevailing winter winds. For instance, if winds generally come from the north, plant your windbreak on the north side of your house, in a row that runs east to west to block the path of the wind.

Make it 20 percent wider. If you have the room, make your windbreak about 20 percent wider than the area you want to protect.

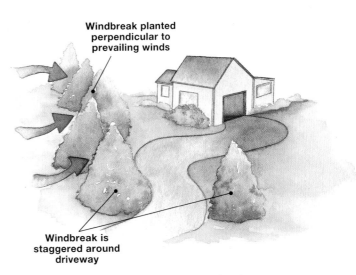

Windbreak planted perpendicular to prevailing winds

Windbreak is staggered around driveway

Winds can accelerate through an opening in a windbreak, such as that for a driveway. Where possible, put a bend in the driveway as shown here so that the windbreak won't be interrupted.

Plant for maximum protection. A windbreak will typically protect a distance that's three to eight times its height. So, if you expect your plants to grow 8 feet tall, you should plant them 24 to 64 feet away from your house (8 × 3 = 24 feet minimum distance; 8 × 8 = 64 feet maximum distance).

Use evergreens. Because they're fully clothed all year, evergreens will give you the greatest amount of protection from wind. You can break up the monotony of all evergreens for greater diversity, more interest, and a place to shelter birds and other wildlife. Just be sure to use evergreens as a base and fill in with deciduous plants.

If possible, plant a windbreak so your home is within the area of maximum protection. If the house is too close to the windbreak, it could be battered by turbulence just downwind from the break.

Stagger the plants. A double row of plants, with the plants staggered from one row to the other, will offer you better protection from wind than a single row of plants.

Use shrubs as a ramp. Plant a row of shrubs on the windward side of your windbreak that are lower than the rest of the planting. These shorter plants will act as a ramp to help deflect winds upward and over your trees and house.

Use windbreaks to reduce snow accumulation. When a windbreak prevents snow from drifting over your driveway, you can reduce the fuel used for plowing—or the labor needed to shovel it!

Don't stake the trees. Surprisingly, trees will grow to stand more firmly in the wind if you stake them only loosely or not at all.

Wind Scoops and Funnels

Winds aren't always an enemy! During hot, sultry summer months, a balmy breeze is a most welcome visitor. You can put nature to work for you, directing desirable winds and breezes to places where they'll be most useful: porches, patios, decks, open windows, or breezeways.

A wind scoop consists of a curved line of trees or shrubs planted quite close together. The gentle curve helps direct the wind so it follows the same curve. Aim your scoop toward your patio or deck and you'll enjoy more refreshing breezes throughout the summer season.

Plant trees close together to form a tight mass and in a gently curving line (called a "wind scoop") so they can direct cool breezes right to your deck or patio—or wherever you want them.

A wind funnel can accelerate and improve an otherwise light breeze. Further constricting and shading the destination with a tree canopy, pergola, or breezeway can make it even more effective.

A funnel, on the other hand, uses two lines of trees that are far apart at one end but that gradually come closer together. Trees or shrubs planted in this cone-shaped formation funnel winds from the wide end though a narrower opening to your house or patio where you can enjoy them.

You can plant wind scoops and funnels either with or without a berm. Choose shrubs or trees based on the size of the area, and plant them in a naturalistic, curving shape to guide the winds with the least amount of turbulence.

A Protective Hedge

In addition to their uses for barriers, privacy, and backgrounds, hedges can help to insulate your home in a cold climate or to protect it from hot winds in an arid one. For instance, a hedge planted on the north side of your house can deflect cold winds upward and create a pocket of insulating dead air space. You'll need to allow plenty of space for growth, though, or you'll lose your air pocket and end up trapping damaging moisture close to your foundation.

If winter's not your problem but hot, summer weather is, you can also use a hedge for protection. Blocking blasts of hot air from reaching windows and doors will improve your comfort and your pocketbook.

Energy-Saving Structures

Trees and shrubs aren't the only way to create some shade or manage the winds. In fact, if you need some shade in a hurry, building or installing a structure may be the fastest and easiest route to take. From a simple trellis to a more complex pergola, you can create some shade in just the few short weeks that it takes to grow a vine. Other ways you can block wind, shade an area, or even reduce the air temperature range from building a fence to installing a pool or water garden.

Arbors, Pergolas, and Canopies

Once of the nice features of arbors and pergolas is that they can give you seasonal shade overhead, yet let the sun shine in to warm things up during the cooler winter months. With a flowering vine or climbing rose, you can cover your structure with the beautiful flowers, and folks sitting in the area below will enjoy their sumptuous fragrance.

Of course, if you live in a climate where you'd like year-round shade, you can plant an evergreen vine such as Armand clematis (*Clematis armandii*) or Carolina jessamine (*Gelsemium sempervirens*).

Another option is to use a fabric canopy that will give you the effect of a covered outdoor room. A fabric canopy is a wonderful choice for a spot where a tree or even a vine just isn't practical. While cotton canvas

Extend nature's beauty overhead with a vine-covered pergola to shade your outdoor dining area.

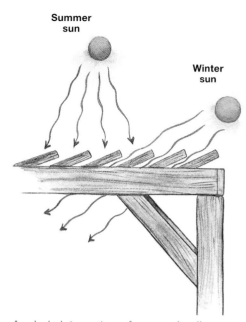

Summer sun

Winter sun

Angled slats on top of a pergola allow morning sunlight to come through. But at midday when the sun is high in the sky and temperatures are soaring, the slats will block the intense light and heat.

fabrics have long been used for awnings and canopies, acrylic fabrics aren't prone to rot and are available in a variety of colors so you can suit your surroundings with something as subtle or festive as you desire.

Arbors can be arching or flat-topped to fit your outdoor decor, and you can buy or build them to suit. Choose wood or metal structures depending on the style of your home and your other outdoor furnishings.

Pergolas normally are flat on top, with horizontal structures for growing vines. Left unplanted, a pergola will let some sun through to an area between the slats on top. This may produce enough shade for your situation. You can even dress up an naked pergola with hanging baskets of potted plants. Choose plants suited for partial shade and you can enjoy a variety of greenery overhead. Just be sure you'll have easy access to the plants for regular watering.

Depending on the placement, an arbor or pergola can help shade an indoor room, too. And their shade will also can help to cool breezes before they enter the house. If you choose a vine that doesn't grow too densely, you'll find that the light it lets through to your patio, deck, or indoor rooms has a warmer, more dappled quality. What a nice way to enjoy the benefits of sunshine without its harsh glare.

Trellises

Trellises are vertical structures used to support growing vines. They can be free-standing along the side of a house, shed, or other structure and can be as decorative or simple as you like. One inexpensive idea is to use simple wood lattice that you can get at any home center.

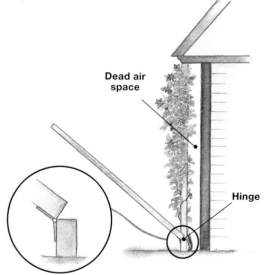

Dead air space

Hinge

To make maintenance tasks on your home's exterior easier, use a vigorous vine that can regrow quickly when cut to the ground, and hinge the trellis for quick and easy access.

To use a trellis for shady comfort, place it where it can cast shade on a porch, deck, or patio. For energy savings, plant an evergreen climber on a trellis to help insulate a cold wall. Using spacers to hold a trellis several inches away from a wall, you create an insulating dead air pocket. Just be sure the trellis is easy to remove for house maintenance.

Fences

If you need a windbreak but don't have the space for a deep planting, a well-designed fence may provide some relief from cold winter winds. Be sure to use a style that allows some air through, however, or the fence may create turbulence downwind that's worse than the original blow! Dress up the interior of your fence with a narrow planting bed for perennials. If you don't even have space for that, try incorporating a mow strip at the base of the fence to eliminate trimming in this tight spot.

In addition to all the noise-reducing and wind-blocking benefits a berm has to offer, you'll also enjoy the view. Here, the evergreen trees and shrubs really help to deaden the noise and soften harsh winter winds, while the deciduous tree adds lovely fall color to the mix of plants.

Berms

Berms can be serious business, so it's a good idea to get help from a landscape architect and an experienced contractor if your project is large. Alone or combined with plants, they can deflect cold wind or help to channel cool summer breezes. Close to the house, a berm can also block the sun's low angles if sun glare is a problem.

Sculpt berms carefully with flowing curved lines that resemble natural land forms and so they can guide the air with a minimum of turbulence. For more ideas on how to use and create berms, see "Reducing Unwanted Noise, Glare, and Wind" on page 43.

The vertical slats on this fence allow some wind through and imitate the performance of a planted windbreak better than a solid fence.

CHAPTER 6

Pulling It
All Together
with Hardscaping

Hardscape elements can be used to **solve** a multitude of
landscape headaches that can steal precious
hours of gardening time—or hours you would rather spend sitting
in the **shade** enjoying a cool drink, playing with your
children, or **sleeping in a hammock.** If you have
all too much experience dealing with overgrown patches
of grass or weeds that require **weekly trimming,**
muddy quagmires around the garbage cans,
or slippery, weed-choked paths, it's time to
take a look at what **hardscaping** can do for you.

Make the Most of Your Yard with Hardscaping

All too often homeowners overlook an essential part of what makes a landscape work—or not work. It's hardscaping. Just what is hardscaping? It is the nonliving part of your landscape, meaning elements constructed of materials such as wood, masonry, plastic, metal, fiberglass, or stone. Hardscape elements consist of everything from walkways, paths, driveways, and steps to fences, retaining walls, and edging strips. Other examples of hardscape elements include decks, patios, play sets, concrete pads for trash cans and recycling bins, and mow strips. Ornamental elements such as trellises and arbors also fall into the category of hardscaping.

It's all too easy to get caught up in the living portion of the landscape—the trees and shrubs, the flowerbeds, and vegetable or herb gardens, for example—and treat the hardscaping simply as an afterthought. That's unfortunate because well-planned, well-constructed hardscape elements make it easier to enjoy the plants that fill your yard. Good hardscaping makes your yard more practical, attractive, and enjoyable to use.

Safety First

You'll also want to take a look at your hardscaping options if parts of your yard aren't safe or convenient to use. For example, if you can't find a level spot to set down a chair outdoors—let alone a picnic table—hardscaping is the answer. For more ideas on how these all-important landscape features can solve problems and make your yard more enjoyable, see the illustration on page 115.

This chapter begins with guidelines for looking at the existing hardscape elements in your yard and determining which of them are working for you and which are not. After that, you will find information on a variety of hardscaping features organized from the house out—starting with "Decks and Patios" on page 118, which typically function as extensions of the house itself. The sections "Walks and Paths" and "Steps and Stairs" follow. These elements function as a network to connect features in the landscape. Next, you'll find discussions of other hardscape features: driveways, retaining walls and terracing, fences and freestanding walls, edging and mow strips, hardscaping for utility areas, play structures, and outdoor lighting. Use the information in these discussions to help you think about ways these nonliving landscape elements could enhance your yard. Throughout the chapter you'll also find ideas for small, straightforward projects to help you get started—look for the "Easy Projects with Great Rewards" boxes—as well as two major projects you may want to tackle.

Evaluate Existing Hardscaping

Begin your hardscaping makeover simply by walking around your yard to evaluate the existing hardscaping and determine which elements are useful to you. Keep in mind if you live in a new house or one with very little in the way of landscaping, you may not have much hardscaping to examine beyond a driveway and a front walk. If this is the case, the illustration below may give you some ideas on elements to add. Once you have evaluated existing features—and looked at your landscape in terms of problems and opportunities that call out for good hardscaping—make a list of top priorities.

While you are examining your landscape's hardscaping, pay special attention to whether or not in-dividual elements are safe. Don't assume elements such as play sets, decks, or retaining walls are safe and functional. This is especially true when a home is new to you, but even when you've owned your home for years, it is a good idea to periodically inspect hardscape elements for safety and function. If you are not particularly handy or knowledgeable about these features, consider paying a professional for a detailed home inspection such as the kind you might have performed before purchasing a house. If you have a professional inspection done, schedule it so that you're available to go along, and wear clothes that you won't mind getting dirty. By tagging along, you'll learn vastly more about the condition of the existing hardscaping than you will from just reading the final report. You are also likely to pick up some great pointers on future maintenance of your existing hardscaping.

BEFORE   **AFTER**

As you examine your hardscaping for safety, think about places where new hardscape might improve an unsafe or unusable area. Here, a grassy slope was transformed from a hazard to a pretty garden supported by a retaining wall. A new deck and railing are also safer than the original crumbling patio.

To do your own hardscaping evaluation, start by making a list of each existing hardscape element in your yard, then jot down notes on its condition. After that, decide whether or not it is a "keeper" or if it should be removed. Use this list for reference and for prioritizing projects. To evaluate a hardscape element, look first at whether or not it is safe. Then consider whether or not it is used by or useful to the members of your household. If it is neither safe *nor* useful, make plans to remove it to prevent potential accidents. If the item is a keeper, the next step is to decide how well it functions for you, whether the regular maintenance it requires is reasonable, and

whether it needs any repairs. The "Evaluate Your Hardscape" flowchart on the opposite page will guide you through this process step by step.

Once you have evaluated hardscape elements, make a list of action items—individual elements that need to be removed or that need repairs or maintenance. List them in order of priority, with unsafe items at the top of the list (cracked, uneven front steps that have been heaved up by tree roots, for example). Next, list elements that simply are not useful and also should be removed. Finally, list hardscape elements that need safety-related repairs and essential maintenance (a deck that needs the railings repaired and sealing to protect the wood, for example). If minor modifications can reduce or ease an item's maintenance demands, list these next because they can free up more time for other important activities in your life.

Take time to think creatively about existing hardscaping, too. If enhancements would make a particular element function or look better or provide more enjoyment, add them to the list as well. (If you have a boring concrete patio with a chipped-up surface, for example, see "Resurfacing a Tired Concrete Patio" on page 124 for ideas on how to improve it.) Look for features that don't have a convenient design, too, even though you may have gotten used to working around the inconvenience. Perhaps there isn't enough space near the back door to step aside when it's open—or room for getting through the door easily with an armload of groceries. A landing or small deck may eliminate an awkward spot like this. Finally, make a plan for any ongoing maintenance your hardscaping requires such as painting, staining, sealing, or safety inspections.

Evaluate Your Hardscape

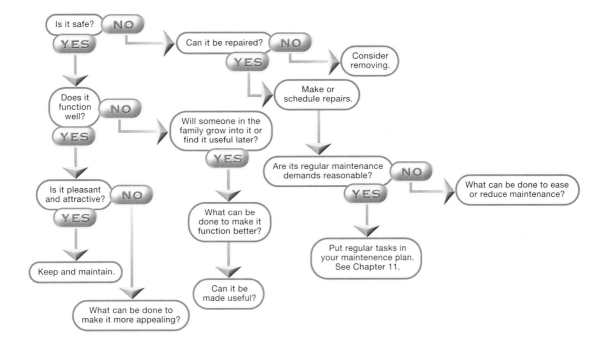

Is it safe? → NO → Can it be repaired? → NO → Consider removing.

YES

Can it be repaired? → YES → Make or schedule repairs.

Does it function well? → NO → Will someone in the family grow into it or find it useful later?

YES

Will someone in the family grow into it or find it useful later? → YES → What can be done to make it function better? → Can it be made useful?

Make or schedule repairs. → Are its regular maintenance demands reasonable? → NO → What can be done to ease or reduce maintenance?

YES

Are its regular maintenance demands reasonable? → YES → Put regular tasks in your maintenence plan. See Chapter 11.

Is it pleasant and attractive? → NO → What can be done to make it more appealing?

YES

Keep and maintain.

Plan a **Hardscape** Makeover

When it comes to planning for and installing new hardscaping, it pays to take the long view. Time and money spent now on well-designed, correctly installed hardscaping will pay big dividends for years to come. The dividends vary depending on the types of projects you are considering—hardscaping may save you time on trimming and weeding, eliminate a spot with compacted soil where nothing will grow, or carve out new spaces to enjoy in your yard. Furthermore, well-designed hardscaping is an essential part of an effective, attractive landscape, which will add to your property value.

One reason the planning process is so essential is that many hardscaping elements can be expensive and time-consuming to install. Also, hardscaping can be very difficult to change if you get a particular element installed—paved paths or a deck, for example—and don't like the result. Keep in mind that major hardscape projects often require a building permit. Check your local building codes before ordering materials or starting work.

If you don't already have a list of new hardscaping elements you would like to add to your landscape, start one now. Once you have a few ideas for new features down on paper, undoubtedly you will need to prioritize projects—and work them in with your action items list. Thinking in terms of a long-range plan pre-

Consider Your *Hardscape Style*

Hardscape elements such as decks, walkways, retaining walls, or fences should complement the style of your house, not work against it. In fact, such elements can be strong forces in unifying the overall design of your house and yard. When planning any element, look for building styles and materials consistent with those featured in your house. For example, a rustic, weathered cedar deck would look out of place attached to a charming Victorian house but would enhance a ranch house in a natural setting.

Repeating particular materials or building styles throughout the landscape is an excellent way to enhance the overall design of your property. If you are planning a patio, consider using flagstones—or rougher stones in a similar color—for pathways or retaining walls. Repetition of materials visually integrates different elements in your yard and makes them work together as a unified whole.

vents wasted effort and helps get you moving in the right direction. For example, if that new deck or patio isn't in the budget this year, you can at least set aside the space for it and avoid planting trees and shrubs on the site that would need to be removed later. And perhaps a simple mulched expanse would suffice as a temporary outdoor living space for a year or two.

Decks and Patios

Classic outdoor living spaces, decks and patios create comfortable spaces for spending time outside that typically are directly accessible from indoors. They are usually located at the back of the house, but in some instances a deck or sitting area at the front door might be a perfect choice. These structures usually are most convenient when connected directly to the kitchen, dining room, or family room, but depending on the layout of your yard, a freestanding deck or patio might be ideal. If you design a freestanding deck or patio out in the yard, be sure to give it the charm of a hideaway with plantings; an arbor, pergola, or sunshade; and perhaps a fire pit. A nicely detailed path leading to the spot can complete the picture.

Wherever they are located, these structures take careful planning. Before you begin to design in earnest, you'll want to take time to decide how you would like to use your deck or patio. Do you expect to read, entertain, sunbathe, barbecue, play with children, grow plants, watch birds? Answering all

This deck, which is nicely proportioned to the size of the house, extends the living space with room for relaxing and dining in a pretty garden setting.

these questions will help you determine essentials such as location, size, features, and surroundings. You also need to determine what utilities, accessories, and furniture you need for those activities. Do you need electricity for lights? Water for cooking or watering plants? A specially designed barbecue or cooking area? Table and chairs? Storage?

Using your base map from Chapter 2, sketch out a deck or patio area to determine the space you'll need. (Begin by assuming that you'll need at least as much square footage as the largest room in your home.) For utilities, consider whether you need (and how you'll supply) essentials such as water, electrical power, and gas. Be sure you've thought about lighting as well. Consider what you want to illuminate and at what level—overhead or in the railings or steps, for instance. Also think about possible lighting styles and where lights should be located. Some other considerations to keep in mind as you develop a functional, satisfying design follow.

Style and Materials

To create a deck or patio that is compatible with your house, use a building style and materials that are consistent with your home. Using a similar style and materials will visually unify your new outdoor living space with your home's exterior. Also look from the inside out: A deck or patio adjacent to your home will look like another room and should harmonize with your home's interior, if possible. For example, a painted deck with turned spindles for balusters would enhance the charm of a house with Victorian

Decks are very popular and look great with contemporary houses or those sheathed in clapboard or cedar siding. But if your home is built of stone or is more formal in design, a flagstone patio may be a more natural choice.

Alternatives to *Pressure-Treated* Wood

Wood is a natural in the landscape, but it doesn't hold up forever! Whether you're using railroad ties, landscape timbers, or dimensional lumber, wood products that home centers recommend for direct contact with soil are likely to have been treated with a chemical wood preservative. While the benefits of using treated lumber where it will come in contact with the ground are clear, so are the risks. Toxic chemicals like creosote, pentachlorophenol, and chromated copper arsenate can leach into the soil. Studies have also shown that these chemicals can potentially be picked up on the skin by wiping or touching treated wood. Although the rate of leaching and the level of uptake in plants is variable and in need of further research, you certainly don't want to expose your children or yourself to these carcinogens. So what should you use instead of treated wood?

Many of the projects described in this section can be made of stone, pavers, or loose fill, but there's no denying that wood is hard to get away from in the landscape. Though you might find good nonwood alternatives for edging, it's hard to avoid wood for decks and gazebos. When wood is the way to go, consider these alternatives to treated lumber.

■ Naturally decay-resistant wood like cedar, osage orange, white oak, black locust, redwood, or cypress

■ Inexpensive untreated wood such as pine treated with linseed oil to deter decay

■ Recycled plastic "lumber"

features—from outside or in—while a brick patio would look great with a colonial house surrounded by a formal garden.

Obviously, wood is the material of choice for decks. Many homeowners use treated lumber for decks, but there are nontreated options, including cypress, cedar, and redwood, that won't be harmful to you and your environment. For the pros and cons of the various choices, see "Alternatives to Pressure-Treated Wood" on this page.

Patios can be constructed of a variety of materials: Look first at a material that will repeat elements on your home's exterior. For a handsome, textured surface, options include brick, tile, flagstone, wood blocks or rounds, commercial pavers, or cobblestones. Both concrete or exposed aggregate are options for a poured surface, and they are available in a variety of colors and textures. If you are unsure of what materials would work best, take a trip to a large distributor of building stone (listed in the Yellow Pages). You may find one in your area that has small "demonstration" patios in a variety of materials that will help narrow your choices.

Terrain and Trees

Decks originally were used to add usable outdoor living space to homes built on hilly terrain. Today, they've become so popular that they now appear in almost every setting, and decks are as common on level lots as they are on slopes. One reason decks

Before installing a patio around a tree, as shown here, it pays to talk to a professional about the steps needed to protect your tree.

are so popular is that their design can be adapted to almost any site. You even can build a new deck over an old patio without the expense and work of removing concrete, and—if you do it very carefully—you can build them around or among existing trees. If you design a deck around trees, it is very important not to make grade changes around existing trees. Also, take steps to ensure that the

original drainage and moisture in root zones isn't drastically changed by construction. To confirm that your existing trees are good candidates for incorporating into a deck design, consult with a professional arborist.

A patio or terrace adjoining the house functions much like a deck does. It offers space for dining, visiting with friends, sitting, or playing outdoors. Patios also can help to make narrow sideyards more useful. You can choose from a variety of materials, from flagstone paving to packed pea gravel or concrete, but whatever their construction, patios and terraces work best on level sites. (You can level out a gentle slope with a low retaining wall.) Because of the construction required to install a patio (including cutting and filling soil to level the site), it takes planning and care to preserve existing trees near a new patio. If preserving trees is a top priority, a deck may be the best choice. For tips on protecting trees during construction, see "Don't Disturb the Trees" on page 26.

Views and Privacy

Consider views carefully as you site your deck or patio. If your home has a stunning view of a mountain or lake, you probably already know how you will site your project. Whether your surroundings are breathtaking or mundane, use a base map like the one in Chapter 2 to record and remember your likes and dislikes as the seasons change. How will the elevation of a deck change the perspective on the views? Are there views to screen? Are there views to open by selectively removing some plants? Is there an undesirable view that your freestanding patio or deck can obscure from the house?

Tips for *Outdoor* Furnishings

Whether you are furnishing a deck or patio or looking for chairs to place on the lawn, thinking about how you enjoy the outdoors may help you narrow down the seemingly limitless choices. Do you garden well into the fall and start again in early spring—or even garden through the winter? Or do you hibernate indoors until the late spring sun is good and warm before venturing out? If you enjoy the outdoors all year and don't want to waste any time on that first sunny day, consider weatherproof furniture that doesn't have to be stored in winter. You'll save storage space as well as the time and effort it takes to move it. You also will get to enjoy it whenever nice weather calls—even if it's February!

The downside of weatherproof furniture is that it tends to be heavy and expensive. Substantial weatherproof furniture is probably not a good idea if you move frequently or if you like to rearrange your outdoor furniture regularly. (The new cast aluminum furniture is an exception; although it is expensive, it is fairly lightweight.)

If you enjoy the outdoors mostly in the warm months and prefer not to invest in the rugged, weatherproof stuff, some of the more portable, storable, functional pieces may be for you. Unlike teak or cedar, furnishings made from heavy plastics or other good-quality materials are sturdy and functional, yet easy to store and adaptable to rearrangement in the yard at a moment's notice. Here are some other suggestions to keep in mind for selecting and getting the most out of outdoor furnishings.

■ Shy away from furnishings or other accessories that have to be brought inside during a rain. Sooner or later, you'll get caught, and you probably have better uses for your time and attention!

■ Look for designs and materials that drain promptly and dry quickly. On solid metal chairs, for example, look for drainage holes. With fabrics, seek out the quick-drying synthetics. Darker finishes and fabrics are great for fast-drying—especially in the sun—but beware of situations where your furniture might overheat and scorch someone.

■ Finally, look for rust-proof materials so you can avoid the sanding, painting, or frequent replacement that comes with the territory.

For items you don't expect to move in your landscape, like heavy picnic tables, substantial benches, or planters, consider creating a "pad" of mulch, pavers, or textured concrete on which to set them. This prevents the hassle of trying to grow grass in their shade, moving them to mow, trying to mow around them, and having to return for a session of hand trimming. Make pads flush with surrounding turf, so you can mow with one wheel on the pad and avoid hand trimming entirely.

Privacy is important when it comes to the location of your patio or deck, but don't give up a good view only because you perceive a lack of privacy. There may be other solutions. Decide whether you can alter the visibility of your deck by screening with either plants or a structure. Designing your space with high railings, screening balusters, an arbor, a pergola, or a trellis can go a long way toward maintaining some seclusion.

Air Currents and Sunlight

Wind and sun can work in tandem to make a space delightfully appealing or appallingly hostile. Your climate, as well as the season or seasons during which you expect to use your deck or patio, will help determine whether you want to take advantage of the sun's warmth or to take refuge from it. Also be aware that the quality and brightness of the light on your

Where privacy is an issue, a screen of plants or a well-placed garden structure can create a cozy nook for reading, romance, or simple contemplation.

deck or patio are likely to be reflected into the indoors in adjacent rooms throughout the day, so plan on manipulating that light with an arbor, pergola, sun shade, or a simple umbrella. See Chapter 5 for more ideas on arbors and other structures for sun control.

Does your deck or patio need protection from or exposure to the prevailing winds? Is there a breeze you would like to catch? If so, make sure your design accommodates that breeze. On the other hand, if winds are a problem, consider locating your deck on the leeward side of your home, where it will be protected from the wind. For ideas on how to catch a good breeze, see "Watching the Winds" on page 106. No breeze at all? Consider installing a ceiling fan suitable for outdoor use and mount it from the bottom of a pergola or other ceiling structure.

Safety

Even the sturdiest, most skillfully built deck presents some danger, particularly to children. Use a reputable, insured contractor or—if you're building it yourself—a set of plans from a reliable source. With a custom design, ask your architect, landscape architect, or designer to review safety options and features with you early in the design process. Before you begin, have a building permit and make sure that the construction plans—whatever their source—are compatible with local building codes. (Stopping construction to acquire needed permits or revising a design to accommodate local codes is frustrating and expensive.) You will find that local building codes often give requirements for key dimensions such as railing heights and widths between balusters. These often are dependent on the elevation of the deck.

Easy Projects with *Great* Rewards

RESURFACING A TIRED CONCRETE PATIO

When the surface of an existing concrete patio has become hopelessly pitted, consider using pavers, slate, flagstone, or tiles to give it a new veneer. It can be a heavy job, but it might be better than that beat-up concrete. Another alternative is to install pavers on a leveled sand base using permanent edging (see the instructions for that project on page 130).

Follow these steps to spruce up your concrete patio with a new surface material.

1. Clean the patio surface. Begin by cleaning the surface of the concrete to remove all loose material and buildup. Treat cracks with patching compound according to the manufacturer's instructions. Also use the patching compound to fill in low spots, as you'll need a level base. To get a good grip between the concrete and the compound, mix latex bonding cement directly into the mortar, or brush bonding cement directly on the concrete in small sections as you go. Whichever you choose, wet the cement for a good bond, but don't leave standing water on it.

2. Install temporary wood edging. You will need wood edging around the patio to contain your mortar base. You'll probably need to dig a shallow trench to position it properly. (If you have plantings around your patio, you may need to move them temporarily.) If you secure the edging with stakes, drive them *below* the height of the edging. That's because you will need to be able to smooth the mortar with a 2 × 4 notched to fit over the edging.

3. Spread the mortar. Because mortar dries quickly, you will want to spread, smooth, and level it in

Storage

Decks and patios present both storage needs and opportunities. A new deck or patio may mean you have to find room to store outdoor toys, furniture, grill implements, and other accessories that will be used there. At the same time, you also can design your deck or patio to include well-placed storage space for other items—perhaps gardening tools and accessories, for example. Screen it with a trellis or enclose it completely to protect items from the elements. If your storage needs are large, plan to take advantage of the space below an elevated deck.

increments: For best results, spread it over no more than 15 square feet at a time. Make the mortar bed ¼ inch thick for ceramic tiles, ½ inch thick for pavers, and 1 inch thick for irregular pieces like flagstones or slate. Fill any low spots with additional mortar.

4. Install the new surface. Still working in small sections, begin to align your new surface material with the edge, pressing each piece gently into the mortar. For tiles and pavers, use spacers to keep the grout lines even. Check to make sure each piece is level and even by laying a board over your work. Gently tap the board over any high units. Continue installing sections and mortaring until you're finished with the entire patio. Be sure to keep the surface wet until you are finished with the entire surface.

5. Grout the pavers. After the mortar has set for a day, come back and grout or mortar the cracks by using a soft wooden or rubber trowel to force a soupy mortar or grout mix between them. Smooth the joints— and make them concave for good drainage—with a piece of ½-inch dowel.

6. Remove excess mortar or grout. When the mortar or grout is almost dry, gently remove the excess with a damp sponge or with a fine spray of water. Spray lightly again with more water, cover the entire patio with plastic and let it cure for a week. After that, remove the temporary wood edging, backfill the soil, restore any plants you had to move, and enjoy!

Walks and Paths

Well-designed landscapes feature a variety of walks and paths that guide people around your yard and let them explore it in comfort and safety. However, not all walks and paths serve the same purpose; there-fore, they do not need to be designed the same way—or constructed of the same materials.

Major routes—like from the street to the front door—should have a clear, well-marked beginning and be designed to make their ultimate destination

(continued on page 128)

MATERIALS FOR PATHS AND WALKS

Materials useful for walks and paths are so varied that you're likely to find one that's just right for your situation. Use the table below to weigh the pros and cons of different surfaces.

Note: In the characteristics column, comments on the unpredictability of the walking surface refer to what that surface could be like to walk on in the dark.

NAME	INCLUDES	CHARACTERISTICS	INSTALLATION COST
GRASS	Existing turfgrass	■ Soft but slow and possibly unpredictable walking surface ■ Shoes get wet from rain or dew. ■ Not for frequent, heavy, or utility use ■ Good for between beds in a lightly used area	None, if it's already there
STEPPING-STONES WITHOUT A BASE	Precast concrete, flagstones	■ Friendly and rustic ■ Walking surface unpredictable; not for utility use or wheelbarrows ■ Easiest to install ■ Subject to frost heave and breakage due to lack of a stable base	Least to moderate, depending on material used
EARTH CONCRETE	Native soil mixed with concrete or stabilizer	■ Earthy and natural-looking ■ Walking surface somewhat unpredictable ■ Follows ground contours well ■ Best on soils with some sand ■ Easy to install but experiment with soil/concrete proportions first.	Minimal
LOOSE FILL ON SAND BASE WITH EDGING	Shredded bark or stone mulch, crushed shells, pine needles	■ Organic materials give a rustic, informal look; stone gives a more formal one. ■ Walking surface fairly predictable ■ Follows ground contours well ■ For moderately used areas ■ Fill can stick to shoes and be tracked indoors. ■ Can wash away in heavy rain	Moderate

NAME	INCLUDES	CHARACTERISTICS	INSTALLATION COST
MASONRY OR WOOD ON SAND BASE WITH EDGING	Bricks, pavers, tile, wood blocks or rounds	■ Masonry choices can go from formal to casual in appearance. ■ Wood choices can be charmingly rustic. ■ Durable and predictable walking surface	Minimal, if you have the wood on hand; moderate to high, depending on the masonry choice
CONCRETE	With or without pebbles or other aggregate	■ Looks can go from formal to casual. ■ Durable, predictable walking surface appropriate for daily and utility use ■ No tracking or wet shoes ■ Contractors can provide custom colors and you can, too (see "Coloring Concrete" on page 132). ■ Seal periodically.	Moderate
WOOD DECKING	Redwood, cypress, cedar, or other rot-resistant woods	■ Looks like a boardwalk and can be elevated above lawn, tree roots, or wet area ■ Warm and casual-looking ■ Good for extensions to or from deck or gazebo ■ Predictable walking surface except for those in high heels ■ No tracking or wet shoes ■ Deck-building experience is helpful. ■ Seal every year or two.	High
MASONRY WITH MORTAR ON A CONCRETE BASE	Bricks, pavers, tile	■ Looks can go from formal to casual. ■ Durable, predictable walking surface appropriate for daily and utility use ■ No tracking or wet shoes ■ Seal periodically.	High

clear. A wide, welcoming walk marked with a lamppost or specimen plant will never leave visitors wondering how to get to the front door, for example. Ideally, two people should be able to walk side by side up the main walk to the house.

Heavily traveled routes, such as utility walkways used to carry trash or groceries—or the path children make as they shoot out the back door to play—should be as straight as possible. Since these paths primarily are used when people are hurrying or carrying a load, anything but the gentlest curve is a recipe for missteps. Curves in utility paths inevitably lead to shortcuts across the lawn and thus to eventual soil compaction.

Both major routes and utility paths need to provide for sure footing and clean, dry shoes. They also should be constructed to accommodate heavy traffic without showing wear and tear and should be well lit if they are used after dark. Finally, keeping a walk flush with adjacent turf ensures solid footing and keeps the need for hand trimming to a minimum.

Ideally, your landscape should also feature walkways and paths designed especially for leisure activities. Consider meandering paths to encourage visitors to wander out to a seat at the back of the yard or through a woodland garden, for example. Use curves in a path to gradually reveal a view, heighten the experience of traveling through the garden, or take visitors around (or past) a particularly interesting feature and see it from more than one side. Avoid using curves willy-nilly, however, because a path that simply wanders aimlessly with no apparent purpose tends to be jarring and unpleasant to use. Finally, always try to design paths that have a destination or feature to enjoy at the end. It can be

frustrating to follow a path to nothing more than a dead end. Keep in mind that meandering paths do not always need to be paved (although heavily traveled ones generally do); grass paths are a practical and inexpensive option for light use.

Tips for Turf Paths

Turf paths are wonderful to walk on, but they can soon become bare, muddy, or compacted with overuse. To keep your turf path looking good and working well, keep these pointers in mind.

- First of all, be sure that turf is the right surface for the use the path gets. Anything heavier than leisurely meandering and garden maintenance might call for a firmer surface.
- When you walk on your turf path, stray to the sides regularly so that the middle gets a rest from wear and tear.
- Consider adding edging strips on either side if the grass spreads into adjacent beds of flowers or groundcovers. Edging strips can echo materials used elsewhere in the landscape. For example, if you have a brick main walk, edge your grass paths in brick to create a unifying element.
- Finally, consider a narrow center strip of bricks or pavers on a sand base if regular trips with the wheelbarrow are taking their toll.

Design Considerations

Walks and paths can be strong unifying elements in the landscape. When deciding what materials to use in their construction, consider repeating materials used elsewhere in the landscape. A flagstone or brick patio, for example, could serve as inspiration for the design of all the walks in your yard. You could pave the main walk to your home in flagstone, for example, and then set flagstone stepping-stones into the ground along the less formal routes. Repeating a material—be it flagstone, brick, or wooden features—visually unifies various landscape elements and creates a more cohesive design. For ideas on materials to use for constructing paths, see "Materials for Paths and Walks" on page 126.

Width is another important consideration. Will your path be used by one person at a time or by two people walking side by side? A minimum width for a path that is going to be used by one person is 3 feet. This is a fine width for a route designed for wandering out and exploring the garden, but you will want to make paths wider if you routinely use a garden cart—at least 4 feet wide. For a major route that will be used by two people walking side by side, a width of $3^{1}/_{2}$ to $4^{1}/_{2}$ feet is best. A front walk should be comfortably wide, for example, so you can walk out, greet visitors, and return to the house with them. It also is a good idea to widen any path at a curve.

If you need a path to traverse a slope that's steeper than a 5 percent grade, it's much safer to install stairs or a ramp. If your design features a wall and a walk that run parallel to each other, buffer them with a planting at least 2 feet wide. If they must be closer, keep the wall as low as possible to make the walk more comfortable to use.

If your new walk or path crosses lawn, plan to have it installed level with the lawn. You'll save mowing and trimming time by being able to take the mower right over it (except for the loose-fill paths) or run a mower wheel along the edging. (See "Edging and Mow Strips" on page 137.)

While a meandering path makes for a nice stroll, pathways that are used frequently, such as from the front door to your car, should be direct. Otherwise, people tend to stray and cut across the lawn.

Easy Projects
with *Great* Rewards

INSTALLING PAVERS ON A SAND BASE

For walks, patios, and even driveways, pavers installed on a leveling sand base offer an alternative to concrete or mortar masonry. They hold up well and require relatively few tools to install. Once you've determined how much square footage you need to cover, you'll be able to estimate the amount of material you need. To avoid unnecessary waste and expense, ask your supplier if you can return any unused units (less some spares for replacements if needed) for a refund.

1. Mark the project area's perimeter. Start with strings and stakes or batter boards for straight lines or a garden hose and temporary marking paint for curved ones. Also prepare spacers to be used between your paving units. Popsicle sticks or tongue depressors work great as spacers, letting you lay your pavers with uniform spacing until sand is brushed into the joints.

2. Clear the site and excavate. Remove sod or other plants, as needed. Then dig trenches to below your frost line for the edging. Excavate between the

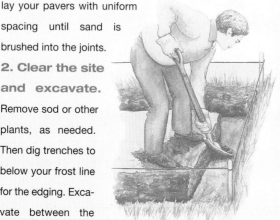

trenches to a depth that will accommodate 1 inch of gravel at the bottom, 2 inches of sand, plus the depth of your paver.

3. Make a firm base. Level the area, then firmly tamp down the soil. Spray the project area with water to make a firm base.

4. Install the edging. Use wood, steel, aluminum, or bricks set on end. (Set bricks on a bed of sand.) Set the edging so that its finished height is at the level where the new surface will be. Check to be sure everything is level, and make adjustments as needed. Backfill the soil as you finish.

5. Spread landscape fabric. For added insurance against weeds, as well as to ensure a stable base, cover the area inside the edging with a permeable landscape fabric, or use heavy plastic sheeting

punched with holes. Overlap sections of your material by at least 1 inch.

6. Spread the gravel. Spread and level a 1-inch layer of gravel over the fabric.

7. Spread the sand. Next pour sand to a depth of 2 inches, level it, and spray it with water to compact it. Continue to spray the sand throughout the project to keep it from drying out.

8. Check the depth. The remaining vertical distance from the top of the sand to the top of the edging, where the surface of your pavers will be, should equal the height of a paver. If it's not, remove or add sand as needed, then level and wet it again. For help with leveling, use a board that you've notched to run over the top of the edging and smooth the sand at the right level.

9. Install the pavers. Press your pavers into the sand in your desired pattern and fit in the spacers

to keep them steady. Level the pavers by adding or removing sand. Work your way out of an area, kneeling only on the sand and not the pavers, which will shift under your weight. For help in leveling, stretch a parallel line across the area for reference and move it as you go. Proceed by laying a section at a time, making sure that everything is level and correcting any individual high or low pavers.

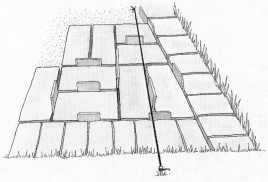

10. Fill the joints. When all the pavers are laid, sprinkle dry sand over them and sweep it into the joints with a stiff broom. Remove the spacers, and spray your new surface with water to flush away excess sand and settle it into the joints. Repeat this a few times, adding new sand as needed, until all the joints are completely filled. Finally, restore any plants or sod disturbed by the edging trench, and enjoy!

Steps and Stairs

On sites that are not level, steps and stairs offer a safe and pleasant transition between one level and another. Although they are commonly an integral part of a walk or path, in some cases steps can also be freestanding. If you have a steep slope in the middle of your lawn, for example, a set of freestanding steps might be a good idea so that visitors can negotiate the slope easily. Ideally, cover the slope with groundcovers or terraced beds on either side of the steps to eliminate the need to mow.

Whether steps are plain or highly ornamental, be sure that they're safe and functional. Use the following guidelines when designing steps and stairs.

Use consistent dimensions. Do not vary the dimensions of the individual steps (the height of the risers or the width of the treads) in a set of steps. When you vary these dimensions, they tend to catch visitors by surprise and trip them.

Highlight steps with design features. It is important that visitors notice steps before they reach the first step, so use design elements that call attention to stairs. If the stairs interrupt a walk, emphasize them with a change in color, texture, or material. In a concrete walk, options might include a different color, a rougher finish, or contrasting steps made of pavers or flagstones. A color that is lighter than the surrounding walk helps emphasize steps in the landscape, but you may want to avoid bright colors in areas where sunlight can bounce off and create a blinding glare.

Coloring Concrete

If you'd like to cut the glare on that new concrete, color it to match your stucco house, or just create a more interesting look, try a trick with latex paint. Use 1 part paint to 4 parts water, making a stain. Apply it in light coats soon after the concrete is poured. A garden sprayer works well for this job; just use one reserved especially for paint, stain, or sealer applications.

Plan for an entrance without steps. Whenever possible, plan on at least one entrance to your home that is accessible without any steps. This not

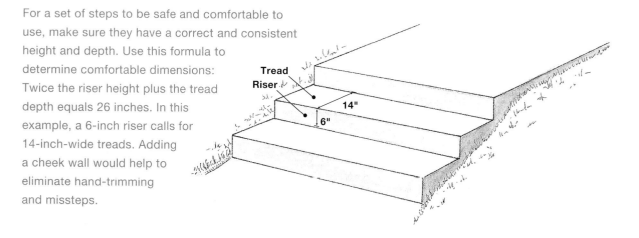

For a set of steps to be safe and comfortable to use, make sure they have a correct and consistent height and depth. Use this formula to determine comfortable dimensions: Twice the riser height plus the tread depth equals 26 inches. In this example, a 6-inch riser calls for 14-inch-wide treads. Adding a cheek wall would help to eliminate hand-trimming and missteps.

Tread
Riser
14"
6"

only makes your home more welcoming to disabled visitors, it also makes it more accessible during an emergency and more accommodating to the very young and the very old. Similarly ramps should slope no more than 1 vertical foot per 12 horizontal feet.

Watch the width. Keep the width of your stairs consistent with the walks they connect. While you can vary tread widths, keep them consistent within a run of steps. Always keep the height of the risers to a standard 6 inches.

Avoid single steps. If possible, avoid installing a single step. In general, people are more familiar with runs of three or more steps, and a single one tends to trip them up. If the grade is that slight, a ramped path may do.

Consider landings. If you are designing a series of steps on a fairly steep grade and your run begins to approach 6 feet in elevation change—plan on a landing of some kind.

Install safety features. In high-use areas, where people might be carrying items or hurrying in the dark, consider a handrail and lighting to help make your steps more safe and useful.

Consider cheek walls for new stairs. These are smooth surfaces on either side of the steps that contain the steps and conceal the corners, which would otherwise protrude and trip people or be damaged by mowers. Cheek walls also can ease mowing along steps that are set in a lawn because they provide a surface for the mower wheel to run along, much like a mow strip.

Plant the edges. If you have steps in a lawn, one of the best ways to add visual appeal, make the site safer, and also reduce maintenance is to plant beds of groundcovers, shrubs, or perennials on either side

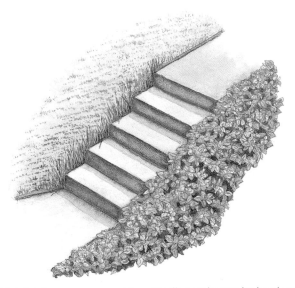

Maintaining grass around freestanding stairs can be hard on you and your mower. Plant a groundcover instead to eliminate the need for mowing and soften sharp edges on the stairs.

of the steps. (This is especially true if the steps have no cheek wall to contain the ends of the steps and conceal the corners.) Not only do the ends of the steps protrude and trip people, they are nearly impossible to mow around—in the process, the mower either damages the steps or the steps damage the mower blade. Beds of groundcovers or other plants on either side of a set of steps not only discourage people from stepping off the sides of the steps, but also eliminate the need to mow or trim right along the edges of the steps. You may want to save even more mowing and plant the whole slope!

Driveways

The driveway is an element that's not quite house and not quite landscape, so it's easy to overlook. Still, a poorly designed driveway can wreak havoc on your landscape and make for unsafe arrivals and departures. Conversely, a well-designed drive that incorporates certain safety and ecological features can be a boon to your family and better for the environment.

If you're designing a driveway for a new or existing home, make sure it's clearly visible from the street and easy to turn into. If you have the space, provide dedicated, out-of-the-way parking that does not conflict with travel or with turning. If you can, give pedestrians a route to and from your front door that doesn't require them to walk on the driveway. Be sure your driveway has adequate lighting, especially for guests and visitors who may not know the lay of the land. Finally, consider a color and material that works with your house, your site, and your climate. For ideas, see "Materials for Paths and Walks" on page 126.

Permeable Paving

Before going ahead with a large paving project, consider whether you can use a more porous option for some or all of the area. Why? Using permeable paving instead of asphalt or concrete is an environmentally sound choice. Unlike conventional asphalt or concrete paving, which quickly sends rainwater to storm sewers or surface channels, permeable paving allows surface water to soak into the soil and recharge groundwater. Because surface water runs off so quickly, conventional paving doesn't allow time for it to soak in and boost groundwater supplies. It also leaves little time for contaminants in the water to break down and for silt to settle out before making its way into rivers and streams.

Permeable paving is suitable for areas that will receive very light use, such as a portion of a driveway that will only be parked or driven on occasionally. For areas like these, turf stabilized with precast concrete or plastic units might be a way to go. In arid climates with sandy soils, earth concrete can be an option for light to moderate use. "Plastic" concrete is a light-to-moderate-use option in areas with no frost. Finally, stones or gravel make a durable, permeable surface if your climate isn't too dry and dusty and your building codes permit. Porous paving (bituminous) is also durable, but good subsurface drainage is critical. Check with a local landscape architect for ideas and suggestions on what permeable paving option will work best for your site, soil, and climate.

Retaining Walls and Terracing

A single retaining wall—or a series of walls that create terraced beds—can transform a sloping site into useful, attractive space suited to any number of purposes. Instead of a frustrating area that is difficult to mow and hard to plant, you can use a retaining wall to create a level playing field or easy-to-maintain lawn. Use a series of walls to terrace a slope, and you can create level beds for flowers, herbs, or other plants. The material you choose to build the walls can either repeat an existing texture featured elsewhere in your landscape (in the walls or paths, for example) or introduce a new one. The size, length, and presence of a wall usually will make it a prominent element in the landscape, so consider the design and materials carefully. That way, you can ensure that it will be a strong unifying element. To keep a large wall from dominating the entire yard, take advantage of the level planting areas it creates at the

Safe, Easy-Maintenance
Retaining Walls

top and bottom. Plantings will soften its effect: Plants at the top can spill over, while the wall will create an interesting backdrop for plantings at its base.

Retaining walls and terracing can be constructed of a variety of materials, including brick, stone, and commercial-locking pavers, as well as wood timbers. It is essential that they be properly designed and constructed—especially if they are more than 1 or 2 feet high. That's because the walls are subject to heavy loads, especially from water accumulating on the high side. With masonry construction, plan on drainage holes; walls constructed with timbers, as well as dry-laid stone, normally are loose enough to allow drainage.

Build retaining walls with a foundation that starts from below the frost line. For large walls carrying heavy loads, tilt the wall back into the slope to reduce outward forces. Limit vertical timber walls to 3 feet in height.

Fences and Freestanding Walls

Both fences and freestanding walls can serve a variety of purposes in the landscape, and when you're planning to install one, it is important to be clear about what purpose you want it to serve. Both types of structures can be used to provide various levels of privacy. They also can be designed to frame or accent plantings or a view. In addition, they can be used as backdrops to plantings, as unifying elements in the landscape, or to keep children and pets in and unwanted visitors

A retaining wall with lawn growing right to the top edge is a dangerous thing for the one who's doing the mowing—or for unwary children or visitors who come upon the edge unexpectedly. Depending on the thickness of the wall, a return trip with hand trimmers may be the safest option to trim an unruly edge, but it certainly is more time consuming. A better solution is to plant the top of the wall with shrubs or perennials that will keep mowers—and others—away from the potentially dangerous drop. The taller the wall, the greater the barrier you'll want to grow. Even on a low wall, make the bed at least 3 feet wide to give the plants a real presence.

By the same token, you'll want to eliminate the need to hand-trim or run the string trimmer at the bottom of a retaining wall. A simple solution is to install a mow strip along the base of the wall. Another option is to create a planting bed at the bottom of the wall. Walls of just about any material make a nice backdrop for perennials and flowering shrubs, so play up the potential! For a retaining wall close to a walk, consider extending the planting to meet the walk and eliminate mowing altogether.

out. As with all other new hardscape elements, check your local building codes early in your planning stages—certainly before beginning the installation.

FENCES

Typically, fences are used to surround the boundaries of a yard, but they also can be used to separate spaces within a garden or to frame, accent, or provide background for plantings. For example, a low picket fence can be a charming accent and also clearly separate a lawn where children play from flowerbeds. Keep in mind that fences can be rather isolating—especially the 6-foot privacy kind—so review your options carefully before you build. Like other hardscape elements, a well-designed fence can be a unifier in your landscape.

Materials for fences can include wood in the form of poles, rails, boards, and lattice, as well as woven twigs called wattle. Other materials can include chain-link, resin, and vinyl-coated steel. The function you want your fence to perform will help determine its design—how tall you want it to be and whether you want a closed design (solid boards, for example) or an open one (such as lattice). Thus, function should help you narrow your choices of materials and designs. For instance, pole, rail, and picket fences have an open design and are low, so they add charm and provide separation but not privacy. Chain-link provides separation, but little charm or privacy. Wattle fences can be tall for privacy or short for separation, and they have lots of character. Board fences can be short or tall, with the tallest designs providing the most privacy, but you can still choose a degree of openness by using a louvered or basket-weave design or one that has a lattice insert at the top.

Keep in mind that a bit of openness in the design of a privacy fence can help make it seem less con-

Wooden board fences are a good choice where privacy is an issue. You can create a more open feeling by choosing one that has a widely spaced treatment at the top.

fining and more airy visually. (Louver-style fences, which have vertical boards set at a slight angle, are attractive and provide ventilation, for example.) A design that has some openness to it—not simply board next to board—will also make your yard more airy in a literal sense because it can help keep the air moving in spots where it might otherwise be still. Even in a low fence, an open design can let in light and air, helping to keep plants healthy.

Gates are an integral part of any fence design, and it is important to consider the placement of your gates as well as their width and style. What is the widest object you'll want to get through it? Will a future project involve a truck with supplies, soil, or a hot tub? Does your property have a utility easement that might require truck access for repairs? Do you use a lawn tractor, garden cart, or riding mower? Keep your options open. If you have an opportunity to put in a utility gate wide enough to accommodate a truck in an inconspicuous but useful spot, do it. For strictly pedestrian access, know that an inconspicuous gate tends to preserve your privacy and a contrasting one tends to extend an invitation to enter.

FREESTANDING WALLS

Use a freestanding wall much like a low fence: to separate spaces, to provide a bit of privacy, or to contain, frame, or define an area. Low walls are great for front yards where you might like some discreet separation from the sidewalk and street but don't want to construct a fence. Low walls made of bricks, stone, or stucco also can form a stately, but neighborly, property line. Regardless of your material, be sure that the foundation begins below your frost line.

A low stone wall separates this property attractively from the road. Adding a planting bed or mow strip in front of it, however, would be a good way to avoid extra hand-trimming.

Edging and Mow Strips

Installing edging and mow strips is a simple, relatively inexpensive way to use hardscaping to reduce landscape maintenance. Use edging strips to separate landscape elements—to keep lawn grass from invading a flowerbed or to discourage groundcovers from spreading into the lawn, for example. By keeping such plantings separate and in bounds, edging strips keep your landscape looking neat with a minimum of intervention from you. (Vigorous groundcovers may be able to overgrow a strip, but you will need to weed out only those few escapees.)

A properly installed edging or mow strip—one that is level with the soil surface or just slightly above it—also makes it unnecessary to make a separate trip around the yard with hand trimmers or a string trimmer. Simply run one wheel of the mower on or just inside the mow strip and trim the edges as you mow. (Choose plants for the bed that can stay a few inches inside the edge of a narrow strip, and spread mulch from plants to the mow strip, so you have an open area to run the mower.)

In areas where you only need to separate competing plants or keep rambuctious growers such as mints in bounds, use narrow edging—made of steel, aluminum, or plastic. Use wider mow strips made of boards, timbers, pavers, or brick where a bed abuts the lawn and you'd like to keep mowing quick and easy. Wider mow strips can also become landscape elements that enhance a design: Brick mow strips can echo brick paths throughout the yard and thus become a unifying element.

Use raised edging—normally formed from concrete—to create a barrier between elements and to channel runoff. Avoid using it next to a lawn where it would create a need for hand trimming.

Easy Projects with *Great* Rewards

EDGING STRIPS TO THE RESCUE!

Spending a few hours installing an edging or mow strip may be the perfect way to eliminate some of your worst maintenance headaches, such as those lawn areas that require weekly hand trimming or regular sessions with a string trimmer to keep them neat looking. Consider installing edging or mow strips in the following locations:

■ In odd corners of the lawn near walks, planting beds, or other features that require lots of backing up and driving forward to mow. Create a simple, easy-to-mow curve or straight line, then install an edging strip to keep the lawn where you want it. Mulch the area you dug up or fill it with groundcovers or other plants.

■ At the base of retaining walls. Position them several inches away from the base of the wall so you can mow and trim in one step. Or, create planting beds at the base of walls.

■ Around pads under utility areas or heavy outdoor furniture such as picnic tables to eliminate the need to mow and trim around them.

■ Along fences to keep lawn grasses out from under the fence and eliminate the need to mow and/or trim. Mulch the area under the fence or, better yet, plant it with low groundcovers, perennials, or shrubs that need little care.

For narrow edging, steel is solid, substantial, and long-lasting. It rusts to a natural-looking brown in time. (Avoid using it next to concrete because the rust can stain the concrete.) Steel is costly though. Aluminum edging has become a reasonable alternative—lightweight but sturdy and makes a good line.

Plastic edging is most commonly available, but it needs to be installed correctly to look attractive and work properly. Since it is difficult to lay a perfectly straight line with plastic edging, it isn't the best choice for formal beds with straight sides. When plastic edging is installed poorly, it heaves out of the ground in winter and can be mangled by mowers.

You will need to start the installation of strips as you would for any other type of edging: by digging a trench along the edge of the bed so you can sink it to the proper depth. Plastic edging has a bead that runs along the top of the strip and a flange that runs along its length. (The flange helps keep the edging from heaving out of the soil.) When the strips are installed, the bead should run along at the soil surface. It is tall enough to discourage most (but not all) creeping grasses from jumping over the top.

To install plastic edging, unroll the plastic in the trench (spreading it out in the sun helps warm it up and makes it easier to keep it flat) and then gradually fill in the trench, checking periodically to make sure the bead is at the right depth. (Edges or ends that are too high will get mangled by mowers.) One disadvantage with plastic is that it's hard to get it exactly straight. To avoid most wobbles, fill the trench in gradually on both sides of the strip, straightening the line as you go. Firm the soil down on either side of the plastic.

Hardscaping for Utility Areas

Every landscape has utility areas, and most cry out for well-thought-out, practical hardscaping. That's because they need to look neat and function well with a minimum of maintenance. After all, utility areas are not the most exciting places to work in— who wouldn't choose planting in the herb garden over cleaning up the weeds around the trash cans?

Whether you have trash cans—or building materials, a trailer, or a boat—that rest on grass or an unmulched patch of soil, the ground around them gradually becomes compacted, weedy or bare, and eventually muddy. Instead of spending time repeatedly mowing, hand-trimming, or weeding around the area, consider installing some sort of a pad to keep the area neat. For trash cans and recycling containers (or other items you store outside), consider building a bin to contain them. All the better if you can

This garbage can can be stowed out of sight behind the low wooden wall, so it won't detract from the lovely view of grasses, shrubs, and flowers.

connect the pad or bin to the house via a walkway (most likely the kitchen door) for easy removal; installing a walkway to the pick-up point (most likely the street) for hauling away is another good idea. Not only will your trash and recyclables holding area be neater and more attractive, it will require less maintenance to stay that way. The fact that shoes and inside floors will stay cleaner (and you may have more helpers willing to take out the trash or recyclables!) is an added bonus. Bins can be made of wood; manufactured ones are often made of plastic or metal. They offer protection from the elements and scavenging animals. If you have to locate a bin in a lawn area, give it a pad or surround it with a mow strip.

Pads for trash cans and other items can be made from a variety of materials. Loose fill such as mulch or stones is one option—in this case, underlay the area with landscape fabric and consider framing it with edging to keep the fill in place. Pavers made of any number of materials also work—consider brick, manufactured pavers, flagstone, or wood rounds. When using pavers, start with a leveling sand base for drainage and stability. You can also have a poured concrete pad.

As a nice finishing touch, you can screen your utility areas: Install a trellis, or erect one or two sections of fence to hide the area from view, and separate them from the rest of the yard. Plant a pretty vine, and you can even make your trash area appealing!

Play Structures

As every parent knows, playing outdoors in the fresh air and sunshine is a great way for kids to learn, explore, and exercise. Backyard play structures help children to develop self-confidence, coordination,

Try siting your children's play area under shade trees so the equipment will stay cool and the kids will be less likely to get sunburned.

strength, and creativity. When they are well designed and in your own backyard, they can also be convenient, private, and inviting for the children to play outdoors whenever they want. Provide activities that accommodate a range of developmental stages, and the equipment is likely to get lots of use— probably to the benefit of your indoor environment!

Use the following guidelines to determine the best location for your backyard play structure:

■ Choose a location that offers privacy and security from the street, even a sense of seclusion.
■ Locate play structures away from hazards like the driveway, power lines, and swimming pool.
■ Look for a location (or plan design features, like fences, for example) that direct kid traffic away from hazardous areas like the street.

Tips for
Safe Play Sets

- Plan on easy access to and from the house over a fairly debris-free surface (path, walk, or lawn) that will help to keep shoes clean or get them clean on the return trip to the house.
- Find or design a direct route between house and play structure that avoids rough areas and planting beds.
- Choose a location with quick and easy access to the nearest bathroom.
- Select a location that is close enough to the house that you can observe and/or supervise either from indoors or from outdoor living areas, but not so close that noise is a problem.
- Plan on close proximity to open play space such as a lawn.
- Select a spot with a mix of sun and shade that's protected from wind.
- Plan on an orientation so that flat or dark surfaces don't get too hot from the sun.
- In addition to space for the structure, keep in mind you also will need clearance for things like swings.

Play structures can be constructed of metal, wood, or plastic, but most combine wood for outdoor ruggedness and plastic for safety on sliding and gripping surfaces. Whatever you choose, be sure it blends with your backyard rather than dominating it. Many play structures are now modular, which allows you to remove and replace pieces as kids' skills develop and interests change.

Whether you're building or buying a play structure, and especially if you're inheriting one from a previous homeowner, consider these safety tips.

- Avoid play sets made from pressure-treated wood so that little hands won't come into contact with the toxic chemicals used to preserve this type of material.
- Smooth sharp or rough edges and splinters, and cover protruding bolts or corners that can scratch.
- Sand off loose rust that can get into eyes.
- Tighten loose bolts and other fasteners.
- See that bolts have smooth heads and covered or ground-off ends that can't catch clothes.
- Check for wear on swing chains and replace them as soon as they are needed.
- Make sure that bases and support posts are firmly anchored in concrete.
- Even though most slides are now plastic rather than metal, check that they and other flat or dark surfaces don't face into the hot sun. Play equipment baking in the sun has been known to burn little hands! In a temperate climate, face slides to the east or north; in a hot climate, face them north only.
- Make sure elements are at usable heights for your child or children, and adjust or change them as needed.
- Seal wooden components as needed with material recommended by the manufacturer.
- Ask your children to report damage or wear as soon as they notice it, and involve them in scheduled maintenance checks.

The surface under a play structure is important because it can make or break its safety. Turf is too hard for children to land on, but even if it wasn't, it quickly dies out under heavy use and the soil becomes compacted in the exact spots where resilience is most needed. (Trimming lawn grass around a play structure isn't a fun job anyway.) Consider using a thick bed of loose fill under a play structure such as bark mulch, wood chips, or pea gravel. You can even find a wood chip mulch made especially for play areas at many home improvement centers. Use sand only if there are no cats around and you don't mind having it tracked into the house on or in shoes. For good resilience, use at least 6 inches of fill, and contain it with edging that's set well away from the play structure. As added insurance against weeds, you can use landscape fabric beneath the fill.

Lighting Your Landscape

Creative, effective outdoor lighting can complement your landscape and make it possible to enjoy your yard and garden during more hours of the day. In fact, if you have a long workday or live in a hot climate, evenings may be the best—or only—time you have for gardening. Outdoor lighting also can help prevent accidents and discourage intruders.

Imaginative outdoor lighting can add drama and intrigue to your landscape at nighttime. You can use it to spotlight a particularly stunning feature, cast dramatic shadows (by arranging lights to shine through an intricate cast-iron fence, for example), or artistically illuminate the branches of a tree or trees. Keep in mind that well-placed lighting is effective both indoors and out: Use it to add warmth and wel-

Well-placed lighting can lend a touch of drama and artistry to the night garden.

come to your landscape whether you're out in the yard or looking out on a rainy or snowy evening.

With all of the choices available for safe, functional, attractive, energy-efficient lighting, avoid confusion and unnecessary cost by assessing your needs before you buy. For safety and security, look first at lighting driveways, walkways, and entrances. Next, focus on other spots where household members come and go, particularly with loads of things like groceries, supplies, items going to the curb for pickup. Do these areas need light for sure footing and a sense of safety? Also consider your need for security lighting. Do you prefer to see the stars in the night sky? Do you feel more secure in darkness, as some people do? Perhaps some manual lighting at entrances is the only security you'll want.

If it's helpful, go outside after dark with a flashlight and do some experimenting. Don't try to simulate daylight unless that's a goal for your security lighting. Instead, try for different effects. Light washing downward can highlight interesting architectural or landscape features. You can make leaves glow in summer and dramatize bare limbs in winter by using lights that point up into the branches of a tree or by positioning lights to backlight the tree. Diffused lighting shining down from trees can be subtle and enchanting. Spotlights on winter-bare plants can cast stunning shadows on walls. For a landscape-in-progress (and whose isn't?), use lighting to feature strong or completed features, leaving unfinished areas in darkness.

Voltage and Other Design Considerations

Once you've done some thinking about your needs and the general types of fixtures that might meet them, tape a sheet of tracing paper on a copy of your base map or landscape plan, and begin to draw the pools, spots, and washes of light that you might want for both safety and enjoyment.

For landscape lighting, you can choose between regular house current (120 volt), low-voltage (12 volt), or solar-powered fixtures. Regardless of your power source, choose good-quality fixtures that won't discolor or degrade in the sun and weather. Furthermore, look for fixtures that either shine down or can spotlight or wash an item with light from a hidden location without blinding you or your neighbors.

House Current: 120 volt

- Even brightness
- Higher-quality fixtures more widely available
- Added costs to electric bill
- Can activate by motion, heat, darkness, timer, or manual switch
- You'll need an electrician to install it.
- Most building codes require wire burial and above-ground conduit.
- Most codes require GFCIs (ground fault circuit interrupters) to reduce shock hazard.
- With hard wiring, a lighting system is less flexible and more permanent.

Low Voltage: 12 volt

- Easy on the electric bill
- Moderately flexible because wires can simply be hidden under mulch or soil
- Can activate by darkness, timer, or manual switch
- Even brightness if you limit wire length and number of fixtures per circuit
- Diminishing brightness with length of line
- Quality fixtures that don't fade or crack in the sun are sometimes hard to find.

Solar

- No impact on electric bill or demand
- No wires
- Landscape lighting is entirely flexible: You can pick up fixtures and move them.
- Wall- or eaves-mounted units for security use
- Your landscape stays lit during a power outage.
- Activates by darkness or switch at each fixture; some have motion and heat detection.
- Cloudy weather may affect brightness.
- Styles of fixtures somewhat limited, but selection is improving.

Hardwired (120 volt) fixtures are still prevalent for security lighting, but solar-powered lighting is now available in house-mounted units. Position switches for 120-volt units indoors when you can so that you'll be able to switch the lights on and off without going outside. In addition, consider whether you want one or several switches to control various security lights. If your only option is to use them all at once—even if you just need one—the impact on your electric bill is likely to be higher. Whether you're using solar or utility power, take advantage of technology—timers as well as light-, heat-, or motion-detection devices— as appropriate to save energy. Finally, be a good neighbor and make sure that your lights don't shine directly into your neighbor's house or yard—or into the eyes of passing drivers or pedestrians.

For low-voltage lighting, transformers reduce the 120-volt house current to 12 volts (the same voltage as car headlights). Most local codes allow low-voltage systems to be installed without an electrician, but there are a few things you'll need to know. First, transformers can support only a limited number of fixtures, and brightness dims with the length of wire, so you may be limited by the number and location of outside electrical outlets. Mount the transformer near the outlet and as close to the fixtures as possible. If the unit has a light sensor so that it will automatically turn on at dusk, be sure it is exposed to daylight but not to artificial light at night. Try out your system before burying the cable in soil or mulch.

If you have a shed or far-off spot where you'd rather not run wires, consider solar lighting. Weatherproof units can mount on an outside wall; others are portable or mountable and can even be placed inside for task lighting.

Maintaining Hardscape Elements

Here are some ideas for protecting your investment in hardscaping and preventing time-consuming and costly repairs. It is a good idea to routinely inspect hardscaping and look for potential problems. Sometimes, a relatively simple solution will delay or prevent the need for costly repairs. For example, if moisture is deteriorating concrete or masonry hardscaping, sometimes all it takes is redirecting water from a gutter with a splash block or correcting a grade to help prevent future problems.

Caring for Concrete and Masonry

Concrete and masonry seem so permanent, but the elements can take their toll. Dampness, standing water from poor drainage, and alternating cycles of

Fun with Hardscaping

Although hardscaping is usually designed to reduce maintenance, change the lay of the land, or keep down weeds, all your hardscaping doesn't need to be simply utilitarian. Consider some of the following options for adding fun to your yard with hardscaping.

Add a Planter

These are great for patios, decks, and any other places where a little waist- or eye-level color would be a plus. Make them from yard-sale finds like old wheelbarrows or wooden boxes, with hypertufa made from sphagnum moss and cement for an aged look, or with upturned concrete drainpipes set in the ground and filled with soil for that post-modern look.

Design a Water Feature

There's nothing like a water feature like a small pond to add interest and a spot of coolness to the landscape. Water not only makes it possible to grow a new palette of plants, but it will also attract wildlife. With a simple fountain, you can even add the sight and sound of moving water to the garden. Great news is that solar-powered pumps and fountains are now widely available, so you don't necessarily need to use electricity. Plan on stocking your pond with fish—they feast on mosquito larvae during the summer months—or, if you don't want fish, float Mosquito Dunks in the water. They contain *Bacillus thuringionsis* (BT), a bacteria that kills the larvae but doesn't harm other garden residents.

Mount a Sundial

Have fun with the sun! Whether mounted on a wall, an old stump, a formal pedestal, or laid out on the ground, a sundial can help you to tell the time and remember what fuels life on our earth. Your sundial doesn't adjust for daylight-savings time, though, and it becomes merely decorative in cloudy weather.

Decorate with Sculpture

Sculpture can be serious or whimsical, obvious or subtly hidden in the shadows. If you have a special item, even a found object that you haven't quite found a home for, consider creating a place for it in your garden. You'll get to enjoy it more, and it's likely to become a great conversation piece.

Support Some Climbing Vines

Plan for some high-flying color by erecting support structures for vines. Vine-covered trellises are effective for adding height and color along the back of borders. They also are ideal when mounted against outbuildings such as the garage or shed or next to the house. Consider a vine-covered arbor as a destination for one of your paths or to add much-needed shade to a patio. A formal wrought-iron pillar—or even a bean-pole teepee—will add height to the middle of your flower garden. Plant permanent structures with hardy vines such as clematis or even climbing roses. Or consider colorful annual vines like bright blue morning glories (*Ipomoea* spp.), red-flowered scarlet runner beans (*Phaseolus coccineus*), or green and purple cup-and-saucer vine (*Cobaea scandens*).

Avoid *Harsh* Deicers

Rock salt and other ice-melting materials can do serious damage to concrete as well as plants, soil, and water, particularly when they're overapplied. In addition, these materials contaminate surface water resources when they wash into storm drains and flow into rivers. When rivers flood and inundate bottomlands with chemical-laden water, the damage spreads even farther.

When possible, consider using alternatives like sand, clean cat litter, or cinders from a wood stove or fireplace. These materials can be messy—they mix with melting snow and ice to make mud and may be tracked indoors—but salt gets tracked indoors, too, and rotting concrete and bare, compacted soil is even messier!

In some spots, it is difficult or impossible to control the use of deicers—many homeowners struggle with the strip of land along the street, for example. If you're planting in an area that will be exposed to deicing salts, check with your local Cooperative Extension office for a list of salt-tolerant plants. Keep in mind that an individual plant can differ in its tolerance to wind-borne versus soil-borne salt. On smaller plants, physical protection—like a loose burlap wrap—may be a practical option for keeping off the salt spray. Also, if possible or practical, all plants will benefit from a good watering to leach away the salts once the snow and ice have gone.

freezing and thawing can wreak havoc as moisture enters tiny cracks and leaches away salts and binders. Add the ravages of ice-melting materials—whether or not applied by you—and even the best construction takes a hit.

If you have new concrete or masonry, use a good paint or a clear sealer to protect it. If you're painting, latex masonry paint protects well on vertical surfaces like walls, but consider alkyd masonry paint for walking surfaces. To apply a clear sealer, use a brush, roller, or garden-type sprayer, depending on the coarseness of the surface. Make an annual application, and your concrete and masonry are likely to weather the seasons and hold onto their good looks.

Algae and Moss on Concrete and Masonry

If you have algae or moss building up on pavers, stones, or concrete, first look for the cause. Is air circulation poor? Is the shade dense? These are usually the major culprits, though acid soil can sometimes have an effect. If it's possible to lighten up or to get the air moving better, do it, or you'll be fighting this particular fight indefinitely. For a quicker but less permanent solution, consider one of the soap-based algaecides or moss killers.

MASONRY REPAIRS

Patching concrete and repairing masonry are worth the effort if the damage isn't extensive. The job mostly takes time, physical strength, and a willingness to follow product directions. If you correct underlying drainage problems before you patch, your hardscaping will look and function better for longer. For tools, count on a 2-pound sledge, a trowel, a wire brush, a brick chisel, and a bucket. Be sure to wear safety glasses to protect your eyes from flying pieces.

- To replace a brick or stone, break away the mortar with the sledge and chisel, then smash the brick or stone and remove the pieces. Apply mortar to the new piece, slip it in, and let it dry.
- To replace grout or mortar between stones or bricks, break it up with a sledge and chisel, then remove all of the loose pieces with a shop vacuum. Make a slurry of the new mortar and carefully pour it into place.
- To patch concrete that has minor cracks or chips, begin by removing all debris from the patch area. Use your wire brush as a final step to remove loose material, then apply a latex, vinyl, or epoxy patching compound according to the manufacturer's directions.
- To repair deeper cavities in concrete, use a bonding agent together with either a patching compound or a conventional cement-sand mixture. (The bonding agent goes down first.) If possible, to help hold the patch in place, undercut the edges so that the hole is wider beneath than on top. Pack in the new concrete and let it dry.
- To patch a concrete step that's crumbling, first remove all the loose concrete. Use stakes to snug a retaining board up against the repair area and fill or pack with a stiff patching compound. Let it dry, then remove the board.

Treating Wood Structures with Care

All too often, wooden decks get lots of use but little care. With time, the wood gets sun-drenched, dry, and thirsty; worse yet, it begins to rot. By preventing damage or catching it early, you can ensure that your deck will continue to provide good times with little care. What follows are some strategies and tips for preventive maintenance and minor repairs.

- Inspect your deck each spring and fall. Look closely for signs of rot where wood comes in contact with soil or concrete or where moisture accumulates.
- Look for boards or other elements pulling loose, and hammer them back in place.
- If nails are popping up and are loose in the hole, remove them. Drill a pilot hole right next to the hole and drive in a galvanized screw. Seal the nail hole with caulk.
- Restain as needed. If you have sap bleeding through the wood, sand it and seal it with shellac or marine varnish.
- If you have mildew or algae, first see how you can restore sun exposure and air circulation to the spot. Solutions involving chemicals or elbow grease will only be temporary if the damp, shade, or stagnant air remains.
- Where posts meet a concrete base or footer, apply caulk as needed to prevent water from seeping down and causing rot.
- Reseal the wood on your deck about every 2 or 3 years. To speed the job, consider using an inexpensive garden sprayer reserved only for that purpose. Apply sealer annually to end cuts—especially those facing upward.

Timesaving Lawn and Garden Techniques

Getting **More** from Your Lawn **with Less**

There's nothing quite like a lawn. It invites you to **play, daydream,** and rest. Its **steady greenness** makes an effective contrast for flowering plants and gives your eyes **a place to pause** while surveying an otherwise busy landscape. Even the scent of newly mown grass may touch off a pleasant sensory memory for you.

But lawns can be big time-consumers, requiring fertilizing, watering, **mowing, and trimming.** You'll find lots of quick tips in this chapter to help you reduce the amount of maintenance your lawn requires, as well as ways to **renovate** problem lawns and develop some of your unused lawn areas into productive, **lower-maintenance** landscape features.

We **Love** Our **Lawns**

Lawns are the mainstay of the American yard. If you walk around your neighborhood, you'll probably spot many yards where the lawn is the prime feature of the landscape. Lawns make great settings for outdoor fun and games, but they're a lot of work to maintain. Not only that, but the American lawn—all 30 million acres of it—has also become an environmental concern. You'll probably want to have *some* lawn, but one of the best things you can do about your lawn is to think smarter and smaller.

How did you learn about taking care of a lawn? Do you do what your parents did, or did you get tips from your neighbors? Maybe you didn't think there was much to learn and just started mowing and watering whenever your lawn seemed to need it. Lawn care certainly isn't brain surgery, but there are a few important things to know about how a lawn grows and how mowing, watering, and feeding affect your lawn grass. Once you learn a little bit about what's going on beneath the surface of your lawn, you can make much smarter choices about how and when to mow, water, and fertilize. The results will be a good-looking, easy-care lawn.

Cutting Down on Lawn **Maintenance**

Like any other plants, grass needs air, moisture, and nutrients to grow. Grass gets most of these things from the soil, in addition to support for its roots.

Healthy soil has lots of life in it, a good balance of nutrients available for plants' use, and a loose, open structure. But the way we manage what's growing on top of the soil can affect the quality of the soil below. Too much chemical fertilizer or pesticides can kill off the soil inhabitants that help chew up and decompose grass clippings, for instance. So while the time and money spent on fertilizing in the spring can give a

quick greening to your lawn, the long-term results are actually detrimental. So it stands to reason that the best way to a healthy lawn is to take care of your soil.

You end up spending more money on fertilizers than you need to, and since the grass can't utilize all those nutrients at once, the excess chemicals run off and contaminate precious groundwater supplies. By rethinking the way you care for your lawn, you can save money and enjoy the benefits of a lawn that works with nature instead of against it. Follow the mowing, fertilizing, and watering tips in this chapter, and you can avoid unnecessary maintenance tasks like applying multiple doses of fertilizer every year and spend more time instead enjoying your yard on the weekends.

By cutting back on the size of your lawn, you can reduce or even eliminate the need for power equipment. A lawn cut with a rotary mower produces no air pollution and very little noise.

The Downside of Lawns

Why are lawns bad for the environment? It's not that turfgrass itself is bad. It's what we do in the name of maintaining it that's harmful.

First of all, when too much area is turned into lawn, there's less habitat for wildlife and beneficial insects. In addition, pollution increases—power mowers belch 10 to 12 times as many noxious fumes as the family car per hour. Plus, folks filling their mowers spill an estimated 18 million gallons of fuel annually, and 70 million tons *each* of fertilizers and pesticides are applied per year.

Add to this picture the contamination of our water supplies caused by excess herbicides and fertilizers running off into groundwater, streams, and rivers, as well as the amount of our drinking water that we devote to keeping our lawns green, and the staggering environmental costs of our national obsession with lawn grass become clear.

Mowing Tips

Mowing your lawn can be one of the most beneficial things you can do for it—if you do it right. When you mow, how often you mow, and how high you mow all have an impact on how healthy your grass will be. And the healthier it is, the less you'll need to water or fertilize it. So just by making a simple change or two in your mowing habits, you can help improve the quality of your yard—and reduce the time you spend working on it.

To get the most from your mowing, you really need to know what type of grass is growing in your yard. If you didn't plant it and you're not sure what it is, you can take a sample to your local Cooperative Extension office where the staff can help you identify it. Once you know the type of grass you have, follow the recommendations below for the kind of care it prefers.

MOW AS HIGH AS POSSIBLE

A lawn that's scalped may look neat and manicured on the day it's cut, but it can quickly take a turn for the worse. It will suffer from heat stress and lack of water and be left wide open to competition from weeds. On the other hand, if you mow your grass higher, the grass blades help shade the soil, keeping the roots cool and reducing water needs. The shade also prevents weeds from growing—they need warmth and light for that process. And longer grass will simply be stronger grass—there's more leaf surface to produce more carbohydrates, which the grass needs for food. While mowing high is always a good idea, it's especially important during a drought. So mow even higher if possible during long dry spells.

Mowing Height Recommendations

The time to cut the lawn is when it's one-quarter to one-third taller than its ideal height. Check the chart below for the cutting height of your type of grass.

COOL-SEASON GRASSES

NAME	IDEAL HEIGHT (INCHES)
Chewings fescue	1½ to 3
Kentucky bluegrass, improved	2 to 4
Perennial ryegrass	1½ to 3½
Red fescue	2 to 4
Turf-type tall fescue, improved	2 to 4

WARM-SEASON GRASSES

NAME	IDEAL HEIGHT (INCHES)
Bahiagrass	2½ to 4
Bermudagrass, improved	¼ to 1
Buffalograss	2 to 4
Carpetgrass	1½ to 2½
Centipedegrass	1½ to 2½
St. Augustinegrass	2 to 4
Zoysia	½ to 2

LEAVE CLIPPINGS ON THE LAWN

Unlike a popular myth may have led you to believe, leaving grass clippings on a lawn doesn't lead to thatch buildup. Leaving clippings on your lawn will actually help your grass grow better, and it's less work for you!

Grass clippings will settle through the grass fairly quickly when they decompose, adding moisture and nutrients to the soil, reducing its water and fertilizer needs. Leaving the clippings where they fall can supply your lawn with a third of its nitrogen needs over the growing season. They also help feed the beneficial microorganisms and give harmful ones something to do. (They're there anyway; better that they work on your clippings than on your live grass!)

If you have a mulching mower, all you have to do is mow and let the clippings lie. These mowers are designed to cut the clippings repeatedly, mincing them so small that they won't clump on top of your lawn. If you have a side-discharge mower, set a mowing pattern so that you'll mow over the just-cut clippings as you cut the next row of grass. Mulching mower or not, if your grass is very tall, you may need to rake and remove it to prevent clumps from smothering your lawn.

CUT ONLY A THIRD AT A TIME

Don't wait until your grass is 6 inches tall then scalp it back to 2 or 3 inches. When you cut off too much of the blade at one time, you'll weaken the grass plants. Besides, by mowing regularly, you'll prevent the grass from getting so tall that it flops and mats, and the clippings will be small enough to decompose readily.

AVOID MOWING WET GRASS

With our busy schedules, it may seem unavoidable to mow occasionally when the grass is wet. But you'll get poor results and create some big problems if you mow when your lawn is soggy.

First of all, wet grass can be too heavy for your mower to cut well. The mower wheels may leave ruts in soft spots, which you'll have to take time to fix in the future. Cutting grass when it's wet can also make it more susceptible to disease problems. Finally, wet grass is slippery—especially on a slope—so mowing it can lead to a nasty spill and serious injury from that sharp, rotating blade. Don't chance it . . . take a break when the grass is wet.

FOLLOW A PROGRESSIVE CUTTING PLAN

To cut really tall grass—the kind that greets you when you return home from a 2-week vacation—follow this simple plan for getting your grass back under control: Make the first cut with the mower set

Mower Selection Chart

The price tag isn't the only cost to consider when you're buying a mower. There are other kinds of costs to factor in—like the impact of using a noisy mower on your hearing and the hidden costs to the environment of using petroleum products. The chart below will lead you to the least-polluting mower options first. Whatever type of mower you choose, look for a dealer who can supply parts and service. For power mowers, consider buying one with an industrial/commercial (i/c) engine. The additional $50 to $75 cost can buy you several more years in engine life. Mulching mowers are beneficial to your yard; if you're in the market for a mower, choose one that can easily convert from mulching to a bagger when necessary.

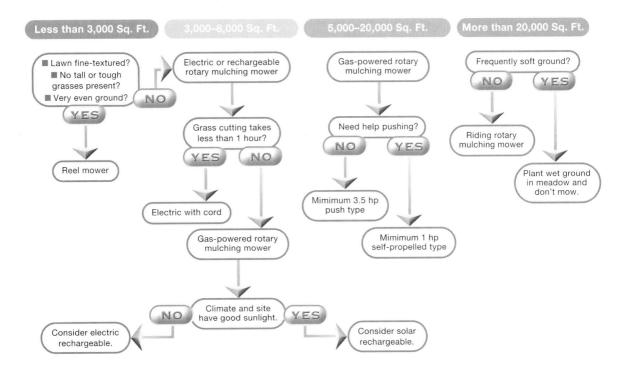

How to *Sharpen* Mower Blades

With just a little mechanical savvy and a few tools, anyone can change or sharpen a mower blade. Give it a try. And remember to keep a spare blade on hand for quick changes or in case of damage.

1. Disconnect the spark plug. This prevents the mower from accidentally starting while you're working near the blade. Secure the wire away from the plug so it can't make contact.

2. Turn the mower on its side. Do this away from your lawn in case gas should spill or leak. Keep the carburetor on the side that's upended to prevent gas from leaking.

3. Remove the blade. Wearing gloves for protection, use a wrench to loosen the bolt.

4. Sharpen the blade's cutting edges. Clamp the blade in a vise, and file *into* the blade rather than away from it, using a medium, flat bastard file. Shy about sharpening? Your local hardware store or lawn mower dealer can sharpen it for you, probably for just a few dollars. If the blade is bent or heavily nicked, replace it.

5. Balance the blade. Using a nail stuck in the wall of your shed, garage, or workroom, hang the blade by its center hole. If the blade doesn't balance horizontally, file or grind off some metal on the heavier end until they do. (A balanced blade prevents vibration, premature engine wear, and hard starts.)

6. Lubricate the blade. Spray both sides of the blade with vegetable-based cooking spray (it pollutes less than petroleum-based products) to prevent grass from sticking.

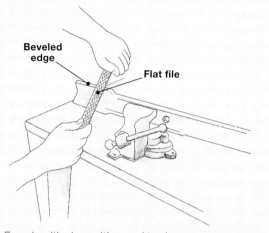

Beveled edge
Flat file

For a healthy lawn, it's good to sharpen your mower blade after 8 to 16 hours of mowing. Learning to do it yourself will cut down on countless errands to your mower dealer or hardware store.

7. Reattach the blade. Be sure the leading edge of the blade is the cutting edge. Most mowers are set up so you can't reattach the blade backward, but do check.

8. Lubricate the mower deck. Spray the whole underside of the mower deck with vegetable-based cooking spray to prevent grass buildup. Don't use a petroleum-based product.

9. Reconnect the spark plug. While you're at it, clean off the spark plug, too, carefully scraping the tip clean.

10. Check the oil reservoir. Make sure the oil is at a safe level. Sometimes it can spill when the mower is turned on its side, which can leave you with a mess to clean up, and it can contaminate your lawn.

at the highest setting. Wait a few days, then lower the setting slightly for the next two mowings until you've reached normal cutting height.

To keep the engine from bogging down, you may have to go slowly, increase the speed of the engine by opening the throttle, or cut only half-widths. *Do* remove clumps of clippings after that first mowing or two because they can block sunlight and promote disease. Don't bag them and leave them on the curbside for trash pickup, however. Dump them on your compost pile, or treat your vegetable or flower garden to a nitrogen-rich grass mulch.

KEEP YOUR MOWER CLEAN

Between emissions and fuel spills, gas-powered mowers can be a significant source of pollution. If you have a small lawn, consider switching to a reel mower, which doesn't create any air or noise pollution. For larger lawns, you'll want to use a power mower, but you can still be kind to the environment if you follow these precautions:

■ Use a funnel or spout when you add fuel to your mower to avoid spills and overfills.

■ Use a gasoline container that's small enough to handle easily; you'll be less likely to spill.

■ Recap both the mower gas tank and the gas container tightly.

■ Keep the mower blade sharp to reduce running time and rpms.

■ Keep the underside of the mower deck clean and clear of grass buildup.

■ Change the oil in your mower at the manufacturer's recommended intervals. Always recycle the used oil—never dump it down a drain or onto the ground.

■ Clean or replace the air filters regularly.

■ Get tune-ups regularly—check your owner's manual for how often to schedule them.

For more on mowers and help in selecting the right one for your lawn, refer to the "Mower Selection Chart" on page 155.

Fertilizing Tips

Each year when spring rolls around, we all seem anxious for the first signs of green. That's probably the reason why so many homeowners are in a hurry to apply fertilizer—and lots of it—to their lawns. That extra nutrient boost really seems to speed things along. But unless you're using a slow-release organic fertilizer, you may be speeding things along too much, which in the end can be harmful to the beneficial soil life in your lawn and damaging to the environment.

Slow-release fertilizers provide just what your lawn needs, when it needs it. It's like feeding your lawn a well-balanced diet. High nitrogen fertilizers, by comparison, force your grass to grow too quickly, which means you'll have to mow more often. But that's not the only problem. Aside from all the time you'll spend mowing, overfertilizing can also kill the soil organisms that munch on your grass clippings. Without them, you'll end up with too much thatch, another problem that leads to more work and more expense. To get rid of that you may need to rent special tools or hire a crew to eliminate the build up.

To feed your lawn without causing these unnecessary problems, use the following low-maintenance fertilizing tips. The result will be a hassle-free, yet lush and healthy lawn.

Test the Soil

Before you apply any fertilizer or other treatment to your lawn, get a soil test. You may find that your grass doesn't need a complete fertilizer (with nitrogen, phosphorus, and potassium) or that adjusting the soil pH level may make more of the existing nutrients in your soil available to the grass. So take the time to have your soil evaluated before you spend time and money on fertilizers you may not even need. You can buy a soil sample bag from your local Cooperative Extension Service or farm co-op for about $10, depending on the tests you request. You dig up the soil sample and mail it in the bag provided. Just be sure to indicate that you're growing lawn and that you'd like organic recommendations. Then use the pH and fertility suggestions you get back as a guide. Do-it-yourself soil-testing kits are also available from garden centers and hardware stores, too, although they may not be as accurate.

Use Only Slow-Release Fertilizers

Slow-release materials tend to produce a lawn with good color yet without excessive leaf growth. They release nitrogen over a longer period of time so they don't have to be applied as often. Also, because the nitrogen isn't released all at once in a big dose, you don't have to worry about the extra that your grass can't use right away getting washed away in the rain. Compost, well-rotted manure, and the various natural organic commercial products that are available are all excellent slow-release options for your lawn.

Compost is a nearly perfect fertilizer that will provide your lawn with the nutrients it needs as well as adding the bonus of disease resistance. It is chunkier than granular fertilizer, though, and may not fit through the openings on some spreaders. (You'll have better luck with a broadcast spreader than a drop spreader.) Another option is to spread a pile of compost as evenly as you can on your grass and rake it to a thin layer. It won't look beautiful at first, but a nice rain will help it break down and seep into your soil.

Let the Clippings Lie

Grass clippings are an excellent source of nitrogen. They work great on a vegetable patch, so why not use them for the same purpose on your lawn, where they'll return small but valuable amounts of slow-release nutrients to your lawn. It sure beats bagging or raking!

Fertilize as Seldom as Possible

Lawn grasses are really quite tough, and with proper high mowing, they'll have enough grass blades to produce their own food. So, by one simple change in habit—adjusting the mowing height—most homeowners can also cut back on the amount of fertilizer they give their lawns. Following my "just once" rule, read below to see when the best time to fertilize your type of lawn is. But even with the most ambitious fertilizing schedule, you should avoid applications that are closer than 8 weeks apart.

Cool-season lawns. Fertilizing in late fall (November) can help you to avoid the questionable spring "green-up" application. If you feel your lawn needs another application, the next best time to fertilize is after spring rains have stopped, and the third time is early fall (September). This strategy will help your lawn to avoid the lush spring growth that, combined with spring rains, requires frequent mowing and invites fungal diseases.

Warm-season lawns. Light, even applications through the growing season are best for warm-season grasses, but avoid fertilizing in late fall. April,

Understanding NPK

Fertilizers are made up of three basic nutrients—nitrogen, phosphorus, and potassium—as well as a bunch of micronutrients. The amount of the three main ingredients are generally indicated by an NPK ratio on a fertilizer package.

Nitrogen (N) helps give a lawn its green color. It generally promotes leaf growth over root growth, which is why too much nitrogen means an ultragreen lawn now, but a shallow-rooted one later. Unless it's formulated for slow release, nitrogen quickly gets taken up by the plants, causing an abnormal growth spurt, or it's leached or washed away.

Phosphorus (P) is critical for root growth. New lawns, whether seeded or sodded, require phosphorus in higher amounts than do established lawns. Both low and high pH levels tend to make phosphorus unavailable to plants. The best pH range for phosphorus intake is 6.0 to 7.0.

Potassium (K) helps plants tolerate stresses, disease, and insect damage. With the exception of sandy soils, potassium is usually plentiful, although a low pH level makes it unavailable.

Be aware that most chemical fertilizers are formulated for lawns growing on dead, chemically dependent soils, and the recommended rates are far higher than you'll need for a lawn growing on a living soil that's constantly releasing nutrients. If you make soil building your goal, you won't have to depend on this method of life support!

The best approach is to time your applications based on your climate, turf type, and goals, and go lightly, especially if you're letting the clippings lie. At an NPK ratio of about 4-1-3, grass clippings are a near-perfect natural lawn fertilizer. Backyard compost varies quite a bit but is generally around 3-1-2. Or you can use a blended organic fertilizer—any product with NPK of around 3-1-2 will be fine. Don't get hung up on the numbers! Make light applications at the most useful times of year, adding more applications at the next most useful times of year if necessary (see page 168).

June, and August are good times to fertilize, with the spring application being the most important.

FERTILIZE BEFORE IT RAINS

You'll have to rely on the weather forecaster for your timing, but if you mow, then fertilize just prior to a predicted rain, the fertilizer will be able to soak into the ground and lie undisturbed by mowing until after that rain.

AVOID HOT, DRY WEATHER

Cool-season grasses go dormant during the hot weather of midsummer. It's a natural defense against hot, dry weather that we often try to prevent by continual watering and fertilizing. If you aren't watering your grass to bring it out of dormancy, by all means, don't apply fertilizer through periods of extreme heat or drought. With rain and cooler weather, your grass will return to its lively green shade.

Applying Fertilizer

If you have a very small lawn, a good eye, and a very steady hand, the best equipment for fertilizing might be no equipment at all. (What you lose in accuracy, you gain in garage or shed storage space!) When scattering lawn fertilizer by hand, you'll find it's easier to spread larger, more visible particles evenly than tiny granular fertilizers.

For liquid and granular fertilizers, sprayers and spreaders offer you a way to get more uniform coverage. Whether you use your hands or an applicator, be careful not to leave any errant fertilizer on sidewalks or driveways where they can wash into a storm sewer and eventually harm rivers and streams.

SPRAYERS

Several types of fertilizers come in liquid form, and you'll need a sprayer to apply them: Compost tea, seaweed fertilizer, deodorized fish emulsion, and liquid cow manure are examples. **Hose-end sprayers** are handy but tend to clog, especially with the particles commonly in many natural organic liquid fertilizers. When they're loaded with a concentrate, though, you can cover a larger area more quickly—if you can avoid the clogs. **Tank sprayers** are more accurate, but you're limited by the amount of material you can mix and use at one time.

SPREADERS

Drop spreaders are very accurate, spreading a consistent amount of fertilizer (or grass seed or lime) in even rows the width of the hopper. In fact, they're so accurate that sloppy applications of quick-release materials leave telltale stripes in the lawn. With natural organic fertilizers, you won't have that problem, although you'll still want to take care to avoid skips and overlaps. Drop spreaders work best with particles of uniform size and do fairly well in the wind.

A **broadcast spreader** has a hopper and a whirling wheel that flings the material out using centrifugal force. You can cover a fairly wide path (about 6 feet) and distribute the material evenly. On better models, the distribution pattern is adjustable for width.

A small hand-held spreader may be just what you need if your lawn is small. A shoulder-mounted broadcast spreader will work for bigger jobs, and the push drop spreader will give even coverage on large lawns. For liquid fertilizers, you can use a hose-end sprayer or a tank model.

When Drought
Strikes

Great on a large lawn but challenging on a small one, some broadcast spreaders come with flaps to lower when you're working alongside a flowerbed or other area where you might not want your fertilizer to go. If you have a large lawn, opt for one with pneumatic tires.

If you don't need a large capacity hopper or if wheels won't work well on your terrain, consider a **handheld** or **shoulder-mounted broadcast spreader.** Look for a model with a plastic cap to protect you from breathing the dust of the material you're applying.

Watering Tips

Lawn grass can actually stand up to some pretty harsh conditions, including dry spells and even droughts. But the only way it can survive such stresses is if it has a substantial root system—one that grows deep enough to tap moisture a few inches down. How do you make sure your lawn develops a good root system? Water it wisely.

When it comes to lawns, watering on a regular basis isn't really necessary—or even a good idea. It's only when grass roots have to reach deep for their own water that they grow strong enough to sustain the grass through tough times. To help your grass develop deep roots and to save time from unnecessary waterings, follow these water conservation tips.

LEAVE THOSE CLIPPINGS!

Grass clippings return small but valuable amounts of moisture to your lawn, so don't waste the effort of raking or bagging them.

All plants suffer during drought—even inherently tough turf grasses. But you can keep your lawn alive through a drought with these water-savvy tips:

■ Water at a rate of ½ inch every 2 weeks if you can. This is enough water to keep the crowns alive but not enough to bring the grass out of dormancy.

■ If you haven't already cut back on fertilizing for the hot, dry months, do it now.

■ Reduce mowing, which causes water loss. When you do mow, choose the coolest hours of the day when your grass will lose the least amount of water.

■ Raise the mowing height even higher than recommended. Taller grass is better able to shade the soil and crowns, reducing water loss and encouraging deeper rooting.

■ Keep mower blades sharp. Dull blades rip rather than cut the grass, which can speed water loss.

■ Pick up clumps of clippings. They increase heat buildup.

■ Reduce or eliminate lawn traffic for the time being. It's a stress on your grass that is avoidable.

■ Don't use herbicides (weed killers)—even the natural ones. They stress the grass and, unless the target weeds are growing rapidly, they're ineffective.

LET YOUR SUMMER LAWN GO DORMANT

Most turfgrasses are beautifully adapted to summer drought. They turn a nice buff brown color, sending their nutrient and water reserves to their roots for safekeeping. Watering, fertilizing, and mowing needs all become minimal, so take a break from yard work while your lawn is resting. Fall rains will restore a healthy lawn to its former soft green condition.

With that said, even a drought-dormant lawn needs a good soak occasionally—not to bring it out of dormancy, but just to keep the crowns alive. See "When Drought Strikes" on page 161 for watering guidelines during drought.

KNOW WHEN AND HOW MUCH TO WATER

Every square foot of your lawn probably doesn't need the same amount or frequency of water. Generally, a lawn needs more water when it's on a sandy or well-drained soil, when it's on a south- or west-facing slope, or if it gets full sun or heavy use. Shady or seldom-used areas require less water. Follow these guidelines to water at the right time in the right amount.

■ Water deeply but infrequently. Deep watering (to 5 or 6 inches down) promotes deep rooting that helps a lawn withstand stresses, including heat and drought. The best way to check your depth is to actually slice the soil with a spade and have a look. You'll quickly get an idea how long your sprinklers or soakers need to run to get a good depth of moisture. Lawn grasses watered lightly on a regular basis become shallow-rooted and weak. Lawns watered too heavily require lots of mowing and extra fertilizer to restore the nitrogen leached away by the water!

■ Look for visible signs that it's time to water, including the beginnings of a gray-green turf color and "tracks" from your footsteps that don't bounce back.

■ Water early in the day when winds are calm and temperatures are lower to avoid evaporation and moisture drift.

■ Let the lawn dry between waterings to prevent fungal diseases. Watering early in the day helps with this potential problem, too.

■ Reduce watering time if water runs off or pools.

■ If you have an automatic watering system, use or add rain- or soil-moisture sensors to avoid unnecessary watering. If your system doesn't have these sensors, you can add them, or simply run your system manually as needed.

Rescuing a Weak Lawn

Some lawns simply need more than what judicious watering, fertilizing, and mowing can provide. If your lawn is weak, bare, or weedy, if it seems prone to damage from summer or winter stresses, or if it's less than 50 percent desirable turfgrasses, your best bet is to replant your lawn. See "Bright Ideas for New Lawns" on page 169 for pointers on reseeding or sodding your lawn. However, if your lawn is more than 50 percent desirable lawn grass, first try these simple strategies to improve what you've got.

■ Test the soil to determine if certain nutrients are lacking, if your soil (and grass) could benefit from a pH adjustment, or if your soil needs more organic matter. When soil is low in fertility, the scene is ripe for weeds like broadleaf plantain to take hold. If the pH level is too high or too low, your grass won't be able to use the nutrients, even if they're present in the soil.

■ Check your soil structure. If it's heavy clay or compacted, consider aerating in the fall. Follow aerating with a topdressing of compost or well-rotted manure. A light coating of about $1/2$ inch should do the job.

A combination of shade-loving groundcovers, bulbs, and perennials will perk up densely shaded areas under trees. It beats having to fight deep shade and surface roots just to try and maintain a so-so lawn.

- Replace areas of densely shaded turf with a shade-tolerant groundcover that won't have to struggle to survive in those conditions.
- Check for thatch buildup. Too much thatch can prevent water, air, and nutrients from getting down into the soil where grass roots need them.

Adjust Soil pH with Lime

The pH level of your soil may be the main reason that your grass isn't growing very well. Even if you fertilize your lawn, you may notice little improvement.

That's because if the pH level is higher or lower than your grass needs, the nutrients will be locked up and unavailable to the grass to use.

Fescues and bentgrasses grow best with a pH between 6.5 and 7.0, while bluegrass, ryegrass, and bermudagrasses like slightly higher pH levels. Compare these ranges with the results of your soil test. If your soil is more acidic (has a lower pH) than these preferred levels, your grass will suffer.

Unless you live in a region where the soil is likely to be alkaline (like the Midwest), it's more common to have soil that's too acidic or sour than it is to have soil that is too alkaline or sweet. To raise the pH level, you need to add lime. Follow the recommendations on your soil test for how much lime to use; they are based upon what pH level you're starting at and how high you need to raise it. In general, you'll need to add more lime to heavy clay soil than to loose, sandy soil. Use a spreader as you would for sowing grass seed or for distributing fertilizer, and wear a dust mask so you don't breath in the small lime particles.

Making even slight changes in soil pH can take sustained effort on your part. You can either keep trying, or choose grasses and other plants that are more adapted to the soil you have!

Aerate to Let Your Soil Breathe

If you're battling heavy, compacted soil and the weeds are winning, you may need to resort to aerating your soil in order to grow a healthy lawn. (You can test for heavy clay soil by squeezing damp soil in your hand. If it forms a tight ball and doesn't easily crumble, it's clay and more prone to compaction than loam or sandy soils.) Aerating is the process of poking holes

Most lawns rarely need aeration, but where compacted soils are a problem, a yearly treatment with a gas-powered aerator will help air, water, and nutrients find their way into the soil.

into the soil to let more space for air, water, and nutrients underground where the grass roots can use it.

While some turf aerators simply push holes in the ground (such as spiked rollers or the spiky sandals you can strap on your feet), the pushing action compacts the soil even further. The best aerator is a gas-powered machine with a reciprocating action that actually *pulls* cores from the ground. The cores (which look like, well, miniature dog droppings) break down on top of the grass and the soil is opened up, leaving more room for root growth and for water and nutrients to penetrate.

Aerating is one of the best things you can do for your lawn if soil compaction is a problem. However,

it's not a practice that you have to do often. Most lawns require aerating only once a year—if that. Whether you're growing a warm-season or a cool-season grass, aerate in the fall and follow it up with a topdressing of natural organic fertilizer, such as compost. Fall rains will wash the fertilizer into the holes, and winter's freezes and thaws will help break down the compacted soil to fill those holes. (Reduced lawn traffic also helps, which is another reason why doing this just before winter is a good idea.) An additional aerating in the spring wouldn't be necessary on most lawns, but if you have heavily compacted soil, it can be helpful.

Aerators are available at tool rental stores, and you can even find a riding model for large lawns. Water the soil the night before so the machine can penetrate as efficiently and as deeply as possible. Go over the lawn at least twice, so you have holes about 4 to 6 inches apart, and apply an organic fertilizer within a few days.

The Catch with Thatch

Oftentimes, grass clippings get all the blame for causing thatch, which is probably why so many people rake them up or catch them in a bagger. However, it takes more than finely mulched grass clippings to make a thatch problem. Thatch is actually a matted layer of grass roots, stolons (the underground grass stems), and clippings that builds up on top of the soil. A little bit of thatch really isn't a problem, but when the layer gets too thick, it prevents moisture and air from reaching the soil, which in turn can kill the grass.

Thatch can develop quickly and is often brought on by the same things that cause many of the other

Strategies for
Busting Thatch

lawn problems I've talked about: using highly soluble chemical fertilizers, cutting the grass too short, light and frequent watering, and compacted soil. The harsh chemicals in quick-release fertilizers, pesticides, and weed killers can especially lead to thatch because they kill the microorganisms and earthworms whose job it is to break down the accumulated clippings, stems, and roots that otherwise become thatch.

In addition to being unsightly, thatch can become thick and spongy, causing the mower to sink in and scalp the grass. Thatch also traps water and nutrients, causing grass roots to grow into it rather than into the soil below. Grass that grows above the soil is more susceptible to the ravages of heat, drought, cold, and heavy use, as well as damaging insects and disease.

How do you know if you have too much thatch? If you can push your finger down through the grass and touch soil, there's probably no problem. However, if you reach a spongy, impenetrable layer of $1/2$ to $3/4$ inch or more, you'll want to use these "Strategies for Busting Thatch" on this page to coax the thatch away.

Sometimes, just knowing when to do lawn maintenance can help prevent weeds from gaining on you. Avoid edging in early spring when annual weeds are germinating. Otherwise your freshly cut edges will be perfect spots for crabgrass or chickweed seedlings to take hold.

If too much thatch is a problem on your lawn, you can reverse the situation by making some changes in your mowing, watering, and fertilizing habits. Using these methods, you can probably avoid the more disruptive process of dethatching (also called vertical mowing), which yanks the thatch up along with a good bit of live grass. Lawns with thatch don't need the added stress!

- Temporarily catch your grass clippings rather than letting them lie. Until you've welcomed the decomposers back, grass clippings will just add to the problem of undecomposed grass parts. Put the clippings on your compost pile or use them for mulch in your garden.

- If you haven't done so already, switch to natural organic fertilizers that help to build a living soil—by that I mean a soil that is alive with microorganisms and earthworms.

- Water deeply and infrequently. If the thatch layer is impenetrable to water, try applying a natural wetting agent like insecticidal soap, which will help the water "stick" to the thatch long enough so it can penetrate rather than run off.

- Core-aerate your lawn, since compacted soil is one factor that can lead to heavy thatch. It's best to wait until fall to perform this step.

Common Chickweed

DESCRIPTION
Cool-season annual that sprouts in fall, flowers in spring, then dies. Flowers disburse thousands of seeds.

PREFERRED CONDITIONS
- Cool, moist weather
- Slightly acid soil

PREVENTIVE MEASURES
- Raise pH by adding lime, according to soil test recommendations.
- Avoid edging in fall, which exposes the soil at a time when conditions are favorable for germination.
- Mow high.
- When practical, pull up what you can.

White Clover

DESCRIPTION
Nitrogen fixer (adds nitrogen to the soil); included in some lawn mixes. Attracts bees to lawns.

PREFERRED CONDITIONS
- Low soil fertility
- Acid soil

PREVENTIVE MEASURES
- Raise pH by adding lime, according to soil test recommendations.
- Maintain nitrogen fertility.
- Mow high.
- When practical, pull up what you can.

Crabgrasses

DESCRIPTION
Warm-season annual grasses that germinate in spring and die in fall, turning brown.

PREFERRED CONDITIONS
- Thin or close-cropped lawns
- Overfertilized summer lawn

PREVENTIVE MEASURES
- Get the lawn growing tall and thick by germination time (normally midspring), and avoid edging then.
- Mow high.
- Water deeply, letting the surface dry between waterings.
- Avoid midsummer fertilizing.
- When practical, pull up what you can.

Dandelion

DESCRIPTION
Perennial with thick, hard-to-remove taproot. Young spring foliage is edible as cooked greens or fresh in salads.

PREFERRED CONDITIONS
- Thin or close-cropped lawns
- Almost any conditions

PREVENTIVE MEASURES
- Prevent germination with a thick lawn that's mown high.
- Invite children to pick the flowers before seed sets.
- When practical, pull up what you can.

Mosses

DESCRIPTION
Bryophytes (nonflowering plants) that spread by spores that are as fine as dust and can blow hundreds of miles through the air.

PREFERRED CONDITIONS
- Shade
- Compacted soil
- Low soil fertility
- Acid soil
- Moisture

PREVENTIVE MEASURES
- If the conditions listed under "Preferred Conditions" describe your overall growing conditions, consider a moss lawn!
- Aerate to reduce compaction.
- Fertilize.
- Apply lime to raise pH level, according to soil test recommendations.
- Consider ways to reduce surface moisture and shade.
- Overplant with shade-tolerant grasses.

Nimblewill

DESCRIPTION
Grasslike perennial that sends out stolons that root at the joints to form new patches.

PREFERRED CONDITIONS
- Wet soil surface
- Close-cropped lawn

PREVENTIVE MEASURES
- Water deeply, allowing the soil surface to dry between waterings.
- Mow high.

Plantains

DESCRIPTION
Perennials that sprout in midspring; can be broad- or narrow-leaved.

PREFERRED CONDITIONS
- Thin lawn
- Compacted soil
- Moist shade

PREVENTIVE MEASURES
- Fertilize.
- Mow high.
- Aerate to reduce compaction.
- When practical, pull up what you can.

Wood Sorrels

DESCRIPTION
Perennials with cloverlike foliage. Young foliage is edible: tangy and high in vitamin C; good in salads.

PREFERRED CONDITIONS
- Compacted soil
- Acid soil
- Shade

PREVENTIVE MEASURES
- Aerate to reduce compaction.
- Apply lime to raise pH level, according to soil test recommendations.
- When practical, pull up what you can.

A MAINTENANCE PLAN YOU CAN LIVE WITH

The easiest way to cut back on lawn maintenance is to follow my "just once" rule. Ask yourself, "If I performed this task (fertilizing, aerating, etc.) just once in a year, when would be the best time to do it?" Then, if you're so inclined, you can build on that single activity by adding a second best time or a third. Following this method puts you in control of how much maintenance you're willing to do. Whether you opt for one or three fertilizer applications, you'll be focusing your time, money, and effort on the times when it will be most beneficial to your yard. Simply refer to the chart below to see what those best times are for your type of lawn (cool- or warm-season grass) and the task you want to do.

LAWN MAINTENANCE FOR COOL-SEASON GRASSES

	Jan	Feb	Mar	Apr	May	Jun	Jul	Aug	Sep	Oct	Nov	Dec
FERTILIZING					B		D*		C		A	
LIMING				B							A	
AERATING				B					A			

LAWN MAINTENANCE FOR WARM-SEASON GRASSES

	Jan	Feb	Mar	Apr	May	Jun	Jul	Aug	Sep	Oct	Nov	Dec
FERTILIZING				A		B		C				
LIMING		B									A	
AERATING		A										

A= the best time to do this task
B= the best time if adding a second go
C= the best time for a third go
D =the best time for a fourth go
*Only if irrigated; not for arid climates

What the Weeds Are Telling You

Weeds are among the biggest indicators that your lawn is having trouble. Some weeds take hold when fertility is low, making it hard for your grass to make a comeback. Others prefer compacted soil or moister conditions than turfgrass.

Learning to recognize the weeds you have in your yard can help you understand the conditions that are going on below the grass. While there's no need to pull out all weeds, you can follow the preventive measures on pages 166 and 167 for each particular type of weed to keep the situation in check.

Bright Ideas
for New Lawns

Sometimes in the rush to give a new home a "finished" look, builders or new homeowners plant grass seed on every square inch that's not paved. (Unfortunately, sometimes it stays that way!)

While lawn is one of the cheapest landscape features per square foot to install, it's also one of the most demanding to maintain. So if you're buying or building a new home and have the opportunity to plan your landscape from scratch, think twice before planting grass seed everywhere just to hold the soil in place. Once that grass is in place, it's a really tough job to remove it, should you decide you'd really rather have an island bed or patio in its place. So before you head out to buy grass seed or hire a contractor to install sod, make a conscious choice about where you really want and need to have grass.

Pare Down to What You Need

Sometimes all a yard needs is a 30 × 40-foot spread of lawn to create an open, inviting feeling. If you have children, you might want a bigger lawn so there's room to play tag, kick a soccer ball, or even round up the gang for a game of croquet. Just remember that lawns are a type of walking surface. If you don't walk or play in a particular

Keeping a lawn concentrated where it's really needed makes room in the landscape for richer plantings. If you design the edge where the bed meets the grass as a smooth flowing line, the planting bed will be a true asset rather than a mowing obstacle.

spot, or conversely, if it gets nothing but heavy traffic, you can probably choose a better surface for the area than turfgrass.

Keeping your lawn small offers benefits to both you and your family, as well as to the environment. A smaller lawn means you might be able to use a less-polluting mower, such as a human-powered reel mower or an electric or solar mower. Even if you have a gas rotary mower, a smaller lawn will help you to reduce emissions by reducing operating time. And, since you'll spend less time mowing, you may find enough time to take up a new hobby or sit down with that book you've been meaning to read!

Places to Avoid Planting Grass

While most homeowners will want some amount of lawn, there are some places where turfgrass would just be too much trouble to maintain. If you have any of the areas described below on your property, avoid planting grass there, and consider other options such as groundcovers, planting beds, or hardscaping features.

- Steep slopes
- Any slope facing south or west
- Heavy traffic areas
- No-traffic areas
- Automobile traffic or parking areas
- Under fences, benches, or plants
- Atop high walls
- Under building overhangs or in sheltered corners
- Where snow, water, or leaves accumulate
- Around rocks or outcrops
- Under trees giving dense shade
- Small, isolated spots

A deck, patio, terrace, or even mulch makes a great surface for heavy and frequently used outdoor furniture. Any of these nonlawn options lets you avoid the lugging, hand-trimming, and other hassles of trying to grow grass beneath each piece.

Reduce Hand-Trimming Up Front

An easy way to cut back on lawn maintenance is to reduce the number of places where you'll have to trim by hand. Mow strips are an attractive yet effective way to do this. Even if you don't have the time or materials to install mow strips at planting time, you can plan for them and install them later. A simple row of bricks that are laid flush with the ground will accommodate your mower's wheels and

Pretty *Alternatives* to Conventional Lawns

Large and small properties each offer their own unique opportunities to break the status quo of turfgrass. Even if you don't have the areas I've listed on the opposite page where you should definitely avoid planting grass, you may simply have too much grass and not enough other enjoyable landscape plants. Here are just a few possibilities you could incorporate into your landscape plans.

- Enlarged beds of landscape plants are interesting to look at and provide habitat for birds.

- Meadow and prairie plantings *(below)* can be right at home even in a residential setting. They usually work best on larger plots, but creative homeowners have tucked them successfully into sunny corners—or even whole front yards—of in-town lots.

- Attractive vegetable gardens *(below)* can work well in yards of any size. Outline them with edible flowers for even more color, and enjoy the flavorful bounty when harvesttime rolls around. Unlike lawn grass, vegetable gardens offer a great return on the real estate space they take up—good eating for the whole family!

- Wooded surroundings often provide the perfect setting for a little wooded area of your own, whether you live in the town or the country. If woods are a backdrop to your property, simply let the pine needles, leaf litter, and wildflowers take over part of your lawn area. (This can happen even more quickly if you give nature a hand!)

Keeping walks and lawns at the same level speeds mowing and eliminates a return trip for trimming.

Choosing the **Right Grass** for **Your Yard**

Today's improved lawn grass cultivars can help you to reduce maintenance as well as water, fertilizer, and chemical use. Many grasses are bred for heat tolerance, and some are endophyte-enhanced, which means they contain fungi that discourage grass-eating insects.

What lawn grass is right for your site? First consider your climate, as grasses are generally categorized as warm season or cool season. Further, you'll want to make note of your soil's type and texture, how the lawn area will be used, how much sun it gets, whether there are south- or west-facing slopes,

give you the space you need to mow close enough to the edges of beds or along walls so that you don't have to return with a hand or string trimmer to finish the job.

To install a brick mowing strip, dig a trench along the edge of the lawn area. The trench will need to be deep enough to accommodate the thickness of a brick, plus about 1 inch of sand beneath for leveling and drainage to avoid frost heave. Lay the bricks in the trench side by side, and backfill the edges with soil as necessary. Level the bricks as you go so you won't have a bumpy surface for your mower to ride on. Pour some more sand over the brick strip and sweep it into the cracks. If you fill the cracks with soil, they'll soon be sprouting weeds.

As long as you don't live in a humid region of the country, our native buffalo grass is a great turf choice that can look great on just a few waterings and mowings a year.

Seed Bag *Primer*

Take advantage of the great information available on grass seed labels. You'll learn what type of specific grass seed you're getting as well as how much weed seed you can expect to get in the bargain. If you're buying in bulk from a hardware store or garden center, ask to see the label from the original bag.

Always look for fresh seed that's been grown for the current year, and beware of bargains. Discount seed isn't such a great deal if it doesn't germinate well or if it contains lots of weed seeds and crop seeds that you don't want growing in your yard.

It's easier to read the labels if you're familiar with the vocabulary and if you know what to look for and what to shy away from.

```
FALL SPECIAL LAWN SEED MIXTURE        TESTED:AUGUST 1999
NET WGT.3.00      POUNDS (1.358 KG)  LOT NO.:48-29970.X23
       PURE SEED                     ORIGIN GERMINATION
34.48%BARON KENTUCKY BLUEGRASS            WA    85%
24.84%STATESMAN II  PERENNIAL RYEGRASS    OR    95%
14.60%CREEPING RED FESCUE *               CAN   85%
14.57%ECLIPSE KENTUCKY BLUEGRASS          WA    85%
 9.85%CHEWINGS FESCUE *                   OR    85%

OTHER COMPONENTS:
   0.00%  CROP SEED        *VARIETY NOT STATED
   1.64%  INERT MATTER
   0.02%  WEED SEED          ITEM NO: 548654
NOXIOUS WEED SEED PER POUND:
NONE

LEBANON SEABOARD CORPORATION    WWW.LEBSEA.COM
P.O. BOX 117 BRISTOL,IL 60512
```

Cultivar. Short for "cultivated variety." Be sure the label lists a cultivar name, such as 'Shenandoah' tall fescue. You'll be getting a specific variety that was bred especially to offer better features than the straight species usually do.

Mixture. Contains two or more grass species; common with cool-season grasses. Some mixtures may include annual ryegrass as a nurse crop that germinates quickly and protects the other slower-germinating grass. Avoid mixtures with more than 5 percent annual grasses or with any amount of bentgrass or rough bluegrass.

Blend. Contains two or more cultivars of the same species. This is often done with bluegrass varieties to maximize resistance to problems like disease and drought.

Straight. Contains a single cultivar; common with warm-season grasses. Buying a straight seed isn't such a good idea for cool-season grasses. If you live in the North, buy a blend or mixture.

Germination rate. The percentage of seed that you can expect to sprout and grow. Look for at least 75 percent for Kentucky bluegrass and 85 percent for perennial ryegrasses, fine fescues, and other turf-type tall fescues.

Weed seed. Percent of seed in the package that will sprout into weeds. Content shouldn't exceed 0.5 percent; 0 percent is even better.

Noxious weed seed. These are the worst type of weeds—ones that may be impossible to get rid of. Content should be 0 percent.

Other crop seed. Percent of seeds that will sprout into plants such as clover that usually aren't considered weeds—unless they're growing in a lawn. Content shouldn't exceed 0.5 percent.

Inert matter. Includes chaff, hulls, and such that won't affect the seed content. While it's not harmful, you don't want to pay for it. Inert matter shouldn't exceed 5 percent.

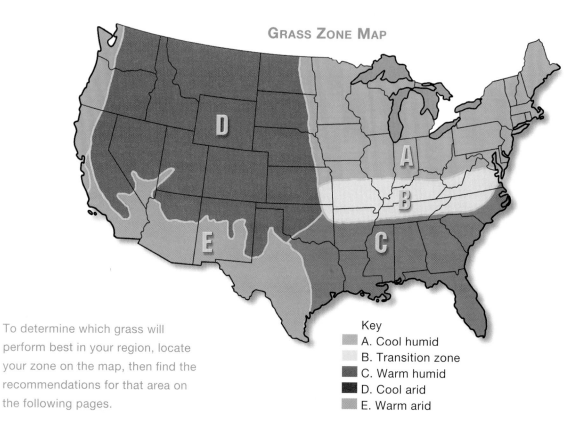

GRASS ZONE MAP

Key
- A. Cool humid
- B. Transition zone
- C. Warm humid
- D. Cool arid
- E. Warm arid

To determine which grass will perform best in your region, locate your zone on the map, then find the recommendations for that area on the following pages.

what the expected rainfall for your area is and whether you plan to irrigate, as well as the kind of greenness, texture, and maintenance you want. To help you sort through all of these criteria, use the Grass Zone Map above to find your region (and thus climate). Then use the "Turfgrass Selection" table on the opposite page to help you to narrow your choices. (For more information on specific lawn grass cultivars for your area, rely on your local Cooperative Extension office or other industry recommendations based on multiyear tests.) Make a short list of your picks *before* visiting the garden center to save yourself time and confusion.

Seed or Sod?

When it comes to starting a new lawn, the least expensive choice—and the one that offers the widest selection—is seed. However, the wait for an established lawn is longer when you start with seed (count on 3 months before exposing it to heavy use).

Sod, on the other hand, provides an almost-instant lawn, but your turf choices will be limited and the cost to start the lawn will be considerably more expensive. Some grass selections, like zoysia, aren't available as seed, so your method may be determined by what type of lawn you choose.

TURFGRASS SELECTION

Once you've located your grass zone on the map on the opposite page, find your zone in this table to identify the turfgrass species and cultivars that are likely to perform well in your yard. Your local Cooperative Extension office or botanic garden can provide further information about specific cultivars to consider.

ZONE A: COOL HUMID

SPECIES TO CONSIDER	ATTRIBUTES	CHOICE CULTIVARS	COMMENTS
BENTGRASS	■ Suitable for Pacific Northwest only ■ Fine-textured ■ Low, ground-hugging ■ Some shade tolerance	'Exeter' 'Prominent'	Shallow root system needs frequent watering.
FINE FESCUE	■ Some drought tolerance ■ Some shade tolerance ■ Some acid tolerance ■ Some salt tolerance ■ Poor traffic tolerance ■ Best mixed with Kentucky bluegrass	'Atlanta' 'Reliant' 'Spartan'	'Reliant' is endophyte-enhanced.
KENTUCKY BLUEGRASS	■ Fine-textured ■ Poor traffic tolerance ■ Best mixed with fescues and perennial ryegrass	'America' 'Liberty' 'Midnight'	Over 100 named varieties to choose from
PERENNIAL RYEGRASS	■ Some alkaline tolerance ■ Traffic tolerance ■ Best mixed with Kentucky bluegrass	'Palmer II' 'Pennfine' 'Repell'	'Palmer II' and 'Repell' are endophyte-enhanced.
TURF-TYPE TALL FESCUE	■ Coarse-textured ■ Drought tolerance ■ Traffic tolerance ■ Often blended with another turf-type tall fescue	'Shenandoah' 'Titan' 'Tribute'	All are endophyte-enhanced.

(continued)

ZONE B: TRANSITION ZONE

SPECIES TO CONSIDER	ATTRIBUTES	CHOICE CULTIVARS	COMMENTS
FINE FESCUE	■ Some drought tolerance ■ Some shade tolerance ■ Some acid tolerance ■ Some salt tolerance ■ Poor traffic tolerance ■ Best mixed with Kentucky bluegrass	'Reliant' 'Spartan'	'Reliant' is endophyte-enhanced.
KENTUCKY BLUEGRASS	■ Fine-textured ■ Poor traffic tolerance ■ Best mixed with fescues and perennial ryegrass	'Blacksburg'	Can mix with a warm-season grass to ensure coverage in this region.
PERENNIAL RYEGRASS	■ Some alkaline tolerance ■ Traffic tolerance ■ Best mixed with Kentucky bluegrass	'Yorktown III'	Endophyte-enhanced
TURF-TYPE TALL FESCUE	■ Coarse-textured ■ Drought tolerance ■ Traffic tolerance ■ Often blended with another turf-type tall fescue	'Rebel II' 'Shenandoah'	'Shenandoah' is endophyte-enhanced.
ZOYSIA	■ Fine-textured ■ Brown in winter ■ Traffic tolerance	'Midwestern'	Goes dormant and turns brown in cool seasons.

SPECIES TO CONSIDER	ATTRIBUTES	CHOICE CULTIVARS	COMMENTS
BAHIAGRASS	■ Traffic tolerance	'Argentine' 'Pensacola' 'Paraguay'	Look for cold-tolerant varieties in northern regions.
BERMUDA-GRASS	■ Drought tolerance ■ Some alkaline tolerance ■ Traffic tolerance	'Tifgreen' 'Tifway' 'Vamont'	Bermudagrass is often overseeded in winter with perennial ryegrass to produce a green lawn when the bermudagrass is dormant and brown.
CENTIPEDE-GRASS	■ Coarse-textured ■ Heat tolerance ■ Poor traffic tolerance	'Oaklawn' 'Tennessee Hardy'	Centipedegrass grows best east of the Mississippi River.
FINE FESCUE	■ Some drought tolerance ■ Some shade tolerance ■ Some acid tolerance ■ Some salt tolerance ■ Poor traffic tolerance ■ Best mixed with another traffic-tolerant grass	'Aurora' 'Reliant' 'Spartan'	'Reliant' is endophyte-enhanced.
ST. AUGUSTINE GRASS	■ Some shade tolerance ■ Some salt tolerance	'Better Blue' 'Floratine' 'Roselawn'	St. Augustine grass grows best in coastal regions.
ZOYSIA	■ Fine-textured ■ Traffic tolerance	'Emerald' 'Meyer'	'Meyer' is coarse-textured.

(continued)

ZONE D: COOL ARID

SPECIES TO CONSIDER	ATTRIBUTES	CHOICE CULTIVARS	COMMENTS
BUFFALO-GRASS	■ Great Plains native ■ Extreme drought tolerance ■ Unmowed buffalo grass grows to only about 5 inches	'Prairie' 'Sharp's Improved' 'Texoka'	'Prairie' is available only as sod.
FINE FESCUE	■ Some drought tolerance ■ Some shade tolerance ■ Some salt tolerance ■ Some acid tolerance ■ Poor traffic tolerance ■ Best mixed with Kentucky bluegrass	'Enjoy' 'Reliant' 'Scaldis'	'Reliant' is endophyte-enhanced.
KENTUCKY BLUEGRASS	■ Fine-textured ■ Poor traffic tolerance ■ Best mixed with fescues and perennial ryegrass	'America' 'Challenger' 'Midnight'	
PERENNIAL RYEGRASS	■ Some alkaline tolerance ■ Traffic tolerance ■ Best mixed with Kentuky bluegrass	'Manhattan II' 'Palmer II' 'Repell'	All are endophyte-enhanced.
TURF-TYPE TALL FESCUE	■ Coarse-textured ■ Drought tolerance ■ Traffic tolerance ■ Often blended with another turf-type tall fescue	'Apache' 'Mesa' 'Mustang'	'Mesa' is endophyte-enhanced.
WHEAT-GRASS	■ Extreme drought tolerance ■ Some alkaline tolerance	'RoadCrest'	Reserve wheatgrass for rough areas. It requires minimal mowing.

Zone E: Warm Arid

Species to Consider	Attributes	Choice Cultivars	Comments
BERMUDA-GRASS	■ Drought tolerance ■ Some alkaline tolerance ■ Traffic tolerance	'Midiron' 'Tifgreen' 'Tifway'	
BUFFALO-GRASS	■ Great plains native ■ Extreme drought tolerance ■ Unmowed grows only to about 5 inches	'Prairie' 'Sharp's Improved' 'Texoka'	'Prairie' is available only as sod.
FINE FESCUE	■ Some drought tolerance ■ Some shade tolerance ■ Some acid tolerance ■ Some salt tolerance ■ Poor traffic tolerance ■ Best mixed with Kentucky bluegrass	'Scaldis' 'Waldina'	
KENTUCKY BLUEGRASS	■ Fine-textured ■ Poor traffic tolerance ■ Best mixed with fescues and perennial ryegrass	'Classic' 'Glade' 'Trenton'	
PERENNIAL RYEGRASS	■ Some alkaline tolerance ■ Traffic tolerance ■ Best mixed with Kentucky bluegrass	'Citation II' 'Palmer II' 'Tara'	'Palmer II' is endophyte-enhanced.
TURF-TYPE TALL FESCUE	■ Coarse-textured ■ Drought tolerance ■ Traffic tolerance ■ Often blended with another turf-type tall fescue	'Arid' 'Mesa' 'Mustang'	'Mesa' is endophyte-enhanced.
ZOYSIA	■ Fine-textured ■ Traffic tolerance		

Grass-Planting
Pointers

Planting a new lawn is something that you can do yourself, or that you can hire out to a landscaper. If you're building a new house, seeding the lawn may even be part of the landscape contract that comes with the house. If that's the case, make sure you have topsoil. It's common practice to scrape away and stockpile topsoil during the grading phase of construction, and sometimes builders fail to put it back. It's a struggle to grow grass—or anything else—on subsoil! If subsoil is what you have, plan to add topsoil at planting time.

Whether you choose to plant your lawn yourself or hire someone to do it for you, follow the steps below for starting a great-looking new lawn.

1. Test the soil. Just like any other plant, grass needs good soil to grow well. If your soil needs improving, now is the time. The better the condition of your soil at planting time, the fewer headaches and hassles later. Take a soil test, and be sure to indicate on the form that you're growing lawn. Pay close attention to pH and organic matter recommendations, and plan on adding any needed materials at soil prep time.

If your home is newly constructed, find out if you've been left with any topsoil. If your home is under construction, require that topsoil be returned when the work is through.

2. Choose your season. For warm-season grasses, seed in spring when daytime air tempera-tures are 70° to 90°F; for cool-season grasses, seed in late August to mid-September when daytime air temperatures are 60° to 85°F.

While some homeowners successfully seed cool-season grasses in spring, it's a chancy proposition because success depends on the weather conditions. If you have to delay spring seeding due to rains and wet soil, you'll be seeding at just the time when annual weed seeds are ready to take off. Avoid the competition and sow cool-season grasses in fall.

Sod can be planted almost any time that the soil is workable and water is available, as long as the weather isn't scorching.

3. Prepare the soil. Add topsoil if yours has been scraped away, then cultivate the soil to a depth of at least 4 inches. If your lawn area is large, you may want to use a rotary tiller. Otherwise a garden fork or cultivator may be suitable for this job. Add organic matter and other amendments as indicated on your soil test results, and rake out weeds, roots, and

Laying sod can be a practical option in high-traffic areas where an instant lawn is needed or on slopes where seed tends to wash away.

LAWN CARE

Once you've begun using the strategies in this chapter, lawn mowing, fertilizing, and cleanup should all be less time-consuming tasks. Most homeowners have the equipment they need to do routine lawn care themselves, but get help if it's worth it to you.

PLANTING GRASS

Whether or not you do this task yourself may depend on how big of a job you have. Homeowners can easily plant grass seed, and even laying your own sod isn't difficult (although it is tedious, grubby, and labor-intensive, depending on the size of your project). But if you need to haul in topsoil or remove old sod or if you have another big hurdle to overcome, then hiring a lawn care or landscaping firm to do the job for you may be a hassle-free way to go. The decision also may depend on your available time: Grass needs to be seeded at certain times for optimal results, and sod needs to be laid as soon as possible after it's delivered so it doesn't dry out.

clods. Till the soil again, and this time roll or lightly tamp the ground to make a firm planting bed.

4. Plant the seed or sod and roll again. Follow the recommendations on the seed package for how much **seed** to spread based on the square footage of your lawn. Use a mechanical seed spreader if the lawn area is large (see "Spreaders" on page 160). Mulch lightly with a weed-free material such as straw (not hay) to protect your valuable seed from being washed away or eaten by birds. Then roll the lawn lightly to make sure the seed is in contact with the soil, and put up barriers, if needed, to prevent anyone from walking on the seed bed.

Though more expensive than seed initially, **sod** is a good solution for high-traffic or sloped areas where you must have grass. Lightly water the soil surface so the sod roots will come in contact with damp soil. Begin laying the sod so that the joints are staggered, and go crosswise along slopes. Use a wide board to protect the row you just laid from your weight as you lay a new one. When you're finished, tamp or lightly roll the sod to get good root contact with the soil. When the grass gets growing, mow perpendicular to the long edges so you don't create ruts.

5. Water like your lawn's life depends on it! For seeded lawns, water two to three times daily for a month and thereafter as needed, depending on how much rainfall you have. For sod, soak daily for about 2 weeks and thereafter as needed. As always, water deeply and allow the lawn to dry completely before watering again.

Turfgrass Is Only Part of the Story

Whether you're starting a lawn from scratch or working on improving the lawn you've already got, you now understand that every inch of your property doesn't have to be covered in turfgrass. There are so many other wonderful plants and design ideas that you can incorporate into your property that will add to your enjoyment and help you keep repetitive maintenance chores to a minimum. So, as you plan your backyard, think judiciously about how much grass your family really needs and what other exciting options you can use.

Great Ideas for
Reducing
Water Use

Whether water is scarce or plentiful where you live, using it wisely makes sense. Developing **gardening habits** that **save water** can also save you time and money, as well as the grief of **battling disease** problems that come from plants being too wet for too long. Water-saving **design ideas,** on the other hand, help you take advantage of the available moisture on your property and help you select plants that are sure to **thrive in** your climate. The result will be a beautiful, **undemanding landscape** that will provide you and your family years of enjoyment.

Water-Saving Tricks

If your tap water comes from a public water system, you pay for every drop you use, so it makes financial sense to use less whenever possible. Even if you don't have to worry about paying a water bill, you may still know the importance of conserving water firsthand if your area has ever suffered a drought. While we'd all like to think there's no limit to this valuable, vital resource, clean water isn't something we can take for granted. We should use it wisely.

The good news is, you can start using the best water-conserving methods right now, without buying anything. In fact, many of my water-saving tricks just require a simple change in habit. Give them a try before you buy a new irrigation system or make big design changes in your landscape. I predict you'll be pleasantly surprised at the difference you'll see on your next water bill. Of course, if you want to see even bigger results, depending upon your situation, you may benefit from using some simple low-tech gadgets. You'll find my favorites on page 187.

Add Organic Matter

My first recommendation for reducing water use is to get in the organic matter habit. Whether you're top-dressing it on a lawn or working it into a vegetable bed, organic matter such as compost will improve the soil structure, creating tiny nooks and crannies that will carry water and nutrients to plant roots. Compost also improve the soil's water-holding capacity and give your plants a steadier souce of moisture. Organic matter also boosts the soil's nutrient levels and makes plants more resistant to disease and pest problems. When organic matter is present in the soil, the microorganisms and decomposers that aid plant health are also sure to be there.

Mulch

A 2- to 3-inch layer of an organic mulch offers many benefits. (By organic mulch, I mean shredded bark, shredded leaves, and grass clippings. Stones and black plastic don't give the same benefits.) Organic mulch slows evaporation by shading and cooling the soil, it slows runoff, and it enriches the soil as it breaks down. Conversely, without mulch, runoff is more rapid, the soil heats up, the decomposers become less active or go away, and you have to water more often or your plants will suffer. Another important benefit is that mulch smothers weeds. So, it's plain to see that surrounding your plants with a layer of organic materials keeps them healthier and means less work for you!

Choose Plants That Don't Need Shearing

Anytime you prune a plant or cut the lawn, it stresses the plant and causes it to lose water more rapidly, particularly in summer heat. If you have plants that you shear regularly, ask yourself why. Can you simply let the plant grow out in its natural form? (Think of the maintenance time you'll save!) If you shear because a plant is too large for the space, consider transplanting or replacing it. If you feel the plant just looks better when it's shorn, try to schedule fewer shearings—especially avoiding the hot months.

Water Deeply and Infrequently

One of the easiest ways to use less water is to water less often! Frequent, shallow waterings make weak, shallow-rooted plants. When a drought hits, plants need to reach deep down for water. Shallow-

rooted plants aren't prepared to do this, and you're likely to lose them. Instead, less frequent, deep waterings that soak the root zone will encourage roots to grow deeply, especially when you let the soil dry between watering times. It's hard to say just how often you'll need to water because so much depends on how quickly your soil drains, what kind of plants you have, whether they're new or established—and on the weather. But instead of watering every other day, try spacing it out to every several days or even weeks, if the weather has been cooperating with some rain.

Water the Soil, not the Plants

Unless a plant is dirty and needs to be rinsed, there's seldom any reason to wet the foliage. Foliage that's regularly wet is ripe for fungal diseases. So when you can, simply soak the soil and let the foliage stay dry. You'll find simple ways to help you do this in "Water-Wise Tools and Gadgets" on page 187, such as using

A hose extension handle, or water wand, lets you get the water where it's needed—on the soil—without having to bend over and reach in and around your plants.

Check Your
Water Quality

Sometimes it's not just how much or how little water your plants get, but what's in the water that can affect them. Each time you water, you may be adding pesky contaminants to your plants. For instance, sodium from your water softener (if it uses salt) can destroy soil structure over time. Use the diverter switch on your softener unit when you water your plants, or collect water in a rain barrel to use instead.

Also be aware of any silt in your water supply, which can crust on the soil surface and prevent water from getting through, especially on lawns. A simple way to test for silt is to put some water in a glass jar and see what settles out. If you find that you do have silt in your water (which is more common in well water than in municipal water supplies), keep an eye out for silt buildup on your soil or lawn surface. You can use a rake to break up the crust.

a hose fitted with an extension (usually called a water wand) and breaker when hand-watering so you can get the hose end down to ground level. You can retire your overhead sprinklers—except when your kids want a chance for water play—and use soaker hoses instead.

Water Only When Needed

While allowing a plant to wilt is never a good idea, your established landscape plants shouldn't require regular watering to keep them in good condition. If you get regular rainfall, that may be all they need,

and chances are, you can cut back on supplemental watering without causing any harm or stress.

How do you know when a plant needs water? Monitor your plants, looking for early signs of water stress such as slight flagging (foliage that's a bit droopy) or normally green foliage that's looking slightly gray. You'll soon know how long your plants can go without water either from Mother Nature or from you. Water as infrequently as possible, but always before wilting begins.

Some plants, however well watered, will wilt like mad in hot weather when the sun hits them. Though this may be alarming, it's not normally harmful. Resist the temptation to keep pouring on the water, but do continue your normal, early-in-the-day watering, and consider transplanting these plants away from the afternoon sun. Morning sun is usually fine. Some common afternoon wilters are bottlebrush buckeye (*Aesculus parviflora*), oakleaf hydrangea (*Hydrangea quercifolia*), morning glories (*Ipomoea* spp.), and ligularias (*Ligularia* spp.).

Water Early in the Day

If you can make time in your schedule to water early, your plants will benefit in three ways.

1. Plants are better equipped to take up water in the morning, before the heat of the day stresses them.

2. You'll lose less water to evaporation and wind.

3. If foliage gets wet, it has an opportunity to dry in the heat of the day, discouraging most fungal diseases.

Water-Wise **Tools** and **Gadgets**

Along with the good watering habits described above, a well-chosen gadget or two can help you make even better use of your time and water. My list begins with items that are likely to give you the most benefit and that you might already own, such as downspout extensions and rain barrels. It ends with products that *may* offer advantages, depending on your property and your needs.

Downspout Extensions

Use your downspouts (if you have them) as the re-source that they are! While it's always a good idea to direct storm runoff away from your house foun-dation with a splash block, extensions can direct the water to where it's needed. Flexible extensions that roll out and sprinkle under pressure make it easy to water your foundation plants, but be pre-pared to unclog them regularly if your gutters

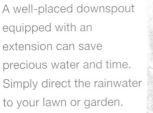

A well-placed downspout equipped with an extension can save precious water and time. Simply direct the rainwater to your lawn or garden.

collect tree debris. Use downspouts as an efficient way to fill rain barrels, too. For tips on that, see "Rain Barrels" below.

Rain Barrels

Recycling rainwater runoff that would otherwise pour out of your downspouts and be wasted couldn't be easier. Simply set a rain barrel beneath your downspouts and you'll have a free supply of water for your yard. Though the wooden ones have a rustic charm, plastic ones are more widely available. Look for a lid to keep out debris and mosquitoes, a hose fitting that will give you easy access to the collected

Rain barrels make great use of rainwater that might otherwise run off your property.

water, and a diverter that lets you switch back to the downspout should the rain barrel get full. Don't expect to be able to water directly from your rain barrel; gravity probably won't give enough pressure to get water through a hose. Instead, use the hose fitting to conveniently fill a watering can or your slow-delivery containers (see below).

Hose Helpers

For hand-watering, an extension handle, breaker, and shutoff is an inexpensive threesome that can't be beat! An **extension handle** (also known as a water wand) lets you get the hose end down to soil level—where the water should go—without having to stoop or wave a floppy hose around. Even if you could hit your mark by holding the hose at waist level, you run the risk of washing away your mulch or eroding your soil from the blast. And if you miss your mark, you end up plastering foliage with unnecessary water. This gadget also makes watering hanging baskets and container plants a snap.

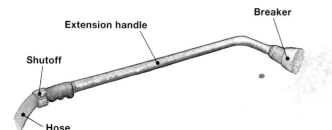

Extension handles are available in a number of lengths, so choose one for the amount of reach you need. Combined with a shutoff and a breaker, it makes hand-watering from a hose more convenient and comfortable and helps you to make good use of your water.

A **water breaker** fits onto the end of a hose extension handle. Its job is to break the water stream into little droplets that have less impact on your soil and mulch than a steady stream or spray from a hose nozzle would. It doesn't reduce the volume of water coming out of the hose. The water will simply hit the ground with much less force. To make watering even easier, a **shutoff** attached to the end of your hose lets you regulate the flow of water that comes through the breaker and turn it off without having to run back to the spigot. Turn it off when you move the hose from one plant or container to another and you'll save water and avoid soaking yourself, paths, and other things that don't need it! A shutoff does put the hose under pressure, though, so check your fittings periodically to make sure they're holding.

Slow-Delivery Watering Aids

Hand-watering plants can mean a lot of repeat trips to the garden, but you can avoid all this fuss, with low-tech, slow-delivery tools like plastic bottles, unglazed flowerpots, or Aqua Spikes. Punch holes in the bottom of plastic milk, water, or soft drink bottles, place them on or in the soil, and fill them with water from your hose as needed. You can use unglazed clay pots in a similar way, but they are very porous so you'll need to set them down in the soil or the water will just evaporate.

Aqua spikes are a clever invention that you can attach to inverted plastic soda bottles and turn them into handy watering devices. Fill a 2-liter bottle with water, screw on the aqua spike at the cap end, then turn the bottle upside down, and poke the spike into the soil. Each of these low-cost or recycled gadgets

When plants are far enough apart, you can bury a soda bottle waterer between them; otherwise, place the bottle toward the front of the bed so you can easily reach it for filling.

sends water directly to your plants' root zones and are especially effective because there's little or no waste from evaporation or runoff.

Soaker Hoses

Soaker hoses are another great yet inexpensive way to water your plants. They're efficient, too. When you keep the water pressure down on these porous hoses, they'll water evenly with no runoff. A soaker hose delivers water directly to plants' root zones, so a minimum is lost in the wind or wasted on wetting the foliage. But, if you turn up the pressure, they *will* spray!

Wind soaker hoses through beds, make a straight run, or use a multirow or Y-connector design for a conventional straight-row vegetable garden (see "Y-Connectors" on page 190). Once you have your course plotted, bury the hoses beneath the mulch to prevent the water from spraying into the air. Hoses buried beneath mulch are also less likely to clog from mineral buildup that can happen as the hose dries between waterings.

Another way to prevent clogs from mineral buildup is to use a filter with a 150 or smaller mesh attached to the spigot before you attach the hose. To remove a clog, turn on the water and bend the hose back and forth until water comes out. (Plan to get wet!) Then open the end caps and flush out the built-up minerals.

Drip Irrigation Systems

Like soaker hoses, drip irrigation systems deliver water to the root zones of plants. Small-diameter tubing and emitters, which are fittings that drip water at an even rate, let you regulate where and how much water to use. You can purchase components at a modest price and assemble your own system. Or, you can have the drip system supplier design a drip system for you. Either way, you can come up with a custom system that fits your bed design—whether it's for flowers, trees and shrubs, or vegetables. As with soaker hoses, it's best to put the tubing and emitters beneath a mulch layer because the mulch can protect the tubing from the weather and preserve the moisture. Besides, if the emitters are on top of the mulch, they'll usually just wet the mulch and nothing more.

Timers

Whether you use a drip system or soaker hoses to water your plants, a timer can help you to make the best use of your time and water. Timers attach in-line with your hose at the spigot and automatically start your watering system during those optimal morning hours while you're busy getting the kids ready for school or rushing off to work. Timers are available in electric, battery-powered, or manual wind-up models. All work fine, so choose whichever type best suits your needs. A manual model is the

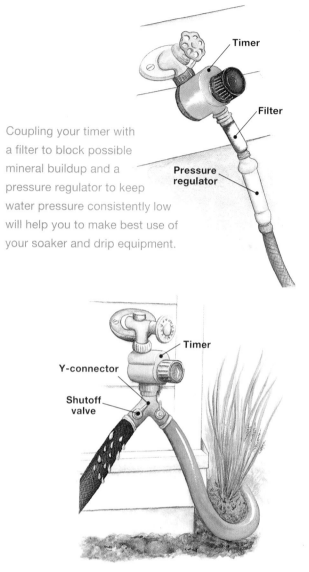

Coupling your timer with a filter to block possible mineral buildup and a pressure regulator to keep water pressure consistently low will help you to make best use of your soaker and drip equipment.

With hoses, a timer, and a couple of Y-connectors, you can water your entire property for a smaller investment and with fewer long-term hassles than you'd have with an automatic watering system.

least expensive, but you'll need to reset it after each use. Battery-operated and electric models offer more convenience and more settings and cost a bit more. An electric model probably lasts the longest, but you need an outlet to use one.

While timers are great timesaving devices, they can't detect rain, so remember to turn them off when wet weather arrives. Adjust them so they keep watering deeply and only as needed.

Y-Connectors

Y-connectors make it easy to extend your watering capabilities, letting you reach all your garden beds at once from one spigot, whether you use hoses, drip systems, sprinklers, or a combination. This handy little gadget attaches at the spigot so you run two hoses from the same spot. If you add a Y-connector to each of those hoses, you now have four hoses that can run simultaneously in different parts of your yard—provided you have adequate water pressure. What's really great about Y-connectors is that they have shutoff valves for each side of the connection, so each time you water, you can water just the sections of your property that really need it.

Water Savvy by Design

If the combination of smart habits and helpful gadgets doesn't get your yard over its water dependency, you may decide that it's time to make some water-saving design changes. Paired with the design advice in Chapter 4, the ideas here should help you to create a water-efficient yard. As a bonus, when you design your landscape for water efficiency, it means you're designing for maintenance efficiency as well. For instance, when you replant a slope with a groundcover that can take the heat, you won't have to bother watering or mowing the lawn in that spot. Other techniques include using native plants that are adapted to your amount of rainfall, limiting planting areas that will need supplemental watering, amending the soil so it will retain more water, and more. You may find that incorporating just one of these ideas (or maybe all of them!) is just what your landscape needs to relieve you of the burden—and expense—of unnecessary watering.

Choose Plants Adapted for Slopes

Avoid high-water-use plants—especially lawns—on south- and west-facing slopes, as these areas tend to dry out most quickly. Other groundcovers such as St.-John's-wort and junipers are better suited to these dry conditions. And since you probably won't be doing a lot of walking up and down the slope, turfgrass just isn't needed there. Or, in these spots where the ground tends to bake, give your plants a fighting chance by using a windbreak, tall hedge, fence, trellis, or shade trees—all of which help to reduce water loss.

Use Native Plants

Native plants aren't the only ones that will be well adapted to your local growing conditions, but they're a good place to start. (Use the advice in Chapter 3 on plant selection to help you determine just what your conditions are.) While not all plants need to be strictly adapted to your local rainfall, you'll want most of them to be. If you choose some plants that will need a bit extra water, group them together and locate them near the house or in another spot where you'll see them often. That way, you'll be able to monitor their water needs more easily, plus you'll get to enjoy them more if they're nearby.

Limit the Irrigated Areas

Now that you're grouping your plants in beds according to water use, plan to limit the number of high-water-use plants so you'll have fewer areas to irrigate. Since lawns are one area that homeowners often water, carefully think about how much lawn you really need and keep it to a minimum, using the design tricks found in Chapter 7. In addition to using native landscape plants, choose locally adapted, drought-resistant lawn grasses as well. The "Turfgrass Selection" table on page 175 is a good place to start, but your local Cooperative Extension agent may be able to offer you even more localized information about the best choices for your area.

Give nearby plants, and yourself, a break from the baking effect of paved surfaces. Plant a tree or hedge to create some shade. The paving will absorb less heat by day and radiate less heat by night.

Fix the Soil

By grouping your plants according to water use, you can also cut down on special soil prep tasks so you can concentrate your efforts where they're most urgently needed. Locally adapted, drought-resistant plants may need very little in the way of soil improvement. (But get a soil test just to be sure.)

For a bed of thirsty shrubs or perennials, add organic matter to the soil to help retain moisture. Sandy soil will drain too quickly for water lovers; compost will slow that process. Heavy clay takes longer to drain but causes other moisture problems, so add compost to that, too. Clay will also benefit from the addition of some sharp sand such as builder's sand. You'll need to add an equal amount of organic matter when you add sand. Start by adding a 1-inch layer of each and mixing it into your soil. Check back in 6 months. If after settling, your soil still drains too slowly, you can always add more sand and organic matter.

Design around Downspouts

If you have downspouts, you have a great source of water, free for the taking without hauling or lug-

Grouping plants together saves water, especially if you cluster them according to their watering needs.

ging. Simply incorporate the downspout locations into bed designs! You can either extend the downspouts (see "Downspout Extensions" on page 187) to reach into planting beds or direct the runoff to where it is needed most. Add a splash block or adapter to slow the water flow and reduce its damaging impact on the soil.

Dig Large Planting Holes

While grouped plants have a better defense against dry conditions, sometimes a solitary plant is just the thing. You can make it easier for the roots of a lone tree to forage for water by digging a wide hole. As the tree sends them out, the new roots will have an easier time getting through that loosened

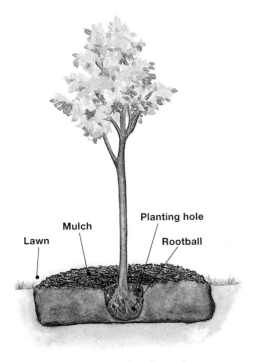

A wide planting hole—five times the diameter of the rootball—is a good rule of thumb to use in any climate.

soil. (Don't dig deeper than the rootball though, or settling could become a problem.) Once you've planted, mulch well to preserve moisture. A mulch ring will also prevent mover damage and discourage foot traffic, which causes soil compaction. If mulch isn't enough of a deterrent, plant groundcovers to keep people away from your newly planted tree.

Advice on New Watering Systems

If you're considering installing a new, automated watering system, my best advice is to proceed with caution. While you might expect that a new system will end your watering woes, it might just as easily spell the beginning of ongoing maintenance expenses or hassles. In temperate climates, automatic irrigation requires an annual fall shutdown and a corresponding spring startup—jobs you most likely will need to hire out. Not only that—repairs are common and they add another layer of expense and bother.

Automatic systems also need constant attention to ensure that the water is going where it should, that it takes rainfall into account (and you're not watering simultaneously with a summer shower), and that it waters on an irregular basis. Then there's that sprinkler head that somehow came off (due usually to mowers, vandals, or joint failure), and you're treating joggers to a 5:00 A.M. shower in the form of a 12-foot geyser. Even irrigation and turf pros say that "set it and forget it" is bad practice, but it's tempting for a busy homeowner to do just that. If you have an opportunity to convert an existing system to a drip or soaker hose system rather than an overhead system, do it.

WHEN TO CALL

A PRO

IRRIGATION INSTALLATION

Irrigation systems can be as simple as a drip system that you can install yourself from a kit or as complex as an automated sprinkler system with underground lines. Drip systems aren't just easier to install and use, they also offer a more sustainable approach to watering. An automated sprinkler system, however, requires plumbing, electrical, and surveying skills, as well as specialty tools such as trenching equipment. A hard look at the hazards of combining water and electricity should lead you right to a contractor—or to a better way to water your plants!

IRRIGATION MAINTENANCE

Irrigation maintenance is as simple—or complex—as the system itself. A drip system, automated or not, is likely to be straight-forward to clean and repair. Parts are easily

replaceable and little, if anything, requires digging up. Annual winter shutdown merely consists of taking up and cleaning the lines and emitters (if your climate is harsh enough to damage them), which you can easily do yourself.

An automated underground system, however, needs skilled attention. If you're fortunate not to have suffered any break-downs or leaks during the growing season, all that remains is winter shutdown: blowing out the lines with an air compressor and disconnecting the system from the water supply . . . year after year. Spring startup often consists of fixing whatever broke over the winter. Unless you like solving mysteries like "the source of the underground leak," and doing outdoor plumbing in the bottom of a muddy hole that keeps filling with water, farm this job out.

Running an Automatic Irrigation System

Automatic systems, especially those with overhead sprinklers, can really be a drain on your water bill or well unless you manage them correctly. If you already have an automatic irrigation system or you've decided that you still want one, follow these tips to make using your automatic sprinkler system as efficient as possible.

■ Use or add rain override. This feature stops your system if it's raining or if it has been raining. Soil sensors are also available and work similarly. If soil moisture is adequate, the system won't water.

■ Measure how much water your plants are actually getting and adjust the system so you use only what you need. To tell how many inches of water an area is getting while the system is running, set out shallow cans to receive water and measure the results. Also, check to see how long each zone has to run before water starts heading down slopes, gutters, and driveways. Keep notes about how long you need to water in each zone, then be sure to set each zone to stop watering before runoff begins.

■ Run your system early in the day when plants are best prepared to absorb moisture. This also gives foliage a chance to dry and to avoid water loss through wind and evaporation. Wind normally picks up as the day goes on, and evaporation increases as temperatures rise. Dry foliage is also less susceptible to fungal diseases.

■ Adjust your system for seasonal changes in plant needs, evaporation, and rainfall.

■ Water deeply and irregularly. (I can't say it enough!) Imitate the unpredictability of rainfall and your plants will root more deeply, especially if you let the soil dry between waterings.

Seasonal Maintenance

Unless you live in a frost-free climate, you'll need to make plans for "spring start-up" and "fall shutdown" of your irrigation systems. Each is a series of tasks to perform repairs and prevent damage to pipes from freezing temperatures and heaving ground during freeze/thaw cycles.

FALL SHUTDOWN

If you suspect your watering system needs repairs, I recommend deferring them until spring unless they're urgent. Even on a well-winterized system, winter weather can do mischief that will need repair in the spring.

1. Turn off the water supply.

2. Disconnect the system from the meter or source.

3. Using an air compressor, blow water out of all lines, one zone at a time.

4. Turn off the controller.

SPRING START-UP

Now's the time to fix the problems you knew about from last fall as well as to search for any new damage that may have occurred over the winter.

1. Reconnect system to the meter or water source.

2. Turn on the water supply.

3. Let the system pressurize and inspect for leaks.

4. Run each zone in turn and make adjustments to the spray patterns.

5. Make any necessary repairs.

CHAPTER 9

Preventive Measures for Pests and Diseases

One of the great benefits of having a **chemical-free** backyard is that pest and disease problems are usually rare. For instance, if you **don't overfertilize** your lawn or landscape beds with synthetic nitrogen, you won't be attracting all sorts of pests that thrive on the excessive, lush new growth it creates. If you don't use chemical pesticides, you won't be killing off all the **beneficial insects** that can help keep the nuisance insects in check. While all this is **good news** for homeowners, it doesn't mean that an occasional uninvited guest won't trouble you. Use the information in this chapter to **prevent and control** any problems effectively and **safely,** should the need arise.

Strategies
for Success

Hearly plants growing in a healthy environment have great natural defenses against invasions by both insect pests and diseases. Stressed plants or plants that are poorly adapted to your growing conditions signal their vulnerability to pests. Conversely, healthy plants discourage infestations and can actually mount their own defenses when they're under attack.

Rather than resorting to chemical warfare against any bug you see, follow my three-prong approach to creating and maintaining a healthy landscape: First, choose plants that are appropriate for your area. When plants are suited to the growing conditions where you live, they're more likely to succeed. Second, Use good gardening practices. A tidy garden and healthy plants will deter pests and diseases from taking hold. My third tip is to give your plants a rich and diverse landscape in which to grow. The more varied your landscape, the more beneficial insects you'll have to eat the pests, and the less likely it will for a particular disease to take hold and run rampant through your entire group of plants. You'll find more details about each of these tactics throughout this chapter.

Start with the Right Plants

You can save yourself—and your plants—from a whole lot of hassles when you simply start with the right plants. If you choose plants that are on the whole adapted to your growing conditions, they'll be less likely to become stressed. And, just like us humans, plants are more susceptible to diseases when they're stressed. In the case of plants, they're also more susceptible to invasion by pests when they're weak or struggling. You can find plant selection tips in Chapter 3 to help you identify your specific growing conditions so you can make the best plant selections for your yard.

In addition to well-adapted plants, choose plant species and cultivars that have been proven to be disease- and insect-resistant in your area. While native plants are frequently a safe bet, many other species are also proven to be resistant to pests and diseases. Some popular plant choices such as crabapples and roses are prone to attracting certain pests and diseases. That doesn't mean you can't grow them. But before you buy, check with your local Cooperative Extension office for lists of pest- and disease-resistant varieties. By choosing resistant plants, you can cut way back on maintenance—and on headaches! Nurseries still often carry disease-prone cultivars—such as

Standard Equipment

Just as new cars come with standard features such as air bags or ABS brakes, some plants come with standard equipment, too. In my area, "standard equipment" on honey locust trees includes spider mites, leafhoppers, honey locust plant bug, and mimosa webworm. While the trees don't typically come home from the nursery infested, the pests are in the environment and quickly find their way to their favorite food. Other examples may include aphids on the new growth of crab apples or scale on mugo pines. Local experts, like the Cooperative Extension Service, can help you learn the standard equipment that comes with the plant you're considering. You can avoid a poor choice or at least know what to look for and how to prevent damage.

'Hershey Red' azaleas—simply because they've been popular sellers in the past. There are plenty of other great cultivars to choose from, so check labels carefully and stick to your list. It's all too easy to get carried away when you see beautiful plants that look healthy in the garden center.

Finally, be sure to purchase only healthy plants and seeds. While nurseries are required by law to sell only pest- and disease-free stock, problems can sometimes escape the attention of busy growers. Check tops and roots (if you can) for healthy, vigorous growth, and also check for signs of trouble, such as brown, rotten roots or pests such as bagworms. If you come across plants that show signs of stress, damage, or symptoms of disease or infestation, put them back and look elsewhere. While you're at it, avoid hitchhiking weeds, too. Look for them in potted transplants, rootballs, or seed mixes.

Keep Plants Healthy

Plants need fertile, living soil (see "Keep the Soil Alive" on this page) with adequate moisture to stay healthy. If you give them these conditions, they'll tolerate insect attacks much better than plants suffering from nutrient deficiencies, water stress, overcrowding, and poor air circulation. Healthy plants also mount their own chemical defenses to fight diseases and insects faster and more effectively than stressed plants do. To keep your plants happy and thriving, give them what they need.

KEEP THE SOIL ALIVE

Thomas Jefferson once wrote in a letter to his sister, "I suspect the insects that have harassed you have been encouraged by the feebleness of your plants; and that has been encouraged by the lean state of your soil." He couldn't have been more right!

Healthy soil contains a dynamic system of soil organisms and mineral and chemical elements that are vital to good plant health. It also contains decomposers—earthworms and beneficial microbes—that eat decaying organic material and turn it into nutrients your plants can use. In fact, certain beneficial fungi turn traitor when organic matter isn't present and attack your live plants instead.

Homeowners often run into trouble when they inadvertently kill or cripple the soil's living components with chemical pesticides and fertilizers.

Without these soil dwellers to churn out nutrients for plants, the soil becomes ever more chemically dependent, needing higher levels of synthetic fertilizer to produce the same quality or quantity of turf, tomatoes, or zinnias. As a result, pests and diseases can run rampant because the beneficial microbes, insects, and animals are absent—either due to chemical poisoning or lack of decent food. In short, maintaining a landscape this way takes ever increasing expense and effort, while the environmental quality decreases.

Keeping the soil alive and thriving isn't hard. After all, it's the soil's natural state. Organic soil components are the key, as they feed the decomposers that break the material into elements that plants can use. You can even assist that nutrient cycle by intentionally returning organic matter to the soil *and* by resisting the temptation to remove it by bagging grass or vacuuming leaves for curbside pickup. You can easily return organic matter to your soil in a number of ways.

- Add compost to beds you're planting or reworking.
- Use organic mulches in tree rings and planting beds. (Avoid plastic mulches or landscape fabrics that tend to keep organic matter, nutrients, and moisture from reaching plant roots.)
- Design planting beds with groundcovers that can "absorb" fallen leaves. (See "Hungry Groundcover, Tasty Trees" on page 82 for ideas.)
- Leave grass clippings on the lawn when you can, and top-dress your lawn with a $1/2$-inch layer of compost in the spring or fall.
- Don't be overzealous in removing thatch or the fungal decomposers that eat thatch will turn their attentions to your living lawn. (If you already have too much thatch buildup, decomposers may have taken a hike and left you with dead soil.)
- Avoid using chemical fertilizers and pesticides. There are plenty of natural materials generated by your own landscape that can do a better job for less cost and less harm to the environment.

It's no wonder some people call compost "black gold." It's highly valuable for keeping soils, plants, and landscapes healthy and thriving.

What's in a Teaspoon of Soil?

While these microscopic creatures may sound like creepy crawlers to you, they're just what your soil—and plants—need!

- 100 million or so individual bacteria
- 50 to 150 meters of fungal threads
- 10,000 to 100,000 protozoa
- 5 to 500 beneficial nematodes

(from *The New Farm*, May/June 1994)

TAKE GOOD CARE OF YOUR PLANTS

When you provide good, basic care for your plants, they'll be able to take care of themselves when insect pests or diseases strike. Good care can be as simple as knowing what your plants' water needs are and then watering accordingly (see "Water-Saving Tricks" on page 184 for tips), or being alert to the plants that are prone to fungal disease if there's not enough air circulation. To improve air circulation, try pruning if it's appropriate for the plant, use suggested spacing between plants, and stake plants if necessary. (See Chapter 10 for pruning strategies.) Finally, applying mulch will do wonders for soil moisture and fertility and can also keep harmful soil microbes from splashing onto plants when it rains. (For advice on mulching, see Chapter 11.)

KEEP A CLEAN GARDEN

One of the easiest ways to keep the spread of pests and diseases in check is by practicing good garden habits. You can limit the spread of harmful pathogens or weed seeds by using the following tips:

- Avoid handling or brushing past plants when they're wet.
- Prevent mower and trimmer damage to plants by using mulches around trees and other plants.
- Remove or clean up damage when you see it, pulling up and destroying diseased herbaceous plants as well as pruning broken or damaged branches on trees and shrubs.
- Clean tools, boots, stakes, and other tools between uses and growing seasons.
- Remove dropped fruit and leaves from plants that are particularly susceptible to disease.

CAST YOUR SHADOW

According to a Chinese proverb, the best fertilizer is the gardener's own shadow, meaning that when you're out in the garden every day, it's hard for problems to slip past your notice and get out of control. When you love gardening, it's hard to ignore your yard for very long. If you're just getting started, however, or you have lots of other demands on your time and attention, you may not get to spend as much time strolling around your yard as you'd like.

Between harvesting, dumping the compost bucket, admiring plants and their progress, and performing various garden tasks, most days I can't stay out of the garden! But if I'm booked up with other demands, I like to take a stroll at least every other day to have a look at things. Whether it's a plant that needs water or a Japanese beetle infestation, you can prevent big losses by checking regularly for the small ones.

Encourage a Healthy Backyard Ecosystem

A diverse landscape—one that has many different types of plants—can help reduce potential pest problems in your yard. When you add more plant variety to your yard, you'll be able to attract a larger quantity and more variety of beneficial animals and insects (ones that eat other pesky insects). From a bug's eye view, fewer plant species mean a more restricted diet. You can't attract beneficials if you don't feed them what they want or give them appropriate shelter plants. The benefit to you, aside from a richer landscape, is that any one pest population is less likely to grow out of control.

Beneficial Bats

If you have the mature trees, old buildings, or water nearby, welcome bats into your backyard. They eat moths, midges, caddis flies, beetles, and mosquitoes in huge numbers, and they're not nearly as threatening as legend or your imagination might suggest. If your neighborhood lacks the good roosting spots bats prefer, you can install a bat house. They're easy to make, and they can frequently be found for sale in bird-feeding catalogs, Internet sites, and stores.

Position bat houses 15 to 20 feet off the ground, on the east or southeast side of a building or post. Avoid mounting them on trees unless you're using a tree-safe mount.

Many beneficial insects and animals aren't particularly attracted to mown lawns and manicured gardens, and they won't stay around if introduced. If you have the space, include a variety of trees of different maturities as well as shrubs, vines, perennial flowers, and herbs in your landscape. Unmown fields or woodlands, ponds, streams, and even outbuildings provide food and habitat for wildlife and add more diversity to the mix. While you may not have all or even some of this richness in your yard or neighborhood, you may be able to develop it. And be alert to any loss of diversity. In an act as simple and seemingly innocent as cleaning out a fencerow, you can easily lose important allies in pest control.

What else can you do to attract beneficial pest eaters? Encourage birds, many of which eat hundreds of insects a day, with food, cover, and water. Perching places in or near a vegetable patch can attract the birds *and* reward you. If you have an infrequently used woodlot, leave logs or dead or dying trees in place. They'll provide a year-round source of food and shelter for various beneficial insects, birds, and animals.

Invite toads and other beneficial amphibians with ground-level water, shade, and spots for sunning. A great water offering is a shallow birdbath or bowl strewn with rocks and filled with just enough water to wet the rocks. If you're not in copperhead snake country, a small pile of large rocks on the ground provides cool shade as well as a basking spot for salamanders, lizards, and toads—voracious eaters of slugs, insects, or both.

Control: The Path of Least Disturbance

One of the hitches with the old chemical means of pest control was that people incorrectly assumed that they could eradicate pests with the right dust or spray. Years of research and practice with these destructive methods have shown that the pest never really goes away—nor would you want it to. (Some pests, as with some turfgrass diseases, actually have important beneficial functions when they exist in different cultural conditions.) Meanwhile, the predators go hungry, go away, or get wiped out by the chemical while the pest slowly develops resistance to the treatment. What could have been a mild problem turns into a serious infestation.

Start with a Plan

Organic gardening offers a simpler, more common-sense approach to pest and disease control. Start by identifying the problem and determining just how damaging it may or may not be. Then evaluate the treatment options, starting with the least disruptive to other insects and animals. Finally, decide on your course of action. Often you'll find that you can get the level of pest or disease control you need without the backlash caused by more disruptive means.

1. Identify the problem. Are you seeing insect damage or disease symptoms? Or have you noticed bugs, but no damage? (If that's the case, there's probably little cause for concern, but you may want to identify the insects just in case.) Either way, you can look in a reference book, or call your local Cooperative Extension office or public garden for help. Many have

Master Gardener hot lines or walk-in hours, and chances are, these folks have seen your particular problem several times already that day or week! If the local experts are stumped, you can send a sample to your state's diagnostic laboratory. For a reasonable fee per sample, your Cooperative Extension office will diagnose the problem. Call the office for details on how to prepare your samples for shipping. They usually respond quite quickly—frequently by fax or e-mail—unless a sample needs culturing. See "Resources for Backyard Ideas" on page 256 for contact information.

2. Understand the potential for damage. Many problems are self-limiting, while others are more likely to continue or worsen. For instance, an aphid infestation—when accompanied by feeding predators like lady beetles or their larvae—deserves a watchful eye but probably no action early on. Let the predators do their job. How much damage can the plant tolerate before the plant is damaged beyond help? This is a judgment call, but urgent warning signs can include defoliation, skeletonizing, wilting, or dead plant parts. How much damage will you tolerate visually? Another judgment call, but the location of the plant on your property and the ugliness of the damage can help you to decide. Answering these questions will help you to sort through the options that you'll identify in the next step.

3. Investigate options for prevention and control. If the problem is one that will most likely go away on its own or the amount of damage is tolerable to you (and the plant), resist the temptation to swing into action. Doing nothing is sometimes a viable option! Besides, those beneficial predator populations may be building enough to take care of the problem for you. If the situation isn't so harmless, you'll need to take action. For details on all your pest control options, see "Organic Ways to Control Pests" below.

4. Choose a method of control. I recommend starting with the least toxic or nontoxic option first. (And remember, remedies are no substitute for prevention!) If the problem still persists, then you may want to move onto the next level of control. Before you take any steps, be sure to identify the times of the year when the pest is most susceptible to the control method. For instance, if you discover a spider mite infestation in July but the damage is minimal, hold off treating it. Defer treatment until the following February or March when applying a dormant oil would be one of the most effective yet least toxic ways of dealing with the mites.

Organic Ways to Control Pests

On page 210 you'll find a handy reference chart that shows the eight most common landscape pests and the best ways to prevent them from doing harm. This chart also explains how you can safely minimize the damage when the pests become troublesome. If you'd like a bit more detail on the specifics of controlling those and other potential pests, read through the various methods below. They range from the most passive (start there!) to the most aggressive. In dealing with any plant problem, be sure to identify the culprits before deciding on your plan of action, and carefully follow label instructions for all products.

AN OUNCE OF PREVENTION

Preventive measures—steps you can take at the choosing and planting stages—can help you avoid pest problems all together. Starting with healthy, pest-resistant plants as described in "Strategies for Success" on page 198 is one of the easiest things you can do. Give your plants the right kind of growing conditions, and make sure they don't get stressed from lack of water. Also, avoid overfertilizing—lush, leafy new growth is just too tempting for some insects and diseases to resist.

In the vegetable garden, you can use other cultural methods to help prevent both pest and disease problems. Time planting for before or after known pests are likely to be around. Rotate crops to avoid last-year's pests that have overwintered in the soil. Practice companion planting—some plants naturally repel insects that would otherwise love to attack their neighbors. And use green manures—crops such as winter rye that you can grow then turn under and work into the soil in spring—to add fertility and improve soil structure and microbial activity.

BARRIERS, TRAPS, AND PEST REMOVAL

If your pest prevention techniques don't leave your plants entirely pest-free, you can use a number of nontoxic pest control measures, such as creating barriers, setting out traps, or simple removal, which don't include spraying or dusting.

Barriers. Floating row covers for vegetable gardens are lightweight pieces of fabric that you stretch over your crops. They let in light and moisture while keeping flying insects out and away from your tasty treats. Place copper bands at the base of plants to prevent soft-bodied insects like slugs from making their way to your plants. Similarly, tree bands prevent invasions of crawling pests like gypsy or coddling moths. All of these tools are pest barriers that prevent the pests from reaching your plants.

DON'T BLAME BUGS FOR EVERYTHING!

When you're investigating a plant problem, don't automatically assume that damage is due to bad bugs or dastardly diseases. Sometimes the culprit that's affecting the plants may be an environmental condition. Some of the more common plant "ailments" and their symptoms are listed below.

PROBLEM	SYMPTOM
NUTRIENT DEFICIENCY	■ Stunted growth ■ Foliage discoloration in a consistent pattern
POLLUTION	■ Distorted, stunted, or stippled foliage ■ Dieback or decline
EXCESSIVE COLD	■ Cracked bark on trunk or major limbs ■ Dieback or decline often delayed but inevitable
EXCESSIVE HEAT	■ Wilting ■ Dieback ■ Marginal scorch on leaves
MOISTURE IMBALANCE	■ Wilting ■ Discolored foliage ■ Sudden or slow decline and death
WIND	■ Scorched or dried-out leaves ■ Discolored leaves
CONSTRUCTION	■ Mechanical damage ■ Slow or rapid dieback and decline from compacted soil ■ Early fall color
HERBICIDES	■ Foliage with burned or distorted appearance
COMPETITION WITH TURFGRASSES	■ Mower blight ■ Slow dieback or decline ■ Early fall color
GIRDLING ROOTS	■ Lack of flare where trunk meets ground ■ Dieback on one or more sides or decline ■ Roots at surface strangling trunk
EXCESSIVE PLANTING DEPTH	■ Lack of flare where trunk meets ground ■ Dieback on one or more sides or decline

Traps with *Questionable* Results

Two insect traps that have questionable results are Japanese beetle traps and electric bug zappers. Japanese beetle traps use pheromones to attract beetles, and that they do! These traps really bring them in, usually attracting the beetles in far larger numbers than you would otherwise have had in your yard. If you decide to use one, locate it well away and downwind from the plants you'd like to protect. Electric bug zappers, on the other hand, may kill lots of bugs, including many unsuspecting beneficial insects.

While both Japanese beetle traps and bug zappers may leave you with a large number of dead insects in the trap, the real test of their effectiveness is the amount of plant damage you have. If you don't see a change, then these traps really aren't helping. If fact, they may make things worse.

Similarly, you can sprinkle diatomaceous earth (DE) on or around plants to act as a barrier to insects. DE is a powdery mineral—the fossilized shells of algae known as diatoms. The material has microscopic sharp edges that pierce soft-bodied pests such as slugs and aphids, causing them to dehydrate. Sprinkle or dust it on plants after a rain or while plants are still moist with morning dew, so it will stick. (While DE is considered nontoxic, the dust is irritating to the skin and potentially damaging to lungs, so wear a dust mask and gloves when applying it.) DE washes off easily, so you'll need to reapply after a rain. If you buy DE, make sure you don't purchase the pool-grade variety. It's chemically treated.

Traps. Traps sometimes have a chemical or biological component such as a pheromone or food lure to attract the pest. Some traps are best for simply monitoring a pest—like dogwood borer. Once you know the pests are around, you can time the release of beneficials insects or sprays to hit the peak of the population. Other traps, like sticky traps for apple maggots or food or shelter traps for slugs, can give you pretty good control. Pheromone lures used alone—without a trap—can cause confusion, keeping pests from finding mates and food.

Trap crops are another great trick, if you have the space. For instance, four o'clocks are a great lure for Japanese beetles. To keep beetles away from your roses and cherry or other fruit trees, locate these pretty annual flowers downwind and well away from the plants you want to protect.

Pest removal. Hand-picking, shaking, vacuuming, or squirting pests off plants when you see them are often practical ways to deal with unwanted insects. While hand-picking and shaking may be tedious, they're pretty effective for small outbreaks of large, ungainly insects like beetles.

With care, you can even use a handheld rechargeable vacuum to evict pests such as Japanese beetles, cucumber beetles, and Colorado potato beetles from your plants. Move the running vacuum lightly over the plant while you support the foliage with the other hand. Don't vacuum the undersides of leaves, though, because beneficials are likely to reside there. When you're finished, open the vacuum well away from the plants and empty it into a container of soapy water.

Finally, squirting or spraying plants with water can injure, disorient, or knock off soft-bodied creatures like aphids and may be enough to control the problem. Be careful not to use too much force or you might injure your plants. Time the water treatment for early in the day when cool temperatures make the insects sluggish and the plant will have a chance to dry before dark but not scorch in the sun.

ATTRACT—AND KEEP—BENEFICIAL INSECTS

If prevention, trapping, and hand-picking pests aren't giving your plants sufficient protection, you can invite living creatures—beneficial insects, animals, and nematodes—to control pests. Some beneficials pollinate flowers, while others decompose organic matter or provide food for other beneficials. Many also eat or parasitize pest insects—all great things for your yard and garden.

While buying and introducing beneficial insects is an understandable impulse, a more effective and permanent approach is to take full advantage of the beneficials that are naturally present. Lady beetles, ground beetles, predatory and parasitic wasps, and green lacewings are all likely to be somewhere nearby without your having to buy them. But you may need to invite them over and keep them happy if you want them to stay. That means planting alter-

nate food sources for them (or keeping the right kind of weeds around!) because their favorite pest food won't always be present. In addition to eating other insects, beneficial insects also dine on nectar and pollen, particularly from members of the carrot, mint, and daisy families. Plant them, but also just let some garden crops—like broccoli, carrots, mustard, parsley— bolt, and you're sure to have a host of beneficials living in your yard.

Attract beneficial insects to your yard with nectar and pollen, and they'll stay around and eat some of your pest insects, too.

Dew and raindrops normally provide sufficient water for beneficials. During a drought you can help out the beneficials with a shallow bowl or birdbath filled with some rocks and a splash of water. (Just clean it out every couple of days!) These small insects also need shelter from wind, weather extremes, and gardening activities such as mowing, tilling, or spraying. Cover crops, hedgerows, flowering shrubs, and fallow areas like water retention sites are ideal spots to host beneficial insects.

MICROORGANISMS CAN MANAGE PESTS, TOO

This form of pest control relies on using highly specific insect diseases to keep down certain pest populations, while presenting little risk to other species. One of the most commonly used biological controls is BT (*Bacillus thuringiensis*), which kills caterpillars. BT, which is available at garden centers, is most effective on young caterpillars. For BT to do its job, the caterpillars must eat it, so only spray BT on plants that are currently under attack. Be aware that BT will also kill the larval stage of butterflies, so apply it specifically when and where you see pest caterpillars in action. Never apply BT to flowers and herbs in your butterfly garden!

Milky disease spores (*B. popilliae* and *B. lentimorbus*) can kill grubs of Japanese and other related beetles. It's usually sprayed on lawns where it won't harm the grass but it can kill the grubs that feed on the grass roots. Milky disease spores stay effective for years under some soil and climate conditions; under other conditions it has little effect. Sometimes it takes several seasons before it

begins to be effective. Check with your local Cooperative Extension office to find out how well it works in your area.

Another plan of attack you can use while the grubs are still in the ground is parasitic nematodes. You simply mix these microscopic wormlike creatures into water and then sprinkle or spray them on your lawn. The nematodes will live in your soil and prey on grubs throughout the growing season. Apply the nematodes during the spring, when your lawn is damp and the soil has reached a temperature above 55°F.

AS A LAST RESORT, TRY ORGANIC SPRAYS

Some of the most powerful forms of organic pest and disease control include horticultural oils and insecticidal soaps. Just as with more toxic chemicals, these materials can be irritating, especially in concentrated form. Follow the label instructions carefully for how and when to use them, and use the recommended protective gear when applying them.

Insecticidal soap. While it can pack a killer punch, insecticidal soap is one of the mildest sprays you can use. If a spray of water isn't enough to dislodge aphids and prevent them from returning, a spray of insecticidal soap can reduce their numbers. Once it has dried, the soap will have no harmful effects on aphids or any other insects. This makes it fairly safe to use around beneficials, but it will still kill soft-bodied insects while you're applying it and while it's wet. Because insecticidal soaps aren't effective when dry, you may need to reapply them every week, depending on how heavy an infestation your plant has.

Homemade Pepper Spray

Horticultural oils. Horticultural oils can help you control pests and block the spread of plant diseases when other methods fail. There are two types of oils—dormant oils and summer oils. Use dormant oils early in the season before new growth starts. They are useful against insects like spider mites that overwinter in bud scales and bark crevices. Because you apply dormant oils before the growing season begins, beneficial insects are less likely to be present and harmed. Dormant oils break down quickly, and as an extra bonus, it's great to be able to get one preventive pest control activity out of the way before spring.

Summer oils are lightweight horticultural oils that are relatively safe to use on plants later in the season when they're actively growing. They help control aphids, beetles, caterpillars, leafminers, and mealybugs without damaging the plant leaves. Summer oils can be phytotoxic (poisonous to plants), however, if you apply them to stressed plants, when the temperature is above 85°F, or when the humidity is high. Some plants, such as Japanese maples and citrus trees, are very sensitive to oils so read and follow the label instructions carefully. Horticultural oils can ruin the blue color of blue spruces and other such evergreens, so follow label instructions about application timing and temperatures strictly.

The "Rule of 140" can help you determine an appropriate day for spraying. Simply add the outdoor temperature (in degrees F) with the relative hu-

Pepper spray is a botanically derived product that's great for shooing pests away, and you can easily make it at home. It works as an irritant and is effective against aphids, thrips, grasshoppers, and rabbits when applied regularly.

   2 to 4 jalapeño, 'Serrano', or 'Habanero' peppers

   3 cloves garlic

   1 quart water

Mix all ingredients in a blender. Put the mixture in a clear quart jar, and let it steep in the sun for several days. Strain the mixture through cheesecloth, and pour the liquid into a spray bottle. Protect yourself from this irritating spray! Wear safety glasses and gloves, and wear rubber gloves when mixing and using it.

midity (expressed as a percentage). If the total is 140 or more, wait for cooler or less humid conditions and you'll avoid the possibility of phytotoxic burn. If hot, humid conditions persist, but the timing is otherwise right for attacking your particular pest, apply the oil during early morning hours. You'll find that the wind is usually calmer then, too, which will prevent unwanted spray from drifting on the rest of your landscape.

The table on page 210 can help you identify the most common insect pests that are likely to visit your landscape—both by sight and by the type of damage they do. For each pest, you'll find a list of ways to prevent them from visiting in the first place and ways to control them if they do arrive.

Aphids

DESCRIPTION

Soft-bodied, small (less than ¹/₁₀ inch), black, green, pink, yellowish, white, or powder gray insects.

DAMAGE

Aphids suck plant sap, causing new growth to be distorted. They also secrete a sticky substance called "honeydew," and a sooty fungus may grow in it. Trees that drop "sap" on cars often are infested with aphids.

PREVENTION AND CONTROL

- Avoid overfertilizing with nitrogen.
- Plant herbs and flowers like alyssum, coriander, and parsley that attract aphid-eating beneficials.
- Introduce or attract predators: Lady beetles and ladybug larvae feed on aphids.
- Spray plants with a strong stream of water.
- Spray with insecticidal soap mixture.
- Dust with diatomaceous earth.

Bagworms

DESCRIPTION

Bagworm larvae, which do the most damage, hatch in late spring. They cover themselves with a tough silk bag and attach pieces of foliage from the host plant to it and continue to feed through the summer.

DAMAGE

Chewing activity can denude an entire plant, leaving it with only bagworms dangling in their sacs. Hungry bagworms will eat almost anything, but their favorites are evergreens such as arborvitae and white pine.

PREVENTION AND CONTROL

- Pick off overwintering bags that hold the pupae.
- By early summer, the new bags are about ½ inch long, and green. Pick them if you can find them and continue doing so through the summer.
- Apply *Bacillus thuringiensis* var. *kurstaki* (BTK)—but only when larvae are actively feeding.

Japanese Beetles

DESCRIPTION

Adult Japanese beetles are about ½ inch long, with blue-green heads and copper-colored bodies.

DAMAGE

Adults feed on leaves, fruit, and flowers of many plants, particularly roses, filberts, lindens, fruit trees, and brambles, leaving them skeletonized. Grubs chew on plant roots, particularly roots of irrigated turfgrasses.

PREVENTION AND CONTROL

- Handpick or shake adults from plants.
- Plant trap crops such as borage, evening primrose, filbert, four-o'clocks, or wild grapes for beetles.
- Plant poisonous crops such as castor beans.
- Apply milky spore disease to control grubs in lawn areas.
- Spray beneficial nematodes in spring or late summer to control grubs.

Pillbugs and Sowbugs

DESCRIPTION

These gray-brown ½-inch crustaceans will roll into a ball when disturbed.

DAMAGE

Pillbugs and sowbugs are largely beneficial insects that feed on decaying plant matter, but they occasionally injure the stems, roots, or foliage of living plants. Give them plenty of organic matter to work on and they'll be inclined to leave living plants alone.

PREVENTION AND CONTROL

- If they're eating your live plants, try to remove their hiding places: surface litter, boards, etc.
- Remove mulch from around tender young plants.
- Surround plants with a protective barrier of diatomaceous earth.
- Water early in the day so the soil will dry out before they emerge.

Scales

DESCRIPTION

Scales can have a hard or leathery covering that makes them look nothing like insects, but more like waxy flecks or bumps. The waxy covering protects them from all but oily substances, such as horticultural oil.

DAMAGE

Euonymus, magnolias, pines, and tulip poplars are regular hosts. The scale insects attach themselves, secreting waxy coverings, sucking plant juices, and debilitating the host plant. Excreted honeydew may cause plants to turn black with sooty mold.

PREVENTION AND CONTROL

- Apply dormant oil in late winter to smother scales overwintering on trunks and limbs.
- Check package label to see which plants can safely be treated in summer with dormant oil applications.

Slugs

DESCRIPTION

Soft-bodied, slimy, nocturnal creatures have eyes at the tips of their two tentacles. They leave a visible slime trail.

DAMAGE

Slugs chew on foliage, fruits, and stems, leaving holes and tattered foliage.

PREVENTION AND CONTROL

- Handpick them.
- Set shallow saucers of beer around your garden. The slugs will stop by for a brew and drown.
- Set out a board for them to gather under, then flip the board over to bake in the sun.
- Spread crushed eggshells or diatomaceous earth around the base of susceptible plants.
- Rely on the aid of predators—ground beetles, toads, salamanders, garter snakes, and ducks.

Spider Mites

DESCRIPTION

Adults are barely detectable—check for them by shaking damaged foliage over white paper. Tiny specks that smear red when squashed are likely to be spider mites.

DAMAGE

Adults suck plant juices causing a bronzing or stippling of the foliage. Damaged leaves may then turn yellow or brown and begin dropping. In hot summer weather, outbreaks can crop up overnight. Arborvitae, euonymus, and honey locust are common hosts.

PREVENTION AND CONTROL

- Avoid planting susceptible plants near reflected heat sources such as cars, pavements, or buildings.
- Smother mites that overwinter in bark and buds with an early-spring application of dormant oil.
- Apply insecticidal soap every 7 to 10 days.
- Wash off with a strong spray of water.

Tent Caterpillars

DESCRIPTION

Caterpillars and their tents appear in tree crotches in spring. In summer, tents on the ends of branches signal the presence of fall webworms.

DAMAGE

On fruit trees, caterpillars will venture out of their tent to feed, devouring leaves and leaving tattered foliage. In times when populations are high, tent caterpillars can fully defoliate a tree. These trees will usually leaf out again later in the season; however, growth may be stunted for several more years.

PREVENTION AND CONTROL

- Prune out and dispose of a tent if you can do so without disfiguring the plant.
- Treat with BT during times of active feeding.
- Attract parasitic wasps by growing small-flowering herbs and flowers such as catnip and alyssum.

Plant Diseases and Controls

A healthy yard and garden are often full of disease pathogens—fungi, bacteria, viruses, and pathogenic nematodes. Animals, insects, wind, rain, and even tools can bring still more of them onto your property. While that may sound frightful, the good news is that many of these pathogens never develop into damaging diseases because the conditions aren't quite right for them. From natural plant defenses to unfavorable weather conditions to beneficial organisms being present, nature is often on the plants' side. But never underestimate the things you can do to keep your yard disease-free. Refer back to "Strategies for Success" on page 198 if plant diseases are a problem in your yard.

Just as with managing pest problems, if you have to take further steps to control a plant disease, it's best to start with the easiest, least toxic methods. Before you take any action, be sure to identify the problem so you know exactly what to treat, and save the sprays for a last resort. Carefully follow the label directions for any products you may use.

PREVENTION IS THE BEST BET

When you begin with hearty, disease-resistant plants, you are doing yourself and your plants a big favor because the plants will be less likely to contract a disease in the first place. You can also do your part to avoid spreading disease pathogens. If you keep your hands clean and disinfect your tools and garden shoes regularly, you'll be less likely to pass diseases from one plant to another.

Pruners in particular are one way you can spread diseases. When you cut away a diseased or damaged part of one plant, always clean the pruners with alcohol before using them to prune something else. Those open cuts are prime areas for infection. Another easy way to inadvertently spread plant diseases is by brushing against plants when they're wet. And, take the utmost care when mowing or trimming your yard so you don't damage plants in the process. One errant move with a string trimmer can mean an open wound where diseases can enter a plant.

BLOCK DISEASES WITH BARRIERS AND GOOD GARDEN CARE

By keeping your garden clean and tidy, you're really taking big steps toward blocking the spread of plant diseases. When you see disease-damaged plants, prune off the damaged parts, or just pull up the entire plant if it's small. Then make sure you eliminate it from your garden by burning it (if your local ordinances allow for this) or sealing it in a trash container. In addition, if the plant has dropped leaves or fruit, clean them up and dispose of them, too, because they may also be infected. Some diseases can overwinter on fallen leaves and fruits, so unless you get rid of the drops, you'll be looking toward another season of the same problem.

If you have a vegetable garden, barriers like row covers can help protect your plants from disease-spreading insects such as leafhoppers and cucumber beetles. Hungry insects have plenty of time to find their way in to the food, so bury the ends of the row covers to prevent infiltration. You will have to lift the covers again when the plants start flowering so that pollinating insects can get in to do their job.

Soil solarization is a barrier method that can kill pest insects, harmful nematodes, weed seeds, and many disease organisms. Clear the target area of any

Compost Tea Recipe

You can make your own disease-prevention mix at home. Put one shovelful of compost into a burlap bag or retired pillowcase. Tie the bag closed and place it in a 5-gallon bucket that's just about full of water. Let the compost steep for 2 or 3 days, then remove the "tea bag" from the bucket (reserving the liquid) and dump the contents onto your compost pile. Dilute the liquid until it looks like weak iced tea—try 3 parts water to 1 part of your concentrate—and spray or sprinkle it on new ornamental transplants. Refrain from using it on edible plants, as it may contain some bacteria you won't want to eat!

existing weeds or plant debris. Then soak the bed thoroughly. (Leave a sprinkler on the area until the soil is wet to a depth of 3 feet.) Next, cover the soil with clear plastic and seal the edges with soil. Leave the plastic on the bed for at least 6 weeks. The high temperatures generated in the top 12 inches of soil can eliminate a load of pests. Obviously, this technique isn't feasible for beds where you have lots of trees or shrubs planted, but it's useful for annual flower or vegetable beds where you've had problems.

"MEDICINES" FOR PLANT DISEASES

While you can find shelves full of products to take care of plant diseases in garden centers, most of them carry personal and environmental risks that may not be acceptable. However, some disease-control products, when used correctly, are safe for use in an organic landscape. These products tend to protect plants rather than eradicate diseases. Regardless of a product's presumed safety, always read and follow label instructions carefully.

Microbial fungicides contain beneficial organisms that can prevent disease-causing organisms from infecting your plants.

Barrier sprays such as vegetable oil or light horticultural oil can help to prevent powdery mildew, which needs direct contact and—believe it or not—a dry surface to germinate.

Teas or infusions made of compost or plant products like garlic or horsetail can protect new transplants from damping-off by keeping invading fungi from finding a hospitable surface for growth.

Baking soda (sodium bicarbonate) can help protect plants from fungal infection and can also help limit the spread of an existing one, such as black spot or powdery mildew. Use 1 tablespoon baking soda with 1 tablespoon horticultural oil in a gallon of water, or try 1 teaspoon each of oil and baking soda in 2 quarts of water. Add a few drops of insecticidal soap to the mixture to help it mix well. Reapply every 5 to 7 days.

The following table will help you become familiar with several common plant diseases that you're likely to run across in the landscape from time to time and suggest what to do about them. If you need further help with identification, find a good plant disease book that features photos of disease symptoms that are common to specific plants, or contact your Cooperative Extension office.

Anthracnose

DESCRIPTION

A fungal disease that attacks flowering dogwood, maple, and sycamore. Spores need water to germinate and are spread easily during wet spring weather.

DAMAGE

Symptoms vary by plant type but generally take the form of watery, rotting spots on foliage, stems, flowers, or fruits. On sycamores, anthracnose is rarely fatal, but it can be devastating on dogwoods as well as annual garden plants.

PREVENTION AND CONTROL

- Choose resistant cultivars and healthy transplants.
- Avoid touching plants when they're wet.
- Remove and destroy infected annual plants as well as infected parts on woody plants.
- Clean up plant debris to prevent overwintering.

Fire Blight

DESCRIPTION

A bacterial disease that affects pears, mountain ashes, pyracanthas, serviceberries, and spireas. It's transmitted during wet spring weather and by insects that visit infected plants.

DAMAGE

Damage spreads from the tips of young shoots toward the center of the tree. Flowers brown and shrivel, as do leaves, which remain hanging on the plant. Cankers form on branches. This disease can be devastating.

PREVENTION AND CONTROL

- Choose resistant cultivars.
- Avoid high nitrogen fertilizing or hard pruning.
- Control insects to prevent spread.
- Remove infected branches along with 6 to 12 inches of healthy wood. Disinfect pruners between cuts and between plants.

Root and Crown Rots

DESCRIPTION

These fungal diseases affect many plants including azaleas, hollies, lilacs, and rhododendrons. Rots overwinter on infected tubers and plant debris and are apt to appear in wet conditions.

DAMAGE

Woody plants will suffer from shoot dieback and stem cankers. Plants can rot and die in wet weather.

PREVENTION AND CONTROL

- Choose resistant cultivars.
- Space and prune plants for good air movement.
- Plant high for good drainage.
- Prune woody plants to remove infected parts.
- Remove and destroy infected herbaceous plants and tubers; clean up and destroy infected leaves.

Powdery Mildew

DESCRIPTION

A powdery white fungal disease common on bee balms, lilacs, phloxes, and many other plants. It's most common during periods of hot days and cool nights with dry conditions.

DAMAGE

Powdery mildew forms white to grayish patches, usually on the upper surfaces of leaves. A serious infection will cause leaves to brown and shrivel.

PREVENTION AND CONTROL

- Choose resistant cultivars.
- Space and prune to encourage air circulation.
- Avoid high nitrogen fertilizing or hard pruning.
- Mist plants daily to prevent spore germination.
- Remove and destroy infected herbaceous plants.
- Spray a 0.5 percent solution of baking soda weekly to protect susceptible plants.

Leaf Spots

DESCRIPTION

Leaf spots include a wide range of bacterial and fungal diseases. While bacterial spot affects a wide range of woody and herbaceous plants, black spot infects primarily roses.

DAMAGE

Spots form in various patterns, depending on the pathogen. Severely infected leaves may fall early.

PREVENTION AND CONTROL

- Choose resistant cultivars.
- Practice good garden sanitation, to prevent overwintering in the soil.
- Mulch to prevent fungi from splashing up from the soil when it rains.
- Prune plants to promote air circulation.
- Apply baking soda spray (see recipe on page 213) to help control the spread of this disease.

Molds

DESCRIPTION

These fungal diseases occur in cool, humid conditions, appearing as powdery or woolly areas on affected plant parts. Spores are easily transported by air, water, and tools.

DAMAGE

Appears as a thick gray mold on fruit or as water-soaked blighted areas on petals, leaves, or stems. It often starts on aging leaves but quickly spreads to entire branches of the plant.

PREVENTION AND CONTROL

- Space, prune, and support plants for good air movement.
- Avoid overfertilizing with nitrogen.
- Remove dead or dying plant parts, which are usually the first affected.
- Pick all fruit as it ripens, whether or not it's edible.
- Remove and destroy infected material.

Rusts

DESCRIPTION

Fungal diseases that often require two different plant species such as hawthorns and junipers to complete their life cycle. Rusts occur most often in moist conditions.

DAMAGE

Typical symptoms include a rust-colored coating on upper leaf surfaces and fruit and gelatinous tentacles growing from gall-like structures on alternate hosts. A serious infection can kill the plant.

PREVENTION AND CONTROL

- Choose resistant cultivars.
- Don't plant both a primary host and its alternate host in your landscape. (A good plant reference book can give you more specifics.) If you already have both, remove the alternate host.
- Space and prune plants to allow air circulation.
- Remove and destroy infected herbaceous plants.

Scab

DESCRIPTION

These fungal diseases affect a broad range of plants and cause serious damage on apples, crabapples, and peaches. Scab is most likely to occur in cool, moist conditions.

DAMAGE

Infected fruits, leaves, and tubers develop hardened, overgrown, and cracked areas, beginning with olive-colored spots that turn to black. Leaves may yellow and drop prematurely.

PREVENTION AND CONTROL

- Choose resistant cultivars.
- Space and prune plants for good air circulation.
- Remove and destroy fallen leaves.

Controlling Animal Pests

Animal pest problems can be vexing. It seems that critters have unlimited time and energy to undo our best work, and they often do their misdeeds at odd hours. We usually wish them no harm, but we do wish they'd find some other way to satisfy their needs. Is there a chance for peaceful coexistence?

As with other pests, the best approach is prevention through thoughtful plant selection. If you're developing a new plan, find out what animal pests are in your environment and then resist the temptation to use landscape plants that your local wildlife is likely to munch on. Combinations to avoid are azaleas with deer and pulmonaria with rabbits. Also consider depriving them of water (if possible) and their favorite type of cover. With a little research and planning, you can avoid giving animal pests exactly what they want or need, and they may go in search of it elsewhere.

For guidance on plant selection—as well as on other measures you can take to control animal problems—your Cooperative Extension office or USDA Wildlife Services office are both great resources.

If your existing landscape is already under attack, you'll have other decisions to make. Many regions that didn't have deer problems when the homes were first built, for instance, now may have thriving herds because deer have lost their habitat to our built-up suburban environment. Do you need to completely overhaul your landscape? Or can you put up some defenses that will eliminate the animal damage? Start by identifying the problem and work your way through the situation before you make an expensive or time-consuming decision!

Viewing nature close up in a backyard setting can be interesting and entertaining, but when visiting critters start attacking your plants, you might not feel so hospitable.

1. Identify the pest. Often, the only clues we have to animal damage are the telltale signs of how they chewed the plants or the tracks they leave behind. If you haven't actually seen what's been eating your azaleas and you're not sure what's causing the destruction, the USDA Wildlife Services, your local Cooperative Extension Service, a nature center, or even your neighbors can probably help identity of the culprits.

2. Assess the damage. If the damage is merely cosmetic, it may be something you're willing to live with. If so, you may choose to do nothing, but I recommend monitoring the situation closely. Feeding habits change with the seasons and your four-footed bandit may soon head elsewhere for other tasty treats. If the damage is a threat to the plant's health, then you want to take steps to stop the situation.

3. Learn your options. Is there a way to control the damage without excluding the animal (as with repellents) or do you need a barrier to keep the animal off of your property to prevent move damage?

4. Choose a method. You may need to try various control methods, and I recommend trying them out one at a time in the spirit of experimentation. That way, you'll know what worked best. Still, animals can be unpredictable—and they don't read books! A method that worked for weeks or months may suddenly be useless. Keep your sense of humor and be willing to vary your course of action, if needed.

Living Peacefully with Animal Friends

While sharing the outdoors with animal inhabitants can make your outdoor experiences more interesting, sometimes the damage they can wreak can be too much for a landscape to bear. The following control methods may help you minimize the damage done by animal pests.

MODIFY THEIR HABITAT

When you remove the food source, cover, or other attractions for animal pests, they're likely to go elsewhere in search of dinner. In the case of deer, the food source might be azaleas, but for skunks it is probably grubs in the lawn. But don't make assumptions about what an animal is after! Get the facts.

EMPLOY SCARE TACTICS

Scare tactics can include a domestic dog or cat prowling around the property—or the smell of one on old throw rugs or carpet remnants. Something as simple as brushing your pet and laying the hair collected in the brush around your landscape plants may do the trick. Visual imitations of predators, like scarecrows or fake snakes, as well as pie plates or shiny old CDs that flash in the sun have been proven to ward off hungry birds and animals. Sounds are another easy way to scare off critters, whether it's the sound of a radio playing or a tape of predator sounds.

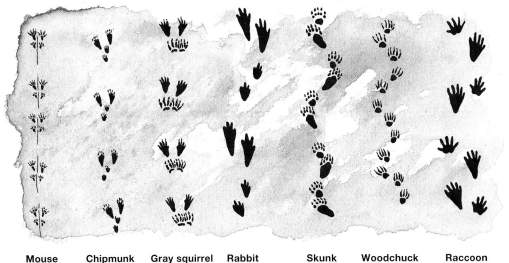

Note the timing and appearance of tracks as well as feeding habits for clues in identifying what's been eating at your house.

Mouse   Chipmunk   Gray squirrel   Rabbit   Skunk   Woodchuck   Raccoon

BLOCK 'EM WITH BARRIERS

Barriers can include fencing (both above and below ground) and netting to control animal access. Check with local experts about specific fencing requirements for individual pests—especially if you live in deer country. Gravel-filled trenches can exclude burrowing animals such as moles and voles.

REPEL THEIR SENSE OF SMELL

You can use animals' strong senses of smell to help keep them off your property, or at least away from your landscape plants. Try commercially made repellents or make homemade varieties; they just need to contain a scent that's repulsive to the pest. A popular goose repellant has concord grapes as the active ingredient. Other repellents include soap bars, human hair, pet hair, and pepper sprays. You'll most likely have to

A purely decorative fence will not keep pests out because deer can jump right over and rabbits, voles, and other small creatures can pass through or burrow underneath it.

reapply repellents after it rains, which can become tedious and time-consuming. Once you find a repellent that seems to be doing the trick, you may not mind reapplying it. Besides, feeding habits change with the season, so you may not have to keep it up year-round.

The Top 8 Animal Pests and What to Do about Them

Your take on whether the wildlife that visits your backyard is a pest or a welcome visitor may largely depend upon what you have planted. Many people enjoy bird watching, for instance, and are grateful for the insect pests they eat. Birds can sometimes be a nuisance, however, especially if you've planted fruit trees, shrubs, or canes. Here are some tricks you can try to limit the damage in your yard.

BIRDS

Many of us enjoy attracting birds to our yards with bird feeders and birdbaths. Some bird species are likely to go after your garden fruits or vegetables, however. Scare them off with fake predators like snakes or owls during the peak season. Or you can distract them by planting mulberries. You can also protect crops with bird netting.

DEER

If you live in an area that's heavily populated by deer, you know the damage they can cause! They like to eat foliage, buds, and young, green twigs. You can try to scare them away with a dog (or the scent of one) or repellents like soap, human hair, or hot sauce. You may even want to resort to electric fencing. Conventional fencing is another option, but deer can jump high, so it will have to be at least 8 feet tall.

CHIPMUNKS

If you find telltale tunnels and uprooted plants in your beds, the culprit may be chipmunks or ground squirrels. They particularly enjoy the tastiness of newly planted seedlings and bulbs. As with deer, you can call your dog (or cat) to aid you, or try repellents. Castor oil spray is another deterrent that works on these small guys. Underground barriers such as wire mesh or hardware cloth around bulbs and new plantings can prevent access to your plants. You can further protect tempting bulbs by putting a handful of gravel into planting holes.

MICE AND VOLES

These creatures eat green vegetation, as well as tubers, bulbs, and the bark and roots of fruit trees when other food is scarce. You can use the same barriers and repellents as described for deer and chipmunks. Also, protect your trees in winter by wrapping the trunks in hardware cloth and burying the ends in the soil. Keep the mulch layer thin near tree trunks so mice or voles won't have a place to hide.

MOLES

The worst damage that moles do is create tunnels where you don't want them. They eat insects like grubs, which is a benefit to you, but if you've ever tripped over a raised tunnel in your lawn, you may not be so thankful. You can simply try to eliminate their food supply by applying milky spore disease or parasitic nematodes on your lawn to reduce the grub population. If you have a particular area where moles seem to be a problem, you can deny them entry by digging a trench around the area. Make sure it is at least 6 inches wide by 2 inches deep, then fill it with gravel. You can top-dress it with soil.

RABBITS

If you have a vegetable garden, you're likely to have a few rabbits visiting for some of their favorite foods: beans, beet tops, carrots, lettuce, and peas. Beyond vegetables, rabbits may chew on tree bark and the buds and stems of woody shrubs. Rabbits aren't apt to hang around for long, however, if you have a dog. In addition, you can use repellents, cover tender young plants, put up a chicken wire fence around your vegetable bed, or use hardware cloth barriers around vulnerable shrubs and tree trunks.

SKUNKS

In addition to the offensive odor skunks can leave behind when frightened, they can also disrupt your yard with their digging and foraging. On behalf of skunks, what they're rooting for in your yard are pests like grubs and other damaging insects. You can pretty much avoid having skunks visit your yard if you control the number of beetle grubs in your lawn. Applying milky spore disease or parasitic nematodes to your turf may help.

WOODCHUCKS OR GROUNDHOGS

Woodchucks like to feed on young garden plants in the spring—everything from flowers and vegetables to shrubs. But worse than their damage or destruction to plants can be their hazardous burrows. If you're not aware they're there, you can easily trip or twist your ankle while mowing or playing in the yard. As with other rodents, dogs are a great way to scare them off. The mere scent of a dog can do the trick, so place dog hair or carpet squares that your dog has slept on around your garden. If you have a vegetable bed that they're after, surround it with a chicken wire fence buried several inches below ground.

CHAPTER 10

Pruning That **Pays:** How, **When,** and **Why** to **Prune**

While **pruning** won't entirely be a thing of the
past in your backyard, my **tips** and **techniques** will help
you avoid the tedious, repeated jobs that often make
pruning a chore. You'll **understand** why, when, and how to
make the pruning cuts needed to keep your plants
healthy and **attractive.** You'll also learn how to choose
the best tools for you and when to farm out the big jobs.
In short, you'll be able to keep pruning chores **manageable**
while getting **admirable results!**

Pruning Priorities

The easiest way to make the most of your pruning time is to start with the right plants. When you plant trees, shrubs, or perennials that are suited to your growing conditions and the right size for the spot where you plant them, you can cut way back on the amount of pruning you'll have to do. An occasional stroll through your property to check for problems such as dead, dying, or crossed branches may be all you'll need to do.

If you have overgrown shrubs or mature trees that haven't been given much attention, you'll need to do a bit more pruning to get your yard back on track. By prioritizing what you need to do, you can start with the tasks that are likely to give you the most mileage. Beyond basic plant health and safety maintenance, you may want to prune to encourage more fruit and flower production on edible and ornamental plants. Or you may need to renew an overgrown foundation plant. And, if you've given in and purchased a plant that didn't quite meet your size requirements, you'll end up pruning it to control its size. Whatever the situation, understanding your goal and the pruning tasks you're facing will help you avoid wasting time and effort.

After you've reviewed the basic reasons for pruning trees and shrubs, you'll be able to establish pruning goals for your yard. Then you can turn to "The Right Time to Prune" on page 231 to find out the best time to do each pruning task. Before you venture out with pruners in hand, read "The Basic Cuts" on page 233, and you'll be ready to tackle any pruning project. Last, if you're in the market for new hand pruners, a pruning saw, or other tool to help make the job easier, see "The Best Tools for the Job" on page 236.

Pruning Trees

Obviously, safety in your backyard is a top priority. On young trees, taking care of potential problems is relatively easy. The pruning you do now will help you avoid serious hazards—and more costly care—later. On large trees, a hazardous situation can threaten property damage or worse, making pruning or any other type of work irrelevant! Taking care of the problem areas to prevent or harm and check trees regularly for any dead, dying, diseased, crossed, rubbing, broken, or cracked branches. On a large, over-mature tree, neglecting pest damage can lead to the ultimate pruning job—the kind that leaves a stump. If you're unfamiliar with pruning techniques, take a look at "Pruning Vocabulary" on the opposite page. It points out the various parts of a tree and explains what they are so you'll be sure to make the appropriate cuts.

Pruning Vocabulary

Just as with other aspects of gardening, pruning has its own terminology to describe the cuts and plant parts. If pruning isn't that familiar to you, take a glance at the definitions below to better understand which part of your tree or shrub to cut.

Branch collar. The place where a branch meets a stem or trunk. Large branches have a bulge at their bases, making the branch collar easier to see, but all branches have collars. Always leave the collar when you make a pruning cut.

Bud break. A place where a new shoot is forming on a branch

Candle. The compact, expanding new growth that appears on pines, spruces, and firs in the spring

Cane. A long, slender branch that usually originates directly from the roots. Shrub roses, forsythia, and twig dogwoods are example of shrubs that produce canes.

Crotch. The place where an angle is formed by two branches or between a branch and the trunk

Crown. The top of the tree or shrub

Heading. Cutting back the ends of branches or stems to produce thicker growth on the outside of the plant

Lateral branch. Any branch that grows out from a larger branch

Leader. The primary or tallest vertical branch originating from a tree trunk

Shearing. Heading cuts (trimming just the branch ends) over the entire plant

Stub. An unsightly branch piece left from a cut that wasn't made at a bud or originating branch

Sucker. A vigorous, upright branch that originates from the base of the tree or shrub

Thinning. Selectively cutting out entire branches or canes to let more air and light into a tree or shrub

Water sprout. A vigorous, upright branch that originates along another branch

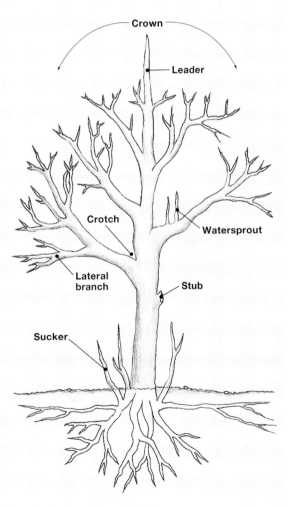

Taking Care of Small Trees

You can handle problem situations on small trees— ones that you can work on from the ground—by yourself. Usually all you'll need to do is make thinning cuts to remove the problems. Here's how.

1. Thin the crown lightly by removing any branches that are growing inward to prevent future breakage from wind, rain, snow, or ice, especially when the tree has its leaves. Be careful not to "clean out" the center of the tree, however, as the major limbs need some of those branches to help build wood for future strength.

2. Next, look for competing branches—branches that originate from the same point—and eliminate all but one of the competitors. This is especially important on the main leader of the tree, where competing leaders—with weight and age—can cause a disfiguring split or worse.

3. During all of your pruning, favor branches with wide crotch angles and, where you have a choice, eliminate the branches that have a narrow crotch angle.

Limbing Up

If you have a young tree that you'll someday want to be able to walk under, it's best to remove a lower limb every year or so until the lowest limb is at the height you want. Doing this gradually over several years will allow those lower limbs to contribute to the growth and taper of the trunk, which is very important for the tree's future strength. I find that lots of homeowners are squeamish about removing lower limbs. You can easily get over the fear that you'll damage your tree once you realize that when large lower limbs conflict with mowing or walking, they're usually exposed to far worse damage than when you make a good pruning cut at the trunk. And waiting to remove a limb until later when it's much larger will

leave a bigger wound that may not close well, exposing the tree to insects and disease problems.

The weight of summer rain on leaves can make branches droop even lower, so try to anticipate the added weight and use thinning cuts to lighten the lowest branches that remain. In addition, if any of the limbs you remove is larger than 3 inches in diameter, use a three-step approach to avoid torn or ragged cuts, as shown below. A good, clean cut will callous over or close much more quickly, leaving your tree less prone to pest or disease invasion.

1. Make the first cut on the underside of the limb, 1' to 2' from the trunk. Saw halfway through the branch.

2. Make the second cut on top of the limb about 1" farther out toward the branch tip and the branch will break cleanly away.

3. Make a clean final cut just outside the branch collar.

When removing limbs that have a 3-inch or larger diameter, use this three-step technique to avoid torn or ragged cuts.

Pruning a Young Shade Tree

You can prevent hazardous situations from occurring in large shade trees by pruning them properly from a young age. Follow these steps to help Mother Nature create a healthy and sturdy mature shade tree.

1. Make cuts to remove dead, dying, crossing, rubbing, broken, diseased, or misplaced branches anytime you see these potential problems.

2. Thin to remove inward-growing or congested branches during the dormant season, as needed.

3. When two branches are competing from the same growing point, remove one. Leave the branch with the widest crotch angle, if possible.

4. If you'll be walking or mowing beneath the tree, remove a lower limb every year or so until the lowest limb gives enough clearance for adults to walk under.

Looking After Large Trees

On large shade trees—those that you can't work on from the ground—look for signs of decay in the crown, the trunk, and at the soil level. Hollows and spongy, exposed wood are warning signs of serious problems. Look also for cracks and splits, especially where two branches form a narrow angle. Wherever significant weight is being held in the air by weak wood—narrow crotch angles, decayed areas, or broken branches—you're looking at a potential danger.

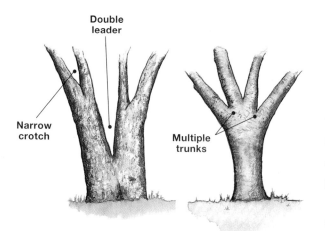

Double leader

Narrow crotch

Multiple trunks

Double leaders with narrow crotches, multiple trunks emerging from one point, and decay or hollows where branches attach to the trunk are all forms of major structural flaws in mature trees that need the attention of a professional arborist.

You may be able to save your tree, but don't try to climb it yourself to find out. Call an arborist for an evaluation. (See "When to Call a Pro" on the opposite page.) Perhaps a crown cleaning or restoration will be necessary, but that's a big job—one that definitely needs to be done by a professional.

Working on trees can be a hazardous enterprise. Make the cuts you feel comfortable making from the ground, but hire an experienced arborist for any work that is high off the ground, requires using a chain saw above shoulder level, or is near electrical lines.

For large shade trees that appear healthy and sound, an annual, visual safety inspection is a good idea. Some arborists will even do this without charge.

Well-maintained shade trees offer benefits and real estate value well worth the expense of occasional maintenance.

It's especially important to inspect trees that are located where they could do real damage. For instance, if your tree is on a large wooded property, you (and the cavity-nesting birds!) may be able to tolerate more risk than if the tree is in the front yard along an active street where a falling limb could harm pedestrians, cars, your house, or the neighbors'.

To reduce the potential risks of a large shade tree, consider pruning it at regular intervals, such as every 3 to 5 years. An arborist can eliminate weak crotches and thin the crown to help keep the tree healthy and everyone below it safe.

WHEN TO CALL
A PRO

FINDING A QUALIFIED ARBORIST

Arborists provide a variety of tree-care services including hazard assessment, pest and disease diagnosis, lab analysis, pruning, removal (including stumps), lightning protection, cabling and bracing, tree moving, cavity treatment (not filling), fertilizing, pest control, and aerating compacted root zones. Unfortunately, in many places anyone with a truck, a chain saw, and a little knowledge can go into business offering arborist services to the unsuspecting.

That's why the International Society of Arboriculture's (ISA) arborist certification program is such a boon to homeowners. By calling the ISA or searching its Web site (see "Resources for Backyard Ideas" on page 256), you can get a list of currently certified arborists by city, county, or postal code. While the ISA certification program offers no guarantees, it provides contact information on arborists who have demonstrated a thorough understanding of tree biology and their skills in tree work.

WHAT TO LOOK FOR IN AN ARBORIST

- ISA certification
- Business telephone listing (indicates a certain level of permanence)
- Proof of personal injury, property damage, and workers' compensation insurance
- Written estimate

WHAT TO AVOID

- Someone who knocks on your door, particularly after a storm (reputable firms will be busy enough without making door-to-door solicitations)
- A tree service that rushes you into making a decision, discourages you from getting a second opinion, or asks you to pay in advance

- A tree service that tops trees or "rounds them over"
- A tree service that climbs living trees with boot spikes

The only way you'll know about these harmful practices is to ask about the company's practices in advance, so don't be shy.

HOW TO GET THE BEST PRICE

For the best possible prices, delay your tree work until the dormant season, unless it's an emergency. Also, get at least two estimates about 1 month or more before you want the work done. Finally, be sure the estimates state exactly what you want done with the wood and that your site will be cleaned up to its original condition.

Pruning **Shrubs**

Just as with trees, anytime you see a problem area in a shrub—dead, decaying, broken, or crossed branches—is the right time to make a pruning cut. But in addition to those "anytime" cuts, there are a bunch of other reasons for pruning shrubs. You can keep shrubs growing happily by pruning to let light and air into the plant's interior to promote natural growth. You can help shrubs bear more flowers or fruit, renew old overgrown shrubs, shape hedges, or (if you must!) trim shrubs to contain their size.

Improve Health and Appearance

On shrubs with canes or branches emerging right from ground level—like abelia, red-twig dogwood, or forsythia—make thinning cuts at ground level. Higher cuts can ruin the natural form of the plant. Remove about one-third of the oldest wood to encourage vigorous new growth that will produce those nice red twigs on the dogwood and abundant flowers on the abelia and forsythia. Do this right after flowering.

Prune shrubs such as orange-eye butterfly bush and blue mist shrub the same way, but make your cuts during the dormant season because these plants bear flowers on the vigorous new growth that emerges in the spring.

For large deciduous shrubs like juneberry or pyracantha—that grow on top rather than at ground level—thin them as needed to expose the interior to light and air. Although you can do this anytime, it's best to prune just after flowering to ensure flowers next year.

On evergreen shrubs like junipers and yews, thin away any congested growth, allowing light and air to penetrate the shrub. Reach inside the plant to make your pruning cuts. It will help hide the cut ends as well as prevent dense growth only on the outside of the plant. Anytime but late summer is fine for pruning evergreens, though you might want to try my "just once" advice described below to keep maintenance to a minimum.

"Just Once" Pruning for Evergreens

If you were going to prune an evergreen plant just once a year, when would be the best time to do it? I like to defer pruning until late fall. Evergreens are pretty forgiving and can withstand pruning just about anytime but in the late summer; this is because any new growth won't have time to harden off before cold weather sets in. But if you wait until November to prune, you can use or give away the trimmings for holiday greenery. If your evergreens—especially yews—need an additional trimming, do it in late spring, following their first flush of growth.

Increase Fruit and Flowers

If you're growing a plant largely for its flowers or fruit—perhaps beautyberry, camellias, hawthorns, shrub roses, or wisteria—you'll want to prune for abundance! For each species, find out whether the plant blooms and sets fruit on the previous year's wood or on new wood. Generally, prune soon after flowering for plants blooming on the previous year's wood so the plant has time to set flower buds before cold weather sets in. Prune during the dormant season for plants that will bloom on new growth, and you'll enjoy blooms on the new shoots that sprout in spring. There's variation even within a genus (as with hydrangeas and hollies), so get information about your specific plants from a good reference book. You can then prune at a time of year when flower buds won't be at risk from your cuts.

On cane-forming shrubs like shrub roses or shrubs that grow directly from the ground like beautyberry, make your cuts close to ground level. This encourages the vigorous growth that keeps the flowers and fruits coming. For larger plants with permanent above-ground structures like camellias or hawthorns, thin them as needed to get good light and air penetration. Flowering vines generally benefit from hard pruning. It promotes vigorous growth and abundant flowers. Similarities stop there, however, so look up the specific pruning needs of your vine in a reputable book.

Renew Growth

If you've inherited overgrown shrubs as part of your property, or if you have one or two plants that have simply gotten away from you, renewal pruning can help you get them back in shape. In some cases, renewal pruning can be as simple as cutting a large or mature shrub entirely to the ground. Other plants may require a gradual process.

The technique you use depends on the plant's inclinations as well as your own. While you might be eager to get a decrepit forsythia blooming again, you may not have the heart to make it all disappear one day. On the other hand, if you don't have the patience to gradually "unshear" yews that have been neatly trimmed into geometric shapes, you may decide one day to thin them out all at once and let the chips fall where they may.

Some flowering shrubs such as this oakleaf hydrangea should be pruned after flowering to promote next year's buds.

PLANTS WITH CANES

The simplest renewal pruning is on those shrubs whose branches or canes emerge directly from the ground, without a permanent above-ground structure. This includes shrub dogwoods, forsythias, deciduous hollies, hydrangeas, lilacs, mock oranges, spireas, viburnums, and many others. For a gradual approach, remove one-third of the oldest branches at ground level each year. In 3 years, you'll have a new plant! For a rapid renewal, you can cut the entire plant to the ground and it will grow back. Do your renewal pruning during the dormant season when the absence of leaves lets you better see what you're doing, or prune just following the bloom time.

PLANTS WITH STRUCTURE

Renewing shrubs with more structure requires a bit more finesse with the thinning cuts and works best when you do it over the course of a few growing seasons. Candidates for this type of pruning include azaleas, bayberries, mountain laurels, rhododendrons,

Plants that are repeatedly sheared are often left hollow because the dense after-growth shades the interior.

Especially on plants that have been repeatedly sheared, the only green growth you find may be on the exterior. Plants in this condition, need to be opened up gradually over two or three growing seasons. That way the interior of the plant has an opportunity to acclimate to the new light levels and form the buds it needs for new growth. Remove just one-third of the old growth by reaching in and making thinning cuts to any foliage or bud that you can find.

Don't be concerned about making holes in the plant. They'll allow light to the interior of the plant, which will spur new growth. When you cut out another third the next year, you'll see that the new growth is beginning to take the form of a newer, smaller, more vigorous plant. When you finally remove the last of the old growth, the holes will be gone. Do this work in late winter when spring's rising sap can energize the new growth and when the sun isn't hot enough to scorch it.

and yews. The plant should be in good condition—just old or overgrown. Begin by getting a look at the structure if you can; you may need to spread the branches apart or even climb inside! On larger plants, look for a basic structure. While you can't do it all in one year, you'll eventually prune the plant back to this shape. On these and smaller plants, also look for opportunities to thin back to even the tiniest wisp of green growth on the plant's interior. Barring that, prune back to a well-placed bud.

Shape Hedges

If you have a clipped hedge in your yard, you'll need to spend more time pruning than if you let the shrubs grow to their natural shape. If keeping that clipped hedge is important to you, use the maintenance tips throughout this book to help reduce other high-

Clip your hedge so it's wider at the bottom than at the top, and you'll be rewarded with a hedge that fills in fully to the ground (*left*), rather than one that's sparse at the bottom (*right*).

maintenance tasks in your yard so you'll have more time to devote to your hedge. But why not consider a more natural-looking hedge? Abelia, forsythia, and spirea can all be used to create a living barrier that doesn't have to be trimmed into a rectangular form.

Just like a lawn, shaped hedges require frequent clipping during the growing season when the growth is soft. As with grass, it's best to cut little but often, never cutting into hardened wood. The frequent shearing encourages bud breaks to form behind the cuts, which will help fill in any gaps.

A common problem with yew hedges is brown needles. You can avoid this situation by shearing or clipping yews while they're still wet with dew—but do this only with manual shears, not electric! Since pruning encourages new growth, stop cutting hedges late in the season because cold weather can easily damage tender new shoots.

Control Size

Trimming to keep a plant small is rarely a permanent solution. If you find yourself going back repeatedly to prune a plant to a more acceptable size, it's a losing battle. If the space is just too small for the plant, a replacement plant that fits the space just makes more sense.

With that said, if you are going to prune for size control, the best candidates are shrubs whose stems originate from ground level, having no permanent above-ground structure. This includes shrub dogwoods, forsythia, deciduous hollies, hydrangeas, lilacs, nandina, spireas, viburnums, and many others. Follow the guidelines under "Renew Growth" on page 229, and follow up annually by removing one-third of the plant's growth at ground level.

The worst candidates for size control are shrubs with permanent above-ground structure. Follow the directions for renewal pruning, then prune regularly to keep the new growth dense and compact.

The **Right Time** to Prune

While you should make some pruning cuts anytime you see the need, there are optional times for most other types of pruning. Just as some trees and shrubs flower in the spring while others are fall showstoppers, your plants have preferred trimming times.

Anytime Cuts

Whenever you see dead, dying, crossing, rubbing, broken, diseased or misplaced growth, it's the right time to make corrective pruning cuts. Where branches are crossing or rubbing, remove the one that's the most damaged or that is heading toward the center of the plant. With diseased growth, be sure to cut all the way back to good wood. Also, rub off unwelcome buds—ones that will sprout shoots that will grow in toward the center of the plant, for instance—to prevent future crossed limbs.

Dormant-Season Cuts

It's easier to prune deciduous plants after they have shed their leaves because you can clearly see what you're doing. Cleanup is quicker, too, because there are few, if any, leaves to pick up when you're finished. Take advantage of the dormant season to do the following dormant-season pruning tasks, and your efforts will go further and your growing season will go more smoothly!

During the Dormant Season

■ Prune summer-blooming shrubs that flower on new growth (see "Summer Bloomers to Prune While Dormant" below).

■ Rejuvenate older, overgrown shrubs with renewal pruning.

■ Prune young shade trees to keep them in good condition so they'll be structurally sound as they mature.

■ Contract out any work that needs to be done on mature shade trees.

Summer Bloomers to Prune While Dormant

Many summer-blooming shrubs produce flowers only on new wood. To ensure that you'll enjoy a full flush of bloom next summer, prune these plants anytime they're dormant. Removing the old wood during the dormant season will promote vigorous spring growth, which will bloom and fruit more abundantly.

Glossy abelia (*Abelia × grandiflora*)

Orange-eye butterfly bush (*Buddleia davidii*)

Blue mist shrub (*Caryopteris × clandonensis*)

Summersweet (*Clethra alnifolia*)

Hibiscus (*Hibiscus* spp.)

Japanese kerria (*Kerria japonica*)

Trees That "Bleed" Sap

Pruning during the dormant season tends to invigorate plants. Plant roots store carbohydrates that will rise up in the spring and support new growth. Because you've reduced the top growth through pruning, the plant is likely to get an extra boost, which is good for flowering, fruiting, and recovery!

Be aware, however, that rising sap can escape from pruning wounds in some species. The dripping sap may be unsightly but isn't damaging, so don't be alarmed. If it bothers you, defer the work on those trees until summer. Finally, know that cuts larger than 2 inches in diameter can close more quickly when a tree is actively growing. Even though the sap may not be pretty, it's better for the tree if you save those larger cuts until late in the dormant season—such as early spring—just before growth is set to start up again.

Maples (*Acer* spp.)

Birches (*Betula* spp.)

American yellowwood (*Cladrastis lutea*)

Dogwoods (*Cornus* spp.)

Walnuts (*Juglans* spp.)

Elms (*Ulmus* spp.)

Go for the Growing Season

While it's best to do some pruning tasks during the dormant season, other pruning tasks are prime for the growing season.

During the Growing Season

■ Prune spring-blooming shrubs such as azalea and viburnum after they bloom, but before they set flower buds for next year.

■ Pinch the candles (the new growth) from pines, firs, and spruces.

■ Remove any dead, dying, diseased, or broken branches as you notice them.

■ Trim evergreen trees, shrubs, and hedges, if necessary; otherwise wait until November.

■ Reduce size (for any type of plant), if necessary.

■ Thin trees that easily form vertical water sprouts, such as crabapples and lindens.

Pruning and the *"Just Once"* Rule

SPRING BLOOMERS TO PRUNE AFTER FLOWERING

Pruning during the growing season tends to reduce a plant's vigor because you're removing growth that the plant has just invested energy to produce. While that may seem undesirable, reducing vigor is useful if your pruning is to reduce size or if you're trying to prevent water sprouts from forming. On spring-blooming plants that will soon set buds for next year, catch them no later than a month following bloom or you may be removing next year's flowers!

Camellias (*Camellia* spp.)

Quinces (*Chaenomeles* spp.)

Forsythias (*Forsythia* spp.)

Rhododendrons and azaleas (*Rhododendron* spp.)

Spireas (*Spiraea* spp., except *S. bumalda*)

Lilacs (*Syringa* spp.)

Viburnums (*Viburnum* spp.)

The **Basic Cuts**

Whether you are pruning to keep plants healthy and looking nice, to encourage more blooms, or to prevent future problems, there are only two types of cuts to make: thinning and heading. Once you're familiar with these two cuts, I'm sure pruning will suddenly seem much less mysterious! Depending on the variety and type of plants you have, you'll most likely need to do each type of cut at one time or another. Knowing the differences between thinning and heading can help you prune any plant with confidence.

Each plant has an optimum pruning time—some in spring, some in fall, some after blooming, some before. You may need to do a little research to find out when that time is. If you're uncertain, check a plant reference book, call your local Cooperative Extension office, or contact a botanical garden. Then devise your pruning plan, follow it, and keep track using a maintenance or gardening calendar. The information in Chapter 11 will help you do just that!

Thinning

Thinning opens up a plant so light and air can reach the center to stimulate new growth. A thinning cut removes an entire branch, or a section of a branch, back to a lateral branch (one that grows out of a larger branch). To thin a plant, selectively remove growth to avoid overcrowding. To remove an individual branch, cut just outside the branch collar to promote healthy closure of the wound. By cutting out entire branches or canes, you can preserve the plant's natural shape while promoting good health.

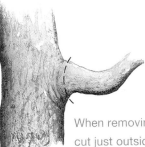

When removing an individual branch, cut just outside the branch collar to promote healthy closure of the wound.

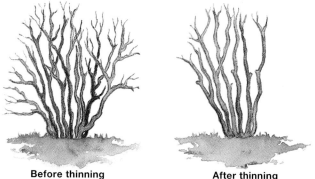

Before thinning   **After thinning**

For shrubs such as forsythias or shrub dogwoods, remove branches or canes at ground level to thin the plant.

Don't Take Thinning Too Far

While thinning is often good for a plant, being overzealous with a pruning saw can be damaging. A good rule is to thin no more than one-third of the branches at a time. Before you head outdoors with your saw, know what common mistakes to avoid:

Lion-tailing is a condition that comes from overthinning the crown of a tree. New branches are thin and weak, with too much weight to support at their ends.

Lion-tailing. When you overthin the crown of a tree or shrub, branches become spindly and weak, and too much growth develops at their ends. The tip of each branch will send out new shoots, making them look bushy, just like a lion's tail.

Removing lower limbs. If you do this too early in a tree's life, the result will be a skinny and weak trunk, rather than one that tapers naturally. However, when the tree gets a little bigger, lower limbs can and sometimes should be removed. (See "Limbing Up" on page 224 for guidelines on removing lower limbs.)

Thinning all at once. When you thin an entire tree all at once, the tree can have a tendency to send up water sprouts—vigorous shoots that grow straight up. Gradual thinning on overgrown trees—especially crabapples—is best.

Heading

A heading cut removes the end from a branch or limb to create denser growth—and often a less natural shape. Generally, it's best to reserve heading cuts for compact, bushy shrubs, perennials, and herbs. When you make heading cuts, new side shoots will emerge from either existing or dormant buds that are just below where you cut. This new, bushy growth tends to fill out the plant and shade the interior of the plant from light and air.

To make a **selective heading** cut, go back to a bud that will grow in a desirable direction, and make an angled cut just above the bud. On plants like ash trees and lilacs, you'll find a pair of buds growing directly opposite one another along a branch. Prune back to the pair and don't hesitate to rub off one of the buds if it's likely to grow in the wrong direction.

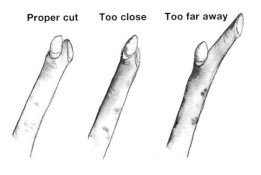

Proper cut   **Too close**   **Too far away**

Make selective heading cuts just above a bud, without cutting too close or too far or leaving a stub.

Pinching is another form of selective heading, though it's done with your fingers on the soft growth of perennials, vines, or young woody plants. It's a great way to encourage bushier growth or more buds on spindly young plants. The tip of the stem contains a hormone. When you remove the tip, you stop the flow of this hormone and send a signal to the plant to start branching along the stem instead of growing longer. Use your pinching skills to avoid more time-consuming corrective pruning later.

At planting time, a quick pinch on young plants like hydrangeas can get them off to a bushier start.

Nonselective heading is another term for shearing, which is trimming back all ends of the plant. Shearing works best on soft, new growth that will quickly close wounds and form new buds. This is the technique that is used to maintain formal shrubs and topiary. Be warned, though, that shearing can be time-consuming, and once you start, you'll need to continue shearing the plant to maintain it, unless you choose to "unshear" using the techniques for renewal pruning on page 229. Sheared plants also become greedy for supplemental water in hot, dry weather. So think twice about including a plant in your landscape—such as a sheared privet or yew hedge—that will need this type of constant attention.

Heading Gone Bad

While heading has its uses, it can be the stuff of pruning nightmares when it's taken to an extreme. Constant heading causes thick growth to occur only at the outer tips of the branches. Air and sunlight are blocked from the interior, which can lead to hollow shrubs that have nothing but woody stems on the inside. Homeowners often do this to shrubs that grow too large for their space, especially when they're located just below a window and they grow large enough to block the view. Instead of spending hours pruning a plant every year and damaging it in the process, pull out the shrub and replace it with one that's a more appropriate size for the location.

Heading (or topping) trees is also damaging. You may have seen trees that have been topped, especially along a street where they can grow into power lines. Topping causes weak branches where new shoots grow out of thick old limbs, which can create potentially dangerous situations in the future.

The Best Tools
for the Job

The right pruning tool for the task can mean the difference between speedy progress and misery on a big job. Your tools can last a lifetime as long as you keep them oiled, sharpened, and clean. When it comes to buying tools, look for ones with the best features, rather than those with a big price tag. Also, you can keep an eye on your budget by just buying the tools you really need. You'll find many options at garden centers and in mail-order catalogs. I'll help you sort through the clutter by starting with the most useful tools for home gardeners and ending with a tool that most homeowners can probably do without.

Start with Safety Gear

Pruning can be a potentially hazardous job. When you combine very sharp cutting implements with things like thorns and heavy branches, there's always a possibility for an accident. Reduce or eliminate the risks by using appropriate safety gear for the job.

GLOVES

Sturdy, pliable gloves are a must to have before you pick up the hand pruners. Leather is a good choice, but fabric gloves with rubber nubs for a good grip are great, too. I use insulated gloves in cold weather.

Gloves' most important function is protecting your hands from an errant cut from the pruners. An accidental cut happens most often when you're hurrying, or rooting around the base of that overgrown shrub, removing old wood and perhaps not quite getting a full view through the tangle. A sliced glove beats a trip to the emergency room for stitches any day! Gloves also protect your hands from blisters on a big job, or scratches from thorny or brushy work. If you're using a power tool such as a chain saw or electric hedge trimmer, gloves are imperative!

SAFETY GLASSES

In professional landscaping, pruning and staking account for the most eye injuries that occur. It's understandable, considering that pointy objects are moving around somewhat unpredictably and quite often just outside your peripheral vision. When you're pruning an overgrown tree, you don't always know how or where that bound-up crossing branch is going to cut loose when you get it free. Safety glasses or even sunglasses can help prevent scratches and other eye injuries.

PROTECTIVE CLOTHING

Similarly, a hat can protect your head from scratches and bumps as you cut branches or handle the brush, especially when the job is a thorny one. If you happen to be using a chain saw or other power equipment, make it a hard hat.

Although the need for a chain saw is rare in most backyards, avid do-it-yourselfers with large or wooded properties may need the power of a chain saw. If that's your case, use additional safety gear to protect your hearing as well as your eyes. Ears, eye, and head protection are available combined in a sturdy hard-hat unit. If you're going to use a chain saw, you'll want one of these.

Depending on the job, you may also want chain-saw chaps to protect your legs and steel-toed boots or boot protectors. Tragic chain-saw accidents happen all too frequently, even among trained and seasoned workers, so use caution and protective gear, and read the manufacturer's instructions.

Use Your Hands

Your hands can be one of your most useful pruning tools—and they're free! From rubbing unwanted buds from the trunk of a honey locust or crabapple to pinching candles from a pine or spent flowers from a rhododendron, your hands can quickly eliminate what might later turn into a larger, more time-consuming pruning job.

Hand Pruners

Hand pruners are one of the most indispensable tools you can own. Use them for small cuts of about a pencil's diameter. For long-term service, invest in by-pass pruners (they have a scissorslike action) rather than anvil-type pruners (they pinch together). Anvil pruners tend to crush stems when they get a bit dull. Look for removable blades that you can replace if they get damaged and that you can remove to sharpen.

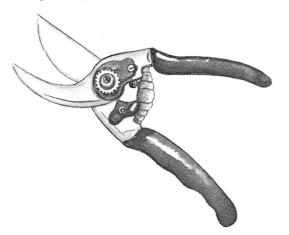

Kept clean, sharp, and oiled, quality hand pruners can provide a lifetime of good service.

A few minutes spent pruning new candle growth from pines can help keep their growth dense and compact and save you from having to come back and prune later.

Buds sprouting on trunks soon turn into pesky and unsightly water sprouts. You can use your hand to rub them off when they're small, but when they've grown this large, reach for your pruners.

Be sure you can replace the spring on your pruners, too, should it break or come loose. A safety lock that keeps your pruners closed when they're not in use is another important feature. Make sure the pruners you buy have one, and use it!

If you have limited hand strength, you may benefit from pruners with a ratchet mechanism, which adds more leverage to your squeezing energy. Be wary, though, because that extra power can cause a stem to crush if the blade is dull or if the cut is just too big for the tool.

Loppers

Most loppers can handle cuts up to about 1¾ inches in diameter, which makes them good for pruning smaller tree branches. If you're in the market for loppers, choose a

Sharp, sturdy loppers with good shock-absorbing features are a pleasure to use and will make your pruning tasks go quickly.

pair with bypass action rather than an anvil cutting mechanism. For shock absorption, choose ash handles rather than metal ones, and look for a pair that features a neoprene disk that makes the loppers bounce—rather than snap—closed. During and after big jobs, your shoulders, neck, back, arms, and hands will thank you.

Loppers are also available with a ratchet mechanism, but I recommend these only if you have limited upper body strength and need all the help you can get to make a regular cut. Under most conditions, difficulty making a cut usually means that your tool needs sharpening or that you're using a tool that's too small for the job. If that's the case, sharpen the blades or move on to a pruning saw.

Pruning Saws

Depending on the model, most pruning saws can make cuts up to 3 inches in diameter. If you're considering a first pruning saw, you may find the folding kind to be the most versatile because you can stash one safely in your pocket. Be sure it locks securely when open and in use, usually with a wing nut or a spring mechanism, so it won't collapse in your hand. You won't have that worry with a fixed-blade pruning saw, which generally can make even larger cuts.

A pruning saw is a different from the saws found in a wood shop. Pruning saws are curved so that you can negotiate tight branch crotches more easily without nicking adjacent wood. They cut on the "draw" (pull) stroke rather than the push stroke because in most pruning situations you have more power cutting in that direction. Some pruning saws cut on both the push and pull strokes, which is handy when space is tight. Just be sure you know which type you have before you take it to be sharpened. A well-meaning saw shop can ruin a good pruning saw by trying to sharpen it as they would a wood saw!

Finally, look for a pruning saw with a blade that has teeth on only one side. Saws with teeth on both sides sometimes nick or damage nearby branches.

Pole Pruners and Saws

Pole pruners are very handy for making overhead cuts and are much safer than using a ladder with regular hand tools. If you can't comfortably make a good cut with your regular tools or with pole pruners, it's time to call an arborist.

These tools normally have either wood or fiberglass shafts. Some of the fiberglass shafts are telescoping so you can extend them to further your reach. Others have unit construction that can reach up to 18 feet. The cutting part may be bypass pruners, operated by rope, or a stationary saw blade. The most versatile pole pruners have sockets that allow you to use the two types interchangeably.

Even when you can reach the work comfortably with your pole saw, you'll find that the lightest model can get heavy in your hand. For safety, cut only those branches you can reach while standing well off to the side, and seriously consider wearing a hard hat and safety glasses. Also, scout for hazards like wasp or animal nests as well as power lines before you make any cuts. If a power line is present, call a qualified arborist or the electric company to do the work.

Other extension pruning tools are available, but eye them warily. The chain-blade-on-a-rope that you throw up and over a limb to begin sawing can be dangerous and damaging, so avoid it. Similarly, extension chain saws (chain saws on a pole!) are questionable for both home and professional use.

Hedge Shears

Hedge shears are best for shearing cuts on soft new growth. Electric trimmers can make a large job go more quickly, but they can also make it effortless to make a mistake. There's also the added hazard of cutting through the cord, and you can't use that moisture-conserving trick of shearing when the plants are still wet with dew or you could be in for a shock. Gas-powered trimmers are heavy, polluting, and probably more powerful than needed for backyard use. If you must shear, favor manual power!

Chain Saws

Chain saws are available in many makes, models, and sizes, and they normally handle cuts larger than 3 inches. Use a chain saw only for cuts you can make confidently while standing on the ground. If you need to reach above shoulder level to make a cut, or if you're tempted to work from a ladder, it's time to call on an arborist!

It's all too easy to cause damage or injury when using a chain saw. Be sure to follow the safety procedures described in the owner's manual, and always wear basic safety gear when using one.

Tree Paint

Although arborists once thought that tree paint would promote healing and reduce decay in pruning wounds, we now know that its effect is neutral at best. Making a good pruning cut just outside the branch collar is the best defense against invaders! So save the tree paint for cosmetic use, when you'd rather not be looking at a bunch of "shiners" (bright new cuts) on that outstanding tree in your yard.

CHAPTER 11

A **Maintenance** Plan You Can **Live With**

Even if your yard is a quarter acre or less, creating a **basic maintenance** plan can be **helpful in** many ways. You can choose ahead of time when you're going to do a particular task, and when you're not, **scheduling certain jobs** for when they work for you. A written plan will help you avoid the all-too-common question, "Now when was I supposed to **prune that shrub?"** as well as resist the temptation to follow harmful but all-too-common practices simply because you've always done them. With a little bit of forethought and organization, you'll be on your way to a more **attractive landscape** that takes less time and cash and uses **fewer resources.**

Know Your Goal

While the ultimate goal is to have a whole-yard maintenance plan that's easy to follow, the way to get to that point is to think about your goal for each individual element in your yard. Not every tree and shrub needs to be pruned at the same time, nor does every perennial need to be deadheaded or divided. So start out with a list of the individual plants, trees, lawn, and even hardscape items in your yard. Then think about your goal for each. Are you growing a shrub for privacy, fruit, flowers, wildlife, or some combination? If privacy is the goal, you may let it grow large and do very little pruning. If you want lots of fruit, annual pruning to encourage new wood will probably be required. Do you want your trees to provide privacy with low branches or will you need to prune them so you can mow beneath them without clunking your head? How do you feel about your lawn? Will you be militant about a few weeds or can you live with some clover and dandelions? Will you let your lawn naturally go dormant during a drought, or will watering be part of your regime? How about your deck? Is it okay for the wood on your deck to fend for itself and turn a natural gray or do you want to protect it and preserve its original color?

Planning Your Priorities

As you can see, for each plant or other element in your yard, there's a range of possible looks, outcomes, and results. If you decide up front exactly what your expectations are, it's much easier to plan what you need to do to achieve the outcome or the look you want.

The following steps—identifying and evaluating maintenance tasks, prioritizing them, and working to economize them—will help you get and keep your yard in shape based on the time and resources you're willing to commit.

Identify Tasks

For each plant, first list the tasks that you can do to promote health and prevent pest or disease problems. For trees and shrubs, this might mean pruning to let in light and air, fall cleanup to prevent the overwintering of diseases or insects, and certainly mulching to hold moisture, suppress weeds, and improve soil conditions. If you're growing perennials, this might mean mulching heavily in winter for some or pulling back the mulch around others to prevent rot. You'll also need to cut back some perennials in spring before new growth begins.

It's helpful to include exterior home maintenance in your plan, too, so you can arrange garden activities around them. For instance, you may want to scrape and paint or clean gutters before mulching nearby ornamental beds, or take down a trellis during the dormant season when the vine growing on it can tolerate being cut back.

Don't leave hardscape items off your list, either. Tasks here can range from seasonal storage to sealing a wood deck to painting a trellis.

List each task separately rather than grouping them, so that each can be assigned to an appropriate time of the year. For help in generating your list, refer to Chapter 6 for tips on keeping hardscape elements attractive, safe, and functional. Also use the ideas on lawn maintenance in Chapter 7, for reducing watering needs in Chapter 8, on preventive pest control in Chapter 9, and for pruning in Chapter 10.

Evaluate and Eliminate

Some of the yard-work tasks many homeowners do are downright unnecessary. And let's face it—who wants to do work they don't have to? Where can you save time and effort? A quick and easy way to eliminate chores is to take a look at your task list and make special note of the jobs where you expect to transport materials to or from your property. Homeowners frequently bag leaves, grass clippings, and prunings, and haul them out for the trash. Meanwhile, they spend time and money at the local home and garden center, buying fertilizers and mulch and hauling them home.

Instead, your property may be quite capable of making its own fertilizer and mulch by using up the stuff that commonly gets discarded. Rather than bagging grass clippings, why not leave them in place to reduce water and fertilizer needs? After all, they're free and you've probably got plenty of them. While you're at it, why not use your fall leaves for mulch or compost them to use as fertilizer? If you have a chipper (or can rent one), you can even turn prunings into mulch. Another option is to leave pruned branches whole and pile them in a back corner of your property for wildlife cover. Other ways to save include turning off the hose or sprinkler system and instead using a rain barrel or two to collect rainwater for your watering needs.

Each time you "close the circle," allowing materials generated on your property to be used on your property, you save time and money. It's rewarding and fun to see how your gardening efforts can become more self-sustaining.

There are other jobs you might be able to do without, too. If you find yourself cleaning out rain gutters regularly, it might be worth your while to

WATER CYCLE

NUTRIENT CYCLE

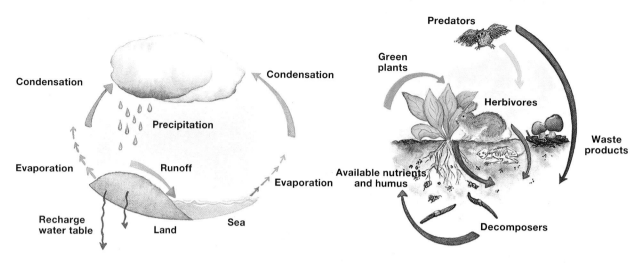

Make your landscape part of the water and nutrient cycles by capturing rain in barrels and turning garden refuse into compost. By recycling these elements, you save time and money while nurturing your surroundings and the environment.

install gutter guards. While they won't eliminate the chore completely, they'll certainly reduce the number of times you'll need to climb a ladder to clean out debris. And with an unclogged gutter, you'll prevent rainwater from gushing over top instead of flowing into your rain barrel where you can recycle it. If you're regularly cutting back a shrub or tree that wants to be larger than its space, it might be time to consider a replacement. Or, if you're treating the entire yard for insect pests (or paying someone else to do it), know that even the safest materials can disrupt beneficial insects. It's better to identify and treat for specific problems on a case-by-case basis. And that way, you won't be spending time and money fighting problems your yard isn't even facing.

Prioritize

After you've identified, evaluated, and weeded out your tasks in a year of yard work, review them one more time to be sure that the most useful and beneficial jobs get top priority. Whether you're working on paper or your computer screen, highlight all the tasks that will promote plant health or help prevent damage. Some examples are spending a few minutes each year training a young tree, a day spent mulching, pruning shrubs for better air and light penetration, and cleaning up in the fall to control pests. When you're pressed for time, choose to do these jobs first because they add value and help to prevent future work.

Prioritize further by using the "just once" rule. Ask yourself "If I do this task just once a year (fertilize the lawn, prune the spirea, or whatever), when

Buying Mulch?
Go Local

would be the most effective time to do it?" Zero in on the best times for each task. Then, if you don't have time to prune or fertilize during the optimal time, you can still get the job done at the next best time.

Economize

You can shave costs even further by economizing whenever you do your garden tasks. First, plan to use the least amount of material possible for each job. And be sure you apply it only where it's needed. Whether you're using fertilizer, pest control supplies, mulch, or a soil amendment, more is not always better! When you're really pleased with the result of a particular application, it's tempting to really pile it on next time. But using just enough material can save more than money. It can also save you the hassles and extra work that often come from overapplication. Here are some consequences of overapplication of certain landscape supplies.

Fertilizers. Too much lush new growth can cause floppy perennials that will need staking (and more of your time). It can also lead to certain diseases and insect infestations in both turf and landscape plants. Too much fertilizer on lawn grass leads to constant mowing and potentially burning—especially in dry or drought conditions. In addition, excess fertilizers that are not used by the plants can run off and pollute streams and groundwater supplies.

Deicers. Too much ice-melting material can be toxic to sensitive plants. Deicers also break down soil

Frequently the best mulches for your area are the ones that are generated locally. Pine needles in the south, hardwood bark in the central hardwoods region, and salt hay in coastal areas are some examples. Like spent mushroom compost from mushroom production, many organic mulches are by-products of local enterprises, and they're often abundant and inexpensive if you live near their source. And don't forget wood chips from your local municipality or tree services. Local mulches blend nicely with the character of the local landscape, and they help us all to avoid the hidden environmental costs of distant production and transportation.

Regardless of your source, always use organic mulches. In addition to suppressing weeds and holding in water, they also have the ability to break down and enrich the soil.

structure and worsen compaction from foot traffic, so try to avoid using them.

Mulch. When piled right next to a tree trunk, mulch provides cozy accommodations for mice and other bark-chewing mammals. It also promotes rotting. Under the right conditions, mulch piled too thickly can go "sour," because oxygen can't circulate through the pile. As a result, the mulch produces toxic substances that leach down to root zones with rain, so be sure you don't overdo it.

Pest control materials. Unfortunately, most pesticides don't work solely on the pest that's bugging you. They also disrupt predator populations, which in turn will promote even greater damage by the pest.

Create Your Own Maintenance Calendar

Now that you've done all the work, simply take your refined tasks list and put it on some sort of calendar. Use whatever sort of calendar that works best for you: a store-bought one that hangs on the kitchen wall, a gardening diary, a computer file, or one like that shown on the opposite page. You can now see how the jobs are distributed over the months, and you can adjust them, if needed, to mesh better with travel, school, work, and other plans.

Of course, you don't have to use your plan as though it's chiseled in stone. One way to really make it work for you is to take a look at how your yard-work season is shaping up. Why not save some precious growing-season time (or time you'll just enjoy being outside with your family) by moving certain tasks to the so-called off-season? Unless the mulch is frozen, you can spend a sunny winter or early spring day outside, getting that heavy job done while it's still cool. Pest protection is another job you can take care of early. For some pests, the single best pest control measure is dormant oil, which you can apply in February or March. That surely beats a spider-mite fight in July! You can take care of many pruning jobs during the dormant season as well. With other duties more pressing during the warm months (such as mowing, planting, watering, weeding, and harvesting), why not move the flexible jobs to other times?

Building a Plan

Building your maintenance plan means assigning the best times to do the specific task you have on your list. Those times can vary depending upon the climate where you live. I've created a sample maintenance plan on the opposite page that you can refer to.

Let's say that my northern garden contains crabapples, winterberry hollies, liriope, and a lawn. My maintenance plan might begin with pruning the crabapple and thinning the holly during the winter months, then cutting back the foliage on the liriope a few weeks later. In late spring, my lawn-mowing regimen begins. During the summer I remove the water sprouts on the crabapple and then clean up the fallen foliage in fall to prevent the spread of diseases. And, as you can see, the tasks are spaced throughout the year so I won't be overloaded with outdoor chores all at once. In fact, I've arranged all my chores so April and May are wide open for prime lawn-mowing time!

Mulching is just one activity that you can easily move to a nonpeak time of the year.

SAMPLE MAINTENANCE PLAN

A calendar is a useful way to keep track of all your maintenance tasks for your yard. While it may be obvious when it's time to mow the lawn, it's still a good idea to list it on your calendar. That way, you'll quickly see when you'll be busiest and when you might have some spare time to fit in other essential tasks. Simply adapt the calendar below to reflect the plants you're growing in your landscape.

JAN	FEB	MAR	APR	MAY	JUN	JUL	AUG	SEP	OCT	NOV	DEC

1
"ANYTIME" PRUNING on crabapples and winterberry to remove dead, dying, diseased, crossing, rubbing, broken, or misplaced branches—anytime you see them.

2
THIN WINTERBERRY before growth begins. Cut ⅓ of the branches back to ground level to keep the plant open to light, and therefore blooming and berrying profusely.

5
MOWING. Use a mulching mower and cut about every 5 to 10 days, only as needed.

3
CUT BACK LIRIOPE foliage before growth begins. The new leaves look so much better when they don't have to struggle up through old, ratty foliage.

6
PRUNE CRABAPPLES to remove water sprouts— those vertical branches that ruin its form and clog up the crown. Summer pruning inhibits their return as will gradually removing them over a few seasons.

7
CLEAN UP CRABAPPLE FOLIAGE to prevent black spot from overwintering, especially if you have a nonresistant variety or if you're expecting a wet spring.

4
MULCH. There are plenty of other things needing attention during the growing season, so as long as the mulch isn't frozen, why not mulch now?

JAN	FEB	MAR	APR	MAY	JUN	JUL	AUG	SEP	OCT	NOV	DEC

Tools: Savvy Selection, Care, and Storage

Few homeowners set out to start a tool collection, but eventually that's what happens! Item by item, it's easy to accumulate tools and gadgets. Rather than spending money on the latest gadget each season, plan to get the most from your tool purchases by looking for quality construction and features. See "Quality Tool Features" below for pointers that can help you make good choices.

If you're just getting started, start with a basic collection of the essentials: a fork and spade for digging, a garden rake and leaf rake, a hoe, trowel, basic pruning tools—hand pruners, loppers, and pruning saw—and a lawn mower, if you need one. For tips on selecting lawn mowers and spreaders, see Chapter 7. You'll find lots of information on watering gadgets in Chapter 8 and specifics about pruning tools in Chapter 10. Other tools you may need are featured here.

Quality Tool Features

Whether you're searching for tools at a hardware or discount store, a garden center, or an estate sale, look first for the features that will be most useful to you. Then compare prices. A quality tool can last a lifetime and be a pleasure to use while a poorly made tool can make any chore cumbersome and even unsafe. It's not a bargain if you won't use it.

LOOK FOR THESE FEATURES

Make sure any tool you buy is comfortable for you to hold and use. Beyond that, I recommend looking for the following features:

- A turned footrest on spades and shovels to distribute your weight when you're standing on the tool (Wear sturdy boots anyway, as tough jobs can cause bruised feet.)
- A handle with a straight grain and no knots, preferably made of the very resilient white ash
- A handle that isn't painted (Paint often covers poor wood.)
- A handle that can be replaced if it splits or breaks
- A blade and socket or strap formed of a single piece of metal for strength
- A sturdy blade that can be sharpened as needed

Hand Tools

When you have a choice, I recommend a hand- or people-powered tool over a power tool. You'll produce fewer emissions and less noise as you work. And think of the benefits you'll receive: You'll protect yourself from hearing loss while getting more exercise. In addition, I think you'll find your gardening efforts to be more rewarding and peaceful—and your neighbors will think so, too!

If you have an occasional need for a power item like a chipper, aerator, or tiller, it might make sense to rent instead of buy. The cost-per-use when you rent is likely to be reasonable compared to owning one, and you'll probably have the pleasure of using a more up-to-date model than one that would be aging and taking up space in your garage.

Hand weeders can be anything from a simple screwdriver or knife for popping out dandelions to one of those flamers that torches offending sprouts. Some gardeners swear by their screwdrivers, but use an old retired one because it will rust eventually. For a weeder with a blade such as a Cape Cod weeder or a Japanese grubbing knife, look for one that can be sharpened. Use it to slice just beneath the soil surface, rather than digging out the entire root system. When weeding, it's best to do so rather gingerly so you won't churn up any new weed seeds!

Hoes are useful in a vegetable garden where they can help you lay out rows, create hills and furrows, and make raised beds. In any type of bed—vegetable or landscape—use a hoe to cultivate around plants. Most have a long handle that allows you to work with minimal bending. One option is a hoe with a narrow blade. It encounters less resistance in the soil, so it's easier on your arms, but it will cover less area at a time. Another popular option is an oscillating hoe that slices weeds on both the push and pull strokes. Regardless of the blade type you choose, get one that's substantial so it can hold an edge, and keep it sharp.

Shovels have a rounded blade that is ideal for scooping materials, mixing cement, and digging rounded planting holes. For most other garden digging, reach first for a spade or spading fork. Shovels typically have a long handle, about 4 feet. Look for one that comes about to your shoulder or higher for comfortable digging.

Spades have a flat, squared blade rather than the scooped blade of shovels. A spade is great for digging, for dividing and moving perennials, and for cutting a neat edge through sod. Spades have a shorter handle than shovels and a D or T grip, which is needed for good control.

Forks come in many forms: The best are forged from a single piece of metal rather than welded. Spading forks, used for digging, help you to loosen the soil rather than lift it. The others are great for handling big piles of compost, straw or mulch where a shovel or spade can't get a bite.

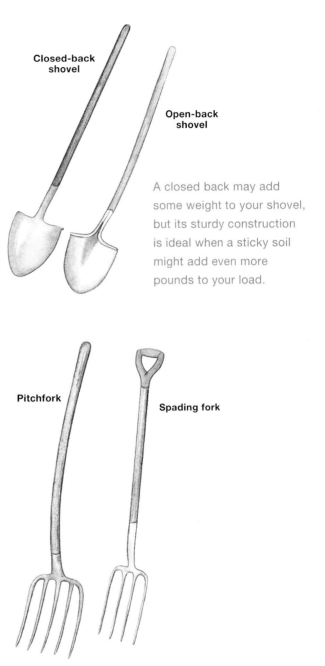

Closed-back shovel

Open-back shovel

A closed back may add some weight to your shovel, but its sturdy construction is ideal when a sticky soil might add even more pounds to your load.

Pitchfork

Spading fork

The pitchfork on the left helps you to spread straw or to handle raw compostables. The spading fork on the right is for digging and mixing, as well as for harvesting root crops.

Garden rakes work well for smoothing a planting bed. Use one to clear debris like roots and small rocks from the bed, for covering furrows and footprints, and even for spreading mulch on top. The handle should be long and the head heavy enough to bite into the soil well.

Lawn, leaf, or fan rakes help you to gather up leaves, grass clippings, and debris. You can find them made of metal, bamboo, rubber, or plastic—all with a long handle. Adjustable-width rakes are great for reaching beneath and around shrubs and perennials. They tend to have a shorter handle and a rubber grip for one-handed use. They're neither comfortable nor durable enough, though, to be an all-purpose tool, so plan to have a full-scale model in your garden shed, too.

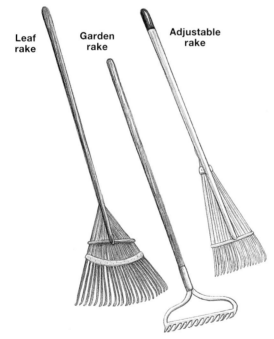

Leaf rake

Garden rake

Adjustable rake

Shown from left to right, the leaf rake, the garden rake, and the adjustable rake. Choosing the right one for the job can make a specific chore go more easily.

Tools for Kids

Little gardeners can lose interest when tools aren't up to the job. Toy-store tools are often made for play and not gardening . . . heads fall off of trowels and rust sets in, making it hard to dig. Plastic items don't fare much better. Consider a small-scale, good-quality tool or two, starting with the indispensable trowel and maybe a hoe or spade. A small wagon or junior wheelbarrow can really instill some pride in helpfulness. Yard and estate sales are great for finding these treasures; mail-order suppliers are listed in "Resources for Backyard Ideas" on page 256 under "Tools and Supplies."

Trowels are indispensable for digging the small planting holes needed for bulbs and small plants and for transplanting seedlings. Trowels are made in a variety of materials, blade widths, shapes, and lengths. The best bet is one-piece construction made with a rust-proof, unbreakable material like aluminum. A cushion grip is great, too!

Mattocks can help to ease the transition from compacted or heavy clay soil to a workable garden bed. The work is hard but a small mattock can make it a bit easier. Use your mattock to help break up the soil before adding your amendments. Look for a nicely balanced one that feels good in your hand. Although they come in larger sizes, a mattock with a 15-inch handle is great for many jobs.

Carts and **wheelbarrows** are great for hauling and dumping soil, mulch, compost, brush, prunings, leaves, and debris. Pneumatic tires, great balance, and a handy dump door all help to make a good garden cart. If you're considering a cart purchase, imagine the heaviest load you might carry in it, then

look at the ones rated for a slightly heavier load. Once you see what a good cart can do, you're likely to give it bigger and bigger jobs!

Power Tools

Sometimes the extra oomph of a power tool is just what you need to speed through a large, tough, or te-dious job. Unless your property is very large or heavily wooded, you may not need one all the time. Often, renting what you need when you need it is a good way to try different models and features—and to save money and storage space. To reduce pollu-tion, favor electric over gas power when you have that option. If gas is the only choice, choose a 4-cycle engine over a 2-cycle engine.

Tillers can make quick work of breaking up the soil, turning, churning, and mixing as well as cultivating. When operating one, be sure to wear safety glasses, hearing protection, gloves, and sturdy work boots.

Chippers can make a great mulch of brush and limbs right there where you need it. Be sure to use one that's rated for the diameter of material you'll be feeding it, and treat it with respect. It can be a dan-gerous piece of equipment. Use the same safety gear when operating a chipper as you would if you were operating a chain saw (see page 236).

Shredders can reduce leaves, soft prunings, weeds, and plant debris into a rich mulch. Because

While the tiller with wheels can handle big jobs, the no-wheel tiller can maneuver in tight spaces easily.

Once You've Got It *Home*

Protect your tool investment by taking a few steps once you're gotten an item home. Inspect and refine wood handles, for instance, by giving them a light sanding (or a good sanding if the tool is used and weather-beaten) and an application of tung oil. For a small tool like a trowel or hand weeder, consider painting the handle a bright and, perhaps, unique color. You'll spend less time looking for it among the vegetation or brush, and it'll make fewer accidental trips to the compost or brush pile. Plus it will be readily identifiable as yours. Many tools now come with padded or ergonomic grips, but if you buy one that's not padded, you can add padding yourself. Pipe insulation makes great padding, and you can cut it to length, snugging and securing the side slit with duct tape. Other options include padded bicycle handle-bar tape or grips.

shredding creates more surface area and air pockets for microbial activity, shredded material can help to jump-start your compost pile. You can move your shredder around the yard to capture and mulch fallen leaves right on the spot, but as with all power tools, use it only as directed and wear protective gear.

Blowers and blower/vacuums have become commonplace in many neighborhoods, easing the cleanup chores but shattering the quiet and belching hourly emissions equivalent to a car traveling 1,500 miles! If you need to use a blower or blower-vac, consider the electric or electric-rechargeable options. They're slightly quieter and less polluting.

Tool Care

Your good tools will serve you well for a long time when you give them regular care. Make it a habit, for instance, to clean and dry an item before putting it away. This prevents debris buildup and the rust that can form when the buildup holds moisture. To scrape off dirt or mud, use anything from a discarded wooden (or plastic) spoon to a dried corn cob. Avoid using another tool, like a trowel, because you'll dull its blade. A handy way to clean most hand tools is to keep a 5-gallon bucket of sand on hand that you can dip tools into to remove bits of dirt and other debris.

When you're storing tools for a longer period—like winter—oil the blades and metal parts after cleaning them. If a tool needs sharpening, do that as well or send it out now. Your tools will get better attention from a sharpening shop in winter than during the growing season. Finally, store your tools in as dry a spot as possible to prevent rust.

Especially when you're storing a tool for winter, take a minute to assess its handle. Replace it if it's split or splitting. If the finish is smooth and oily from steady use, good for you! If it's dry, splintering, or weather-beaten, sand and seal it with some tung oil to maintain its resilience and friendliness to your hands.

Tool Storage and Access

There's nothing like being able to put your hands right on the tool that you're after. Avoid rummaging

Reducing Pollution from Power Equipment

for your tools by finding a system that works for you. You don't have to purchase hangers, racks, and other gadgets to create a good storage arrangement. You can simply rely on a bit of forethought, ingenuity, even your sense of fun, as with the mailbox storage idea shown below.

As much as possible, try to locate your storage close to the action with easy access in and out. If you have a lot of garden areas to tend to, there may be some trade-offs. For instance, our storage is central to our front- and backyards, but inconvenient to our vegetable garden and compost. Our long-term plan is to locate a small shed near the veggies, but for the short term, we're using a caddy to carry numerous small items and toting the big ones. It works for now!

Keep small items handy by storing them in the garden! A rural-style mailbox is great for labels, marking pen, seeds, string, or trowel.

Astonishingly, small engines pollute at rates higher and faster than most cars. Homeowners are frequently proud of their green landscapes but don't realize that the power tools used to maintain them can be causing environmental harm. Few people realize that a poorly tuned lawn mower running for 1 hour puts out a quantity of hydrocarbons comparable to a car traveling 340 miles or that a chain saw or leaf blower operating for 1 hour is equivalent to 1,500 miles of highway driving. Power tools provide great capacity to accomplish work in the landscape, and their convenience has made them indispensable to many. If you must use power tools, you can give your environment a break when you make the following practices part of your maintenance routine:

■ Recycle used oil, coolant, and hydraulic fluid, making sure none gets spilled on the ground. Recycle their containers, too.

■ Maintain engines and have them tuned, regularly clean or chang air filters, replace oil and spark plugs, and lubricate as recommended by the manufacturer.

■ Use fuel containers that are easy to handle and designed to prevent vapor loss and to reduce the chance of a spill.

■ Check the oil pan and the gas and oil ports regularly to make sure they're snug and not leaking.

■ Check the pressure of pneumatic tires regularly to reduce wear and to keep operating efficiency high.

■ Replace mufflers as needed to reduce noise and to protect your hearing.

■ When purchasing a new piece of power equipment, consider one that's not powered by gasoline, such as a solar-rechargeable mulching mower.

Do-It-Yourself Sharpening

Gardening tasks go more smoothly when blades are sharp! If you like to work on things yourself, here are some tips for sharpening your bladed tools.

- Sharpen single-beveled tools such as spades, shovels, and traditional hoes only on the beveled side; don't sharpen the flat side.

- Choose a file that matches the contour of the surface—a flat file for a garden spade and a half-round one for a curved shovel.

- Sharpen by pushing the file forward and across the tool's blade. Press down hard and use the file's full length on each stroke. At the end of the stroke, lift the file—don't go backward—and return it to the beginning of the stroke. Continue until you can feel a burr—a slight buildup of metal along the full width of the blade's opposite side. Finish the edge by running your file lightly across the burr.

- Sharpen the blade at the original angle of the bevel unless a slightly different angle would suit you better. A shallow angle gives a sharper edge, which is good for slicing weeds, while a wider angle is longer-lasting and good for tough jobs like digging and chopping.

- Sharpen your tools as often as it takes to keep them useful and efficient. You often know that a tool has dulled when it no longer slices through the soil, and you find yourself chopping at things.

If your storage area is a bit remote, think about the small items you'll need to use regularly as you do yard work and gardening. Can you fit everything in your pockets or a holster? If not, perhaps a tool belt, roofer's apron, tool caddy, or on-site mailbox can help to keep items convenient.

When you need to move a group of larger tools like a shovel, spade, hoe, and rake, consider what means you have on hand to move them before you start schlepping. While you might not think it's a big deal to go and get each tool as you need it, you may find that you'd prefer to put them back in one trip, especially when you're pooped from a big job. A wheelbarrow or garden cart can be pressed into service. Or a wheeled storage cart may be handy for you. Weatherproof plastic models are now available that will hold a range of tools, or you can try your hand at making one from wood, as shown on the opposite page. You might even be able to recycle an old golf bag on wheels into action to wheel your long-handled tools around.

A tool caddy is great way to both store and carry small tools. You can find old and new wooden ones, heavy- and light-duty plastic models, and canvas outfits you can hang over a 5-gallon bucket.

Storage and transport in one! You can make a simple tool caddy from plywood and scrap lumber. Add casters or wheels, and you're set to go. For more durable construction, use screws rather than nails.

For your home-base storage area, consider a reach-and-grab system that minimizes moving things out of the way to get to what you need. While all of your digging tools might be on one rack, perhaps you keep your favorite spade at the front. A simple hanging system can be made with scrap 2 × 4s and nails for hanging tools, so don't be lured in by expensive storage systems. Label each spot so you know where each tool goes. You'll be able to see at a glance if one is missing. For an inexpensive way to conveniently hang pruning tools, trowel, weeders, and other small items, use perforated hardboard and hooks.

One final storage tip: For materials on shelves, make a habit of storing the liquid items *below* the dry items. If your liquid seaweed extract should spring a leak, it won't soak your bonemeal.

All the Tools You Need

Of course, the tools in your shed aren't the only ones you'll need to revamp your backyard. It takes your creative ideas, energy, and know-how to turn your landscaping dreams into reality. But you're well on your way. Armed with the information in this book—including the helpful resources that begin on page 256—you'll be able to tackle any project in your yard. Whether your goal is to create your first planting bed on the property, pruning what you've already got, or giving the whole yard an overhaul, a new backyard is just as close as the next growing season. Dig in and enjoy the process!

Resources for Backyard Ideas

Sources

Plants

Brent and Becky's Bulbs
7463 Heath Trail
Gloucester, VA 23061
Phone: (804) 693-3966
Web site: www.brentandbeckysbulbs.com
Rare, unusual, and tropical bulbs

Prairie Nursery
P.O. Box 306
Westfield, WI 53964
Phone: (800) 476-9453
Web site: www.prairienursery.com
Native wildflowers, perennials, and grasses

Sandy Mush Herb Nursery
316 Surrett Cove Road
Leicester, NC 28748-5517
Phone: (828) 683-2014
Web site: www.brwm.org/sandymushherbs
Herbs, perennials, trees, shrubs, and native plants

Song Sparrow Perennial Farm
13101 East Rye Road
Avalon, WI 53505
Phone: (800) 553-3715
Hostas, daylilies, peonies, and other perennials

Van Bourgondien and Sons
P.O. Box 1000
Babylon, NY 11702
Phone: (800) 552-9996
Bulbs and perennials

Wayside Gardens
1 Garden Lane
Hodges, SC 29695
Phone: (800) 845-1124
Web site: www.waysidegardens.com
Fine and rare plants and bulbs

White Flower Farm
P.O. Box 50
Litchfield, CT 06759
Phone: (800) 503-9624
Web site: www.whiteflowerfarm.com
*Annuals, perennials, bulbs, shrubs,
   and houseplants*

Woodlanders
1128 Colleton Avenue
Aiken, SC 29801
Phone: (803) 648-7522
Web site: www.woodlanders.net
*Southeastern U.S. and warm-temperate native
   plants*

Seeds

W. Atlee Burpee
300 Park Avenue
Warminster, PA 18991-0001
Phone: (800) 888-1447
Web site: www.burpee.com
Annual, perennial, vegetable, and herb seeds

The Cook's Garden
P.O. Box 535
Londonderry, VT 05148
Phone: (800) 457-9703
Web site: www.cooksgarden.com
Seeds and supplies for kitchen gardens

Johnny's Selected Seeds
1 Foss Hill Road
Albion, ME 04910-9731
Phone: (207) 437-4301
Web site: www.johnnyseeds.com
Vegetable, herb, and flower seeds

Park Seed Company
1 Parkton Avenue
Greenwood, SC 29647-0001
Phone: (800) 845-3369
Web site: www.parkseed.com
Seeds for new and unusual flowers and vegetables

Prairie Ridge Nursery
RR 2, 9738 Overland Road
Mt. Horeb, WI 35372
Phone: (608) 437-5245
*Native seed for prairies and meadows as well as
some bareroot and potted natives*

Seeds of Change
P.O. Box 15700
Santa Fe, NM 87506-5700
Phone: (888) 762-7333
Web site: www.seedsofchange.com
*Certified organically grown seeds, bulbs, and
perennials*

Shepherd's Garden Seeds
30 Irene Street
Torrington, CT 06790-6658
Phone: (869) 482-3638
Web site: www.shepherdseeds.com
Vegetable, herb, and fruit seeds and plants

Tools and Supplies

Gardener's Supply Company
128 Intervale Road
Burlington, VT 05401
Phone: (800) 863-1700
Web site: www.gardeners.com
Innovative gardening products

Gardens Alive!
5100 Schenley Place
Lawrenceburg, IN 47025
Phone: (812) 537-8650
Problem-solving products for lawns and gardens

Harmony Farm Supply
3244 Gravenstein Highway North
Sebastopol, CA 95472
Phone: (707) 823-9125
Web site: www.harmonyfarm.com
Tools, seeds, organic fertilizers, and pest controls

Lehman's Hardware and Appliances
1 Lehman Circle
P.O. Box 41
Kidron, OH 44636
Phone: (877) 438-5346
Web site: www.lehmans.com
*Traditional farm and garden tools, reel mowers,
and nonelectric appliances*

A. M. Leonard
241 Fox Drive
P.O. Box 816
Piqua, OH 45356
Phone: (800) 543-8955
Web site: www.amleo.com
Gardening and landscaping tools

The Natural Gardening Company
P.O. Box 750776
Petaluma, CA 94975
Phone: (707) 766-9303
Web site: www.naturalgardening.com
*Organic nursery, seeds, beneficial insects, tools,
and equipment*

Nitron Industries
P.O. Box 1447
Fayetteville, AR 72702
Phone: (800) 835-0123
Web site: www.nitron.com
*Fertilizers, soil amendments, insect controls,
and seeds*

Peaceful Valley Farm Supply
P.O. Box 2209
Grass Valley, CA 95945
Phone: (530) 272-4769
Web site: www.groworganic.com
*Propagation, irrigation, and pest management
tools and supplies*

Smith & Hawken
117 E. Strawberry Drive
Mill Valley, CA 94941
Phone: (800) 776-3336
Web site: www.SmithandHawken.com
Garden tools, furniture, structures, and workwear

Recommended Reading

Edibles

Creasy, Rosalind. *The Complete Book of Edible Landscaping.* San Francisco: Sierra Club Books, 1982.

Garden Projects

Cook, Ferris. *The Garden Trellis: Designs to Build
and Vines to Cultivate.* New York: Artisan, 1996.
Freudenberger, Richard. *Woodworking Projects for
the Garden.* New York: Sterling Publishing Co.,
1994.

Gardening

Benjamin, Joan, ed. *Great Garden Shortcuts.*
Emmaus, PA: Rodale, 1996.
Bradley, Fern Marshall, and Barbara Ellis, eds.
*Rodale's All-New Encyclopedia of Organic
Gardening.* Emmaus, PA: Rodale, 1992.
Medic, Kris. *Rodale's Successful Organic
Gardening: Pruning.* Emmaus, PA: Rodale, 1995.
Rodale, Maria. *Maria Rodale's Organic
Gardening.* Emmaus, PA: Rodale, 1998.
Shapiro, Howard-Yana, and John Harrisson.
Gardening for the Future of the Earth. New
York: Bantam Books, 2000.

Inspiration

McHarg, Ian L. *Design with Nature.* Somerset, NJ:
John Wiley & Sons, 1995.
Pollan, Michael. *Second Nature: A Gardener's
Education.* New York: Dell Publishing, 1991.
Potts, Michael. *The New Independent Home:
People and Houses That Harvest the Sun,
Wind, and Water.* White River Junction, VT:
Chelsea Green, 1999.
Stein, Sara. *Noah's Garden: Restoring the Ecology
of Our Own Back Yards.* New York: Houghton
Mifflin, 1993.

Landscape Design

Blume, James D., ed. *Better Homes and Gardens
Step-by-Step Landscaping.* Des Moines:
Meredith Corporation, 1991.
Collins, John F., and Marvin Adleman. *Livable
Landscape Design.* Ithaca, NY: Cornell Univer-
sity Cooperative Extension Service, 1988.

Lawns

Franklin, Stuart. *Building a Healthy Lawn.*
Pownal, VT: Storey Communications, 1988.
Hill, Lewis, and Nancy. *Rodale's Successful Or-
ganic Gardening: Lawns, Grasses, and
Groundcovers.* Emmaus, PA: Rodale, 1995.
The Natural Lawn and Alternatives. Brooklyn:
The Brooklyn Botanic Garden, 1993.

Pest Control

Drzewucki, Vincent, Jr. *Gardening in Deer
Country.* New York: Brick Tower Press, 1998.
Ellis, Barbara, and Fern Marshall Bradley, eds. *The Or-
ganic Gardener's Handbook of Natural Insect
and Disease Control.* Emmaus, PA: Rodale, 1996.
Logsdon, Gene. *Wildlife in Your Garden, or
Dealing with Deer, Rabbits, Raccoons, Moles,
Crows, Sparrows, and Other of Nature's
Creatures in Ways That Keep Them Around
but away from Your Fruits and Vegetables.*
Emmaus, PA: Rodale, 1983.

Plants

Appleton, Bonnie Lee, and Alfred F. Scheider. *Rodale's Successful Organic Gardening: Trees, Shrubs, and Vines.* Emmaus, PA: Rodale, 1993.

Hightshoe, Gary L. *Native Trees, Shrubs and Vines for Urban and Rural America.* New York: John Wiley & Sons, 1987.

Hodgson, Larry. *Perennials for Every Purpose.* Emmaus, PA: Rodale, 1999.

McClure, Susan, and Cole Burrell. *Rodale's Successful Organic Gardening: Perennials.* Emmaus, PA: Rodale, 1993.

Odenwald, Neil, and James Turner. *Southern Plants for Landscape Design.* Baton Rouge: Claitor's Publishing Division, 1987.

Sustainable Home Horticulture

*Home*A*Syst: An Environmental Risk-Assessment Guide for the Home.* Ithaca, NY: The Northeast Regional Agricultural Engineering Service, 1997.

Hynes, Erin, and Susan McClure. *Rodale's Successful Organic Gardening: Low-Maintenance Landscaping.* Emmaus, PA: Rodale, 1994.

Moffat, Anne Simon, and Marc Schuler. *Energy-Efficient and Environmental Landscaping.* South Newfane, VT: Appropriate Solutions Press, 1994.

Mollison, Bill. *Introduction to Permaculture.* Tyalgum, NSW, Australia: Tagari Publications, 1991.

Weinstein, Gayle. *Xeriscape Handbook.* Golden, CO: Fulcrum Publishing, 1999.

Tree Care

American National Standard for Tree Care Operations —Tree, Shrub and Other Woody Plant Maintenance —Standard Practices, ANSI A-300. New York: American National Standards Institute, 1995 and 1998. (Available from the International Society of Arboriculture; see address on page 260.)

Matheny, Nelda, and James R. Clark. *Trees and Development: A Technical Guide to Preservation of Trees during Land Development.* Champaign, IL: International Society of Arboriculture, 1998.

Organizations and Web Sites

American Society of Consulting Arborists
15245 Shady Grove Road, Suite 130
Rockville, MD 20850
Phone: (301) 947-0483
Web site: www.asca-consultants.org
Referrals to registered and member consulting arborists

American Society of Landscape Architects
636 Eye Street NW
Washington, DC 20001-3736
Phone: (202) 898-2444
Web site: www.asla.org
Referrals to registered landscape architects

Associated Landscape Contractors of America
150 Elden Street, Suite 270
Herndon, VA 20170
Phone: (800) 395-2522
Web site: www.alca.org
Referrals to certified contractors

Association of Consulting Foresters of America
Phone: (703) 548-0990
Web site: www.acf-foresters.com
Links to members by state and province

Bio-Integral Resource Center
P.O. Box 7414
Berkeley, CA 94707
Phone: (510) 524-2567
Web site: www.birc.org
Publisher of Common Sense Pest Control Quarterly for homeowners and IPM Practitioner for professionals

Co-op America
1612 K Street NW
Washington, DC 20006
Phone: (800) 58-GREEN
Web site: www.coopamerica.org
National Green Pages—printed and online—
includes listings for environmentally
friendly landscape services.

Cooperative Extension Service
Web site:
www.reeusda.gov/1700/statepartners/usa
Web site can help you to find your state's Coop-
erative Extension Service with a click-on
map of the United States and territories.

International Society of Arboriculture
P.O. Box 3129
Champaign, IL 61826-3129
Phone: (217) 355-9411
Web site: www.ag.uiuc.edu/isa
Referrals to certified arborists

National Wildlife Control Operators
   Association
Web site: www.wildlifedamagecontrol.com
Web site is oriented more toward members than
customers at present but offers links
through board members to contractors who
have agreed to meet specified ethical and
standard practice guidelines.

Natural Resources Conservation Service
Attn: Conservation Communications Staff
P.O. Box 2890
Washington, DC 20013
Web site: www.nrcs.usda.gov
The NRCS (formerly the Soil Conservation Ser-
vice) provides information on backyard con-
servation as well as resource conservation
for farms and urban development.

Professional Lawn Care Association of America
1000 Johnson Ferry Road NE
Suite C-135
Marietta, GA 30068
Phone: (770) 977-5222
Web site: www.plcaa.org
Referrals to certified turfgrass professionals

Rodale Inc.
33 E. Minor Street
Emmaus, PA 18049
Phone: (610) 967-5171
Web site: www.organicgardening.com
Publishers of *Organic Gardening* magazine and
   many garden books

Society of American Foresters
5400 Grosvenor Lane
Bethesda, MD 20814
Phone: (301) 897-8720
Web site: www.safnet.org
Referrals to certified foresters who work in a variety
of categories, including residential wood lots

University of Minnesota
Sustainable Urban Landscape Information Series
Web site: www.sustland.umn.edu
Design, implementation, and maintenance
practices for sustainable landscapes

University of Rhode Island
Sustainable Landscapes Program
Web site: www.uri.edu/research/sustland
A plant list and special lists for demanding
situations such as deer, drought, wind, pH
extremes, power lines, and urban conditions

USDA Wildlife Services
Nuisance Wildlife Hotline (800) 893-4116
Web site: www.aphis.usda.gov
Web site can help you to locate the USDA Wildlife
Services office in your state.

Acknowledgments

The seeds for this book were planted nearly 20 years ago when I assisted with a seminar at the Morris Arboretum in Philadelphia on what was then called "appropriate horticulture." So much of my life and work have led from there to this book and to my work in sustainable landscape practices. I thank Paul Meyer and my colleagues at the arboretum—both living and gone—for opening that and so many other doors.

I regard with gratitude my Croatian relatives and ancestors who gave me my earliest and most enduring vision of sustainable cultivation of the land. I hope that the coming generations will continue to value and find new meaning in that tradition as their civilization advances and recovers from the traumas of war.

Closer to home and to the present, I wish to express my deep gratitude to my husband, Bruce Thomason, for his boundless love, support, and encouragement, and to our son Campbell Thomason for his own brand of exuberant good cheer.

I also thank my parents, Ellen and the late Kristijan Medic, for their interest, support, and pride in my work. My father passed away during the writing of this book. Had he lived, he would have proudly trotted the finished product around to show it to anyone standing still long enough. I'll miss that.

I thank Jean Thomason for giving up more than a week of Asheville springtime to help us out as deadlines loomed and Mel Thomason for cheerfully going without Jean's fine company during that time.

I am thankful for my 8 years working with the Columbus, Indiana, Parks and Recreation Department where Chuck Wilt and others gave me the respect and the latitude that I needed to use and develop many of the sustainable landscape practices that appear in this book. The benefits continue to move well beyond the more than 600 acres of city parkland.

Others who have helped with this work include Jon Cain, Kim Coder, Tim Julien, John Kinsella and Meg Storrow, Judy Loven, Lucinda Mays, Rob McGriff, Rita McKenzie, Stephanie and Patrick McKinney, John McMahon, Nick and Cathy Rush, Bill Stalter, Hank and Opal Winters, Sarah and Paul Zmick, and the wonderful staff at Asbury CMO. I also thank the garden clubs of Columbus and Bartholomew County, Indiana, for their enthusiastic support, and Harrison Flint for his encouragement over the years.

Finally, I have the Rodale Organic Living staff and organization to thank, particularly Karen Soltys, Marta Strait, Nancy Bailey, Fern Bradley, Diana Erney, Lyn Horst, and Ellen Phillips. I have the deepest admiration for their care and effort in advancing the causes of safe food, a healthy environment, sustainable agriculture, and healthy, productive, and beautiful landscapes. Rodale's message of personal empowerment around these and other ideals is clearly working within and beyond the organization. May it ever be so.

Photo Credits

Ian Adams ii, 105

Frederick D. Atwood 167 (*bottom right*)

Matthew Benson vii (*Chapters 1, 4, 6, 7, and 11 photos*), x–xi, 3 (*top*), 17, 55, 118, 119 (*bottom*), 140, 163, 170, 172 (*top and bottom*), 187, 192, 200, 226

Jim Block vii (*Chapter 2 photo*), 19, 24, 26, 58, 63 (*top middle*), 74 (*bottom*), 77 (*bottom*), 88 (*top and bottom*), 95 (*top*), 96 (*top*)

Crandall and Crandall 79, 214 (*top left*)

Betty Crowell 227

R. Todd Davis 86 (*top*), 89

E. R. Degginger 66 (*bottom*)

Alan and Linda Detrick 3 (*bottom*), 71 (*bottom*), 82 (*top*), 91

James F. Dill 166 (*top left*), 167 (*bottom left*), 215 (*bottom right*)

Andrew Drake 6, 10, 18, 44, 47 (*top*), 63 (*bottom right*), 64 (*top*), 103, 139, 164, 166 (*bottom right*), 182, 220, 238, 240, 246

Ken Druse 81, 96 (*bottom*), 97 (*bottom*)

Garden Picture Library/John Glover 71 (*top*)

Garden Picture Library/Neil Holmes 63 (*top left*), 76 (*top*)

Garden Picture Library/Mayer Le Scanff 47 (*bottom*), 56, 60

Garden Picture Library/J. S. Sira 94 (*bottom*)

Galen Gates 63 (*top right*), 68 (*top*), 74 (*top*), 215 (*top right*), 215 (*bottom left*)

Gnass Photo Images/ Bruce Jackson 171 (*left*)

Saxon Holt vii (*Chapter 10 photo*), 63 (*middle*), 69, 84 (*top*), 86 (*bottom*), 95 (*bottom*), 166 (*bottom left*), 214 (*bottom left*), 237 (*top*)

Dency Kane 65 (*bottom*), 77 (*top*), 82 (*bottom*), 92 (*bottom*), 98

Kit Latham 180

David Leibman 167 (*top right*)

Janet Loughrey 23, 92 (*top*)

Mitch Mandell vii (*Chapter 8 photo*), 14 (*both*), 49, 111, 160, 185

Kris Medic ix, 67, 80 (*top*), 90 (*bottom*)

Alison Miksch 4

J. Paul Moore 63 (*middle right and middle left*), 65 (*top*), 72 (*top and bottom*), 76 (*bottom*), 78 (*top*), 90 (*top*), 93 (*top*), 229

Leonard Phillips 218

Photodisc 207

Richard Pomerantz 100, 109, 112, 119 (*top*), 135, 136, 137, 167 (*top left*), 171 (*right*), 243

Susan Seubert vii (*Chapters 3 and 5 photos*), xii, 48, 104, 148–149, 150, 166 (*top right*), 169, 191

Richard Shiell 70 (*top*), 75, 84 (*bottom*), 85 (*top*), 94 (*top*), 215 (*top left*)

Michael S. Thompson 63 (*bottom middle*), 64 (*bottom*), 66 (*top*), 70 (*bottom*), 78 (*bottom*), 80 (*bottom*), 83, 85 (*bottom*), 93 (*bottom*), 99, 153, 165, 237 (*bottom*)

Mark Turner 142

Unicorn Stock Photos/Doug Adams 196

Visuals Unlimited/Wally Eberhart 214 (*top right*)

Visuals Unlimited/Joe McDonald 216

Visuals Unlimited/John Schelden vii (*Chapter 9 photo*), 214 (*bottom right*)

Richard Warren 63 (*bottom left*), 68 (*bottom*), 73, 87, 121, 230

Kurt Wilson 97 (*top*)

Index

Cockscomb (*Celosia argentea*). 94, **94**
  'Apricot Brandy', 94
  'Century', 94
Color, as design element, 22–23, **23, 24,** 50
Companion planting, 204
Compost
  as lawn fertilizer, 158
  as soil amendment, 200, **200**
  in sustainable landscape, **4, 244**
  water conservation and, 184
Compost tea, 213
Concrete
  coloring, 132
  maintaining and repairing, 145–47
  "plastic," 134
  resurfacing, 124–25
Construction
  new, makeover for, 30–31, **30, 31**
  protecting trees during, 26–27, **26, 27**
Cooperative Extension Service
  disease or pest diagnosis, 203, 213
  plant selection information, 174, 191, 216
  soil testing, 53
  woodlot information, 18
Coreopsis verticillata. 91, **91**
  'Moonbeam', 91
  'Zagreb', 91
Cornus florida. 65
Cornus kousa. 65, **65**
  'Milky Way', 65
Cornus spp., 229, 231
Cosmos (*Cosmos bipinnatus*), 98
Cosmos sulphureus. 98, **98**
  'Bright Lights', 98
  'Cosmic Orange', 98
Courtyards, 39, **39**
Crabgrasses, 166, **166**
Creeping juniper (*Juniperus horizontalis*).
  86–87, **86**
  'Bar Harbor', 87
  'Blue Rug', 87
Creeping lilyturf (*Liriope spicata*). 85, 86, **86**
  'Variegata', 86
Crop rotation, 204
Crotch, defined, 223, **223**
Crown, defined, 223, **223**

Crown rot, 214, **214**
Cypress vine (*Ipomoea quamoclit*). 80, **80**

D

Dandelion, 166, **166**
Decks
  maintaining, 147
  materials for, 120
  planning, 118–23, **119, 123**
  safety issues, 123
  storage and, 124
Deer, 216, 218
Deicers, 146, 245
Design process, *13. See also* Landscape plan
Dethatching, 165
Diatomaceous earth (DE), 206
Disease control. *See also specific diseases;*
      specific plants
  fertilizing and, 158
  organic methods of, 204, 209, 212–13
  plan for, 203–4
  plant care and, 200
  plant selection and, 57, 198–99
  soil condition and, 199–200
  watering and, 56, 162, 185
Dogwood, flowering (*Cornus florida*). 65
Dogwood, kousa (*Cornus kousa*). 65, **65**
  'Milky Way', 65
Dogwood, shrub (*Cornus* spp.), 229, 231
Dormant oils, 209
Downspouts, water conservation and, 187, **187,**
      192–93
Drainage, 53
Drip irrigation systems, 189
Driveways
  designing, 133–34
  materials for, 134
  pavers on sand base, 130–31, **130, 131**
Drop spreaders, 160, **160**
Drought, lawns during, 161
Dwarf boxwood (*Buxus* spp.), 48
Dwarf fragrant sumac (*Rhus aromatica* 'Gro-low'),
      48, 74, **74**
Dwarf Hinoki false cypress (*Chamaecyparis obtusa*).
      70, 105
  'Nana Gracilis', 70, **70**

Sumac, dwarf fragrant (*Rhus aromatica* 'Gro-low'),
  48, 74, **74**
Summer oils, 209, 213
Summersweet (*Clethra alnifolia*), 71, **71**
  'Hummingbird', 71
  var. *rosea*, 71
Sun
  decks or patios and, 123
  energy efficiency and, **103**
  plant selection and, 53
Sundials, 144
Sweet autumn clematis (*Clematis terniflora*),
  63, 78, **78**
Sweetshrub (*Calycanthus floridus*), 105
Sweet woodruff (*Galium odoratum*), 84, **84**
Swimming pools, makeover for, 34–35, **34, 35**

T

Task checklist, 25
Taxodium distichum, **63**, 68–69, **68**
  'Prarie Sentinel', 69
Taxus spp., 105, 230, 231
Teas, for disease control, 213
Tent caterpillars, 211, **211**
Terracing, 134–35
Texture, as design element, 23–24, **23**, 50
Thatch, 154, 164–65
Thinning cuts
  defined, 223
  technique, 233–34, **233, 234**
Threadleaf coreopsis (*Coreopsis verticillata*),
  91, **91**
  'Moonbeam', 91
  'Zagreb', 91
Thuja occidentalis, 47, 75
  'Emerald', 47, 75, **75**
  'Holmstrup', 75
  'Smaragd', 75
  'Techny', 75
Thunbergia alata, 77, **77**
  'Alba', 77
Tillers, 251, **251**
Timers, for watering, 189–90, **190**
Tithonia rotundifolia, **63**, 95, **95**
  'Fiesta Del Sol', 95
  'Torch', 95

Tools. *See also* Lawn mowers
  buying, 248
  hand, 248–51, **249, 250, 251**
  maintaining, 252, 253
  power, 251–52, **251**
  pruning, 236–39, **237, 238**
  sharpening, 254
  storing, 252–55, **253, 254, 255**
  watering, **185,** 187–90, **187, 188, 190**
Tracks, animal, **217**
Traffic flow
  as growing condition, 55
  as planning element, 20–21
  plants for, 48
Trap crops, 206
Traps, insect, 206
Tree bands, 204
Tree paint, 239
Trees
  decks or patios surrounding, 120–21, **121**
  existing, 17, *17*
  grass underneath, 41, **41**
  planting, 25, 193, **193**
  professional help with, 227
  profiles of, 64–69, **64, 65, 66, 67,**
    68, 69
  protecting, during construction, 26–27, **26, 27**
  pruning, 222–26, **224, 225, 226**
  shade, **103,** 106
  stress-susceptible, 26
  stress-tolerant, 26
Trellises, 110–11
Trowels, 250
Turf. *See* Lawns; Paths, types

U

Unifers, plants used as, 48
USDA Plant Hardiness Zone Map, 52, **276**
USDA Wildlife Services, 216
Utilities, locating, 16
Utility areas, 139–40, **140**

V

Vancouveria hexandra, 83
Variegated bishop's weed (*Aegopodium
  podagraria* 'Variegatum'), 82–83, **82**

Vegetable gardens, 171, **171,** 204
Vertical mowing, 165
Viburnum prunifolium, **63,** 68, **68**
Viburnum rufidulum, 68
Viburnum (*Viburnum* spp.), 229
Views
    controlling with plants, 48
    from decks or patios, 121–23
    small lots and, 38, **38**
Vinca major, 82
    'Variegata', 82
Vinca minor, 82, **82**
    'Alba', 82
    'Gertrude Jekyll', 82
Vines
    for beauty, 144
    for energy efficiency, 109–11, **109, 110**
    profiles of, 76–81, **76, 77, 78, 79, 80, 81**
Virginia creeper (*Parthenocissus quinquefolia*), 79
Voles, 219

W

Walkways. *See* Paths and walkways
Walls
    freestanding, 137, **137**
    retaining, 134–35, **135**
Water breakers, 188
Water features, 145
Watering
    automatic systems for, 193–95
    landscape plan and, 190–93, **191, 192, 193**
    lawns, 161–62
    as plant selection criteria, 55
    with sprinklers, 56
    tools for, **185,** 187–90, **187, 188, 190**
    water quality and, 186
    water-saving techniques for, 184–86
Water softeners, 186
Water sprout, defined, 223, **223**
Water wands, **185,** 188, **188**
Weeds, in lawns, 166–67, **166, 167,** 168
Wet areas, solutions for, 42, **42,** 53
Wheelbarrows, 250–51
White clover, 166, **166**
White fringe tree (*Chionanthus virginicus*), 65, **65**

Wild geranium (*Geranium maculatum*), 90–91, **90**
Wildlife
    growing conditions and, 55
    habitat for, 4, 49, 50
Wind
    decks or patios and, 123
    as growing condition, 55
Windbreaks, 43, **43,** 49, 107–8, **107,** 111, **111**
Wind funnels, 49, 108–9, **108**
Wind scoops, 49, 108–9, **108**
Woodchucks, 219
Woodlots
    makeover, 36–37, **36, 37**
    professional help with, 18
Wood sorrels, 167, **167**
Wood structures, maintaining, 147

Y

Y-connectors, 190, **190**
Yellow barrenwort (*Epimedium* × *versicolor* 'Sulphureum'), 83, **83**
Yellow bedstraw (*Galium verum*), 84
Yellow cosmos (*Cosmos sulphureus*), 95, **95**
    'Bright Lights', 95
    'Cosmic Orange', 95
Yew (*Taxus* spp.), 105, 230, 231

Z

Zelkova serrata, **63,** 69, **69**
    'Green Vase', 69
    'Halka', 69
    'Village Green', 69

American Horticultural Society Heat Zone Map

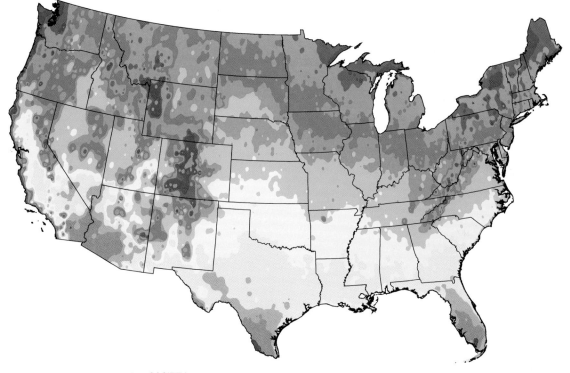

AMERICAN HORTICULTURAL SOCIETY

7931 East Boulevard Drive
Alexandria, VA 22308 U.S.A.
(703) 768-5700 Fax (703) 768-8700

Coordinated by:
Dr. H. Marc Cathey, President Emeritus

Compiled by:
Meteorological Evaluation Services Co., Inc.

Underwriting by:
American Horticultural Society
Goldsmith Seed Company
Horticultural Research Institute of the
American Nursery and Landscape Association
Monrovia
Time Life Inc.

Average Number of Days per Year Above 86°F (30°C)	Zone
< 1	1
1 to 7	2
> 7 to 14	3
> 14 to 30	4
> 30 to 45	5
> 45 to 60	6
> 60 to 90	7
> 90 to 120	8
> 120 to 150	9
> 150 to 180	10
> 180 to 210	11
> 210	12

USDA Plant
Hardiness Zone Map

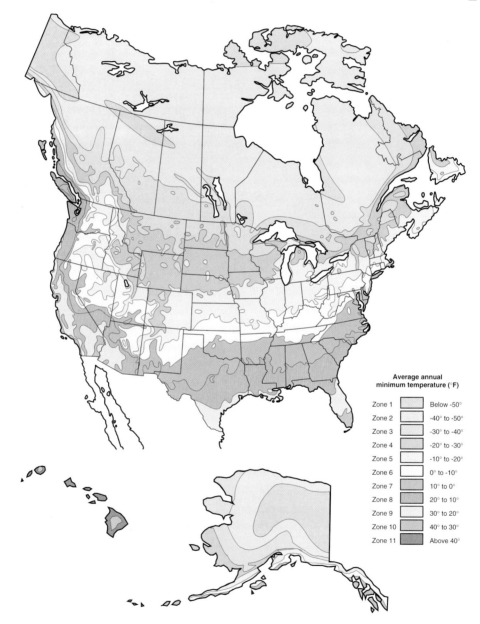

**Average annual
minimum temperature (°F)**

Zone 1		Below -50°
Zone 2		-40° to -50°
Zone 3		-30° to -40°
Zone 4		-20° to -30°
Zone 5		-10° to -20°
Zone 6		0° to -10°
Zone 7		10° to 0°
Zone 8		20° to 10°
Zone 9		30° to 20°
Zone 10		40° to 30°
Zone 11		Above 40°